Securing 'the Homeland'

[This book] provides a thorough, engaging and much overdue account of the key issues at the intersection between critical infrastructure and the field of Security Studies.

(Lene Hansen, University of Copenhagen)

This edited volume uses a 'constructivist/reflexive' approach to address critical infrastructure protection (CIP), a central political practice associated with national security.

The politics of CIP, and the construction of the threat they are meant to counter, effectively establish a powerful discursive connection between the traditional and normal conditions for day-to-day politics and the exceptional dynamics of national security. Combining political theory and empirical case studies, this volume addresses key issues related to protection and the governance of insecurity in the contemporary world. The contributors track the transformation and evolution of critical infrastructures (and closely related issues of homeland security) into a security problem, and analyse how practices associated with CIP constitute, and are an expression of, changing notions of security and insecurity. The book explores aspects of 'securitisation' as well as at practices, audiences, and contexts that enable and constrain the production of the specific form of governmentality that CIP exemplifies. It also explores the rationalities at play, the effects of these security practices, and the implications for our understanding of security and politics today.

This book will be of much interest to students of Security Studies, Terrorism Studies and International Relations in general.

Myriam Dunn Cavelty is lecturer and head of the new risks research unit at the Center for Security Studies (CSS), ETH Zurich. **Kristian Søby Kristensen** is a PhD candidate working with the Research Unit on Defence and Security at the Danish Institute for International Studies.

CSS studies in security and international relations
Series editors: Andreas Wenger and Victor Mauer
Center for Security Studies, ETH Zurich

The *CSS Studies in Security and International Relations* examine historical and contemporary aspects of security and conflict. The series provides a forum for new research based upon an expanded conception of security and will include monographs by the Center's research staff and associated academic partners.

War Plans and Alliances in the Cold War
Threat perceptions in the East and West
Edited by Vojtech Mastny,
Sven Holtsmark and Andreas Wenger

Transforming NATO in the Cold War
Challenges beyond deterrence in the 1960s
Edited by Andreas Wenger,
Christian Nuenlist and Anna Locher

US Foreign Policy and the War on Drugs
Displacing the cocaine and heroin industry
Cornelius Friesendorf

Cyber-Security and Threat Politics
US efforts to secure the information age
Myriam Dunn Cavelty

Securing 'the Homeland'
Critical infrastructure, risk and (in)security
Edited by Myriam Dunn Cavelty and
Kristian Søby Kristensen

Securing 'the Homeland'

Critical infrastructure, risk and (in)security

Edited by Myriam Dunn Cavelty and Kristian Søby Kristensen

Routledge
Taylor & Francis Group

LONDON AND NEW YORK

First published 2008
by Routledge
2 Park Square, Milton Park, Abingdon, Oxfordshire OX14 4RN

Simultaneously published in the USA and Canada
by Routledge
711 Third Avenue, New York, NY 10017
First issued in paperback 2014

Routledge is an imprint of the Taylor & Francis Group, an informa business

Typeset in Times by Wearset Ltd, Boldon, Tyne and Wear

British Library Cataloguing in Publication Data
A catalogue record for this book is available from the British Library

Library of Congress Cataloging in Publication Data
Securing 'the homeland': critical infrastructure, risk, and (in)security /
edited by Myriam Dunn Cavelty and Kristian Søby Kristensen.

p.cm. – (CSS studies in security and international relations)

1. Terrorism–Prevention. 2. National security. 3. United States–Politics
and government. 4. United States–Foreign relations. I. Dunn Cavelty,
Myriam. II. Kristensen, Kristian Søby.

HV6431.S423 2008

363.325'160973–dc22

2007048589

ISBN 978-0-415-44109-4 (hbk)
ISBN 978-0-415-76193-2 (pbk)
ISBN 978-0-203-09265-1 (ebk)

Contents

Contributors

Philippe Bonditti is a PhD candidate in Sciences Po in Paris and research assistant at the Centre d'études et de recherche internationales (CERI). He currently works on the redefinition of the modalities of sovereign power through an analysis of US policies against transnational political violence. He is the author of 'From territorial space to networks. A Foucauldian approach to the implementation of biometry' (*Alternatives*: 29/4, 2004) and co-author, within the C.A.S.E. Collective, of the paper 'Critical approach to security in Europe: a networked manifesto' (*Security Dialogue*: 37/4, 2006). He is a member of the Editorial Board of the French journal *Cultures & Conflits* and of the Editorial and Communication Team of the journal *International Political Sociology*, and is also involved in the European research programme CHALLENGE.

Elgin M. Brunner is a PhD candidate at the Institut für Politikwissenschaft of the University of Vienna and a researcher at the Center for Security Studies (CSS), ETH Zurich. She holds a degree in International Relations and Political Science from the Graduate Institute of International Studies in Geneva. She specialises in gender issues in security studies, information operations, the changing nature of warfare and the societal implications thereof.

Stephen J. Collier is an Assistant Professor in the Graduate Programme in International Affairs at the New School University, New York. He is the co-editor of *Global Assemblages: Technology, Politics, and Ethics as Anthropological Problems* and is completing a manuscript entitled *Post-Soviet Social: Neoliberalism and Biopolitics in the Russian Mirror*. His research interests include urbanism, neoliberalism, planning, security, infrastructure and social modernity. His current projects include a genealogy of vital systems security with Andrew Lakoff.

Maura Conway is a lecturer and the Director of MA Programmes at the Department of Law and Government at Dublin City University. Her research interests are in the area of terrorism and the Internet. She is particularly interested in cyberterrorism and its portrayal in the media, and the functioning and effectiveness of terrorist websites. Along with a number of book chapters, she has also published in *Current History, Parliamentary Affairs, Disarmament Forum*, and elsewhere.

James der Derian is a Watson Institute Research Professor of International Studies. In July 2004, he became the director of the Institute's Global Security Programme. Der Derian also directs the Information Technology, War and Peace Project in the Watson Institute's Global Security Programme. Der Derian was a Rhodes Scholar at Oxford University, where he completed an M.Phil. and a D.Phil. in international relations. He has been a visiting scholar at the University of Southern California, MIT, Harvard, Oxford and the Institute for Advanced Study at Princeton. He is the author of *On Diplomacy: A Genealogy of Western Estrangement* (1987) and *Antidiplomacy: Spies, Terror, Speed, and War* (1992); the editor of *International Theory: Critical Investigations* (1995) and *The Virilio Reader* (1998); and co-editor with Michael Shapiro of *International/Intertextual Relations: Postmodern Readings of World Politics* (1989). His most recent book is *Virtuous War: Mapping the Military-Industrial-Media-Entertainment Network* (2001).

Myriam Dunn Cavelty is a lecturer and the head of the New Risks research unit at the Center for Security Studies (CSS), ETH Zurich and coordinator of the Crisis and Risk Network (CRN). Dunn Cavelty holds a degree in political science, modern history and international law from the University of Zurich. She specialises in security studies and the impact of the information revolution on security policy issues in particular. Along with articles and book chapters on the topic, she is the author of *Cyber-Security and Threat Politics: US Efforts to Secure the Information Age* (2008) as well as co-editor of two recent volumes: *The Resurgence of the State: Trend and Processes in Cyberspace Governance* (2007) and *Power and Security in the Information Age: Investigating the Role of the State in Cyberspace* (2007).

Jesse Finkelstein graduated from Brown University in 2005 and was subsequently recruited by a major technology company to participate in its homeland security business division. Focusing on wearable computing and biometric design, he left that technology company and started his own design business, JF & SON. Now in its first year, JF & SON is a multidisciplinary design group that specialises in textile innovation, fabric engineering and apparel production.

Kristian Søby Kristensen is a PhD candidate working with the Research Unit on Defense and Security at the Danish Institute for International Studies. Previously, he had been a research assistant also at the Danish Institute for International Studies, as well as at the Department of Political Science at the University of Copenhagen. His research interests include transatlantic security policy, the concept of war in international relations, military transformation and the changes in both practice and theory of security, especially the blurring of the domestic/international delimitation. He is a Cand.scient.pol at the University of Copenhagen.

Andrew Lakoff is an Assistant Professor of Sociology and Science Studies at the University of California, San Diego, and is currently serving as programme officer for the SSRC project, 'Preparedness, Vital Systems and Security'. He received a PhD in anthropology at the University of California, Berkeley and was a post-doctoral fellow in the department of social medicine at Harvard Medical School. Lakoff's research involves the social analysis of systems of expertise. His recent book, *Pharmaceutical Reason: Knowledge and Value in Global Psychiatry* (2005), examines epistemological debates around the source of mental disorder. He is also co-editor of *Global Pharmaceuticals: Ethics, Knowledge, Practices* (2006), and has published articles on the history of the behavioral sciences, on methodology in the interpretive social sciences, and on the concepts of risk and security. His current work focuses on the development of techniques to enhance preparedness among security experts in the US.

Julian Reid is a lecturer in International Relations at King's College London, UK and a visiting professor in International Relations at the University of Lapland in Finland. He is the author of *The Biopolitics of the War on Terror* (2006).

Ole Wæver is a Professor of International Relations and former senior research fellow at COPRI, Copenhagen Peace Research Institute (1985–99). He has published and broadcast extensively in the field of international relations, and is one of the main architects of the so-called Copenhagen School in International Relations. Ole Wæver was a member of the Danish government's Commission on Security and Disarmament Affairs between 1993 and 1995 and of the Danish Institute of International Affairs (DUPI) between 1995 and 2002. He is a member of the editorial board for *European Journal of International Affairs*, *Security Dialogue*, *International Studies Perspective* and the *Cambridge Review of International Affairs*.

Foreword

Ole Wæver

'Critical infrastructure protection' seems yet another buzzword in security studies, a field prone to linguistic hyperbole. Since it also features a catchy acronym, CIP, it is likely to be embraced by security experts. But, while it is certainly true that CIP is one aspect among many in a boom of 'security' concerns, industries and practices since September 2001, CIP is more than that. This book shows convincingly that CIP is an ideal lens through which to read broader changes in security – and in society at large. Ultimately, the book engages the question of what is defended by security policy in this day and age.

The novelty of the term 'homeland security' has been noted by many, but it is still too easily perceived as being relatively traditional, due to its accompanying nationalist and statist discourse. The US version of 'homeland security' may, at a superficial glance, appear to be simply another term for 'territorial defence', which almost all other states already had in place – only the US had thought it could do without such measures, since it could push its defence perimeter across the seas. Alternately, the term was perceived as referring to no more than a slightly more novel further step in the merger between internal and external security. However, upon closer examination, the matter becomes much more intriguing – and interesting. 'Homeland security' is not practiced through the category of 'homeland', but operates more often through logics focused on individuals or networks. Also, the fact that a large part of the practical preparations for securing 'critical infrastructure' and the 'homeland', respectively, are the same, regardless of whether the cause of disruption is a foreign enemy or a technical system failure or a natural disaster, raises quite radical questions concerning established conceptions of 'security'.

The issues covered by this book are much more familiar to practitioners than to academics. During the second half of the 1990s, and greatly accelerated by the 11 September 2001 attacks in New York and Washington, a new field of action emerged that connected classical disaster protection and rescue services with concerns traditionally associated with international security. The vulnerability of modern society has become the focal point of a functionally defined set of concerns and responses, where the intermediate problems and the necessary responses define a unified field, irrespective of whether the first cause is a hostile act by a foreign state or violent political movement, a natural disaster, a technical breakdown, or a domestic intentional disruption. But to theorists, this blanket approach is not easy to handle – it does not fit in. Or rather: it fits very well into new storylines, but not the established ones.

Policy researchers whose work reflects practical fields have obviously written about (and advocated) CIP, and sweeping theorists have dropped the term into their generalisations, but so far, there has been no sustained analysis of this field by people who are seriously engaged with the conceptual, theoretical and political debates that are underway in security studies and in society in general. One of the great qualities of this book is that it takes a focused and sustained look at a very specific and, in some senses, highly technical field, and simultaneously presents a very illuminating examination of fundamental changes in dominant dangers and the concurrent countermeasures. All societies define themselves through their categorisation of the crucial subjects and objects to be defended, so the book speaks to nothing less than the question 'who are we?' (or 'what are we?'). It does so through empirically grounded analysis.

When I first took the initiative as part of CHALLENGE, the EU Sixth Framework Programme research programme on the changing landscape of liberty and security in Europe, to plan 'a small workshop bringing together experts on critical infrastructure protection from both sides of the Atlantic', nobody predicted how productive this project would be. This is very much to the credit of the two editors, who – in addition to their fine job of shaping a coherent publication – were the main forces in organising the two workshops where drafts were presented and thoroughly discussed. When reading this volume, it quickly becomes clear that it is not the typical compilation of pieces produced separately, but the result of actual interaction. It is precisely through this process of very lively discussions of a new phenomenon that it became possible for this combination of younger and more experienced European and North American scholars to penetrate this highly technical realm and politicise these CIP practices, and thereby produce a book that brings back 'critical' to 'critical infrastructure protection'.

Acknowledgements

Edited volumes are often faulted for being inevitably uneven in terms of quality or for being nothing more than idiosyncratic collections of chapters. But they can also be valuable additions to our understanding of particular research fields, precisely *because* they look at issues from a variety of perspectives. In fact, some issues seem particularly prone for being addressed in such a manner. In our opinion, critical infrastructure protection (CIP) is such an issue. CIP is becoming an increasingly central, but not yet well-investigated political practice associated with securing societies. CIP plays an important part in strategies to reduce societal vulnerability and to mitigate the perceived threat from terrorism on both sides of the Atlantic. Simultaneously the practice of CIP questions our theoretical understanding of a range of concepts as it introduces new technologies and new knowledge to the practice of security that are not easily grasped from the perspective of traditional security studies or with an overly monolithic approach.

This volume emerged from an initiative undertaken by 'Challenge: The Changing Landscape of European Liberty and Security', a Sixth Framework Research Programme of the European Commission. We greatly acknowledge the financial support provided by 'Challenge', which made possible the first of two intense authors' workshops on CIP. At this initial gathering, which took place in Copenhagen in September 2005, the foundations for this anthology were laid. In order to take the discussion one step further, a second workshop was organised approximately one year later in Zurich. This was made possible by the generous financial and logistical support provided by the Center for Security Studies, ETH Zurich. Both workshops were invaluable instances both in developing our collective thinking on CIP and associated subjects and in focusing the arguments of the individual chapters.

We want to express our thanks to our fellow contributors for their enthusiasm and commitment in making this book possible. We would also like to thank colleagues not represented in this book that have, in some way or another, contributed to it on its journey to completion: Ralf Bendrath, Christopher Daase, Lene Hansen, Jorgos Kolliarakis, Ronnie Lipschutz, Mikkel Vedby Rasmussen and David Wood. Special thanks go to two staff members at the Center for Security Studies: to Christopher Findlay for proofreading all the chapters and to

Susanne Schmid for taking such care that the bibliographies are consistent. Furthermore, we thank two external reviewers for very helpful comments and the editors at Routledge for helping to turn the manuscript into a book.

Myriam Dunn Cavelty, Zurich and
Kristian Søby Kristensen, Copenhagen

Abbreviations

ACTS	Aviation Corps Technical School
AFIWC	Air Force Information Warfare Center
AHV	America's Hidden Vulnerabilities
AWPD	Air War Plans Division
CAPPSII	Computer Assisted Passenger Prescreening System
CART	Computer Analysis and Response Team
CF	Critical Foundations
CGI (Script)	Common Gateway Interface
CIA	Central Intelligence Agency
CIITAT	Critical Investigations and Infrastructure Threat Assessment
CIP	Critical Infrastructure Protection
DARPA	Defense Advanced Research Projects Agency
DCPA	Defense Civil Preparedness Agency
DEPA	Defense Electric Power Administration (in DCPA)
DHS	Department of Homeland Security
DIA	Defense Intelligence Agency
DNI	Director of National Intelligence
DoD	Department of Defense
EMP	Electromagnetic Pulse
EPC	Electronic Product Code
EU	European Union
FBI	Federal Bureau of Investigation
FDCA	Federal Civil Defense Agency
FEMA	Federal Emergency Management Agency
FISA	Foreign Intelligence Surveillance Act
GAO	General Accounting Office
HF/E	Human Factors Engineering
HSDN	Homeland Secure Data Network
IDA	Institute for Defense Analysis
IT	Information Technology
JDD	James Der Derian
LIC	Low-Intensity Conflicts

MAA	Maximum Availability Architectures
MARSOC	Marines Special Operation Command
NCTC	National Counter-Terrorism Center
NGA	National Geospatial Agency
NIPP	National Infrastructure Protection Plan
NORTHCOM	United States Northern Command
NSA	National Security Agency
NSDD	National Security Decision Directive
NSEERS	National Security Entry–Exit Registration System
ODM	Office of Defense Mobilization
OEP	Office of Emergency Preparedness (White House)
OHS	Office of Homeland Security
PCCIP	Presidential Commission on Critical Infrastructure Protection
PDD	Presidential Decision Directive
RFID	Radio Frequency Identification
SED	Systems Evaluation Division (in OEP)
TIA	Terrorism Information Awareness Program
TIS	Trusted Information-sharing
TIW	Transnational Infrastructure Warfare
TSP	Terrorist Surveillance Program
US	United States
USA PATRIOT Act	Uniting and Strengthening America by Providing Appropriate Tools Required to Intercept and Obstruct Terrorism (Act)
USCD	United States Civil Defense
USCENTCOM	United States Central Command
USSOCOM	United States Special Operations Command
WMD	Weapons of Mass Destruction

Introduction

Securing the homeland: critical infrastructure, risk and (in)security

Myriam Dunn Cavelty and Kristian Søby Kristensen

For a number of years since the end of the East–West bloc confrontation, a lot of effort, both political and scholarly, has gone into debating various aspects of how to understand and to react to 'new' threats posed to Western societies. From this plethora of threats, international terrorism was propelled by the attacks of 11 September 2001 to the attention of an anxious public and gave rise to political action. Since then, a lot of brainpower has been expended on critically evaluating a variety of state reactions to this particular threat. In the broader environment of this debate, one political practice associated with securing vulnerable societies and 'the homeland' against the threat of terrorism has been remarkably salient: the practice of critical infrastructure protection (CIP).

Etymologically, 'infrastructure' is the combination of the Latin prefix *infra* meaning below, underneath and the suffix *structura* meaning 'the way in which an edifice, machine, implement etc. is made or put together' (Oxford English Dictionary 1993, Vol. X: 1165). This etymology recalls the context in which the word was used in the first instance – to describe part of the construction of buildings, roads, etc. – and has come to signify an 'underlying base or foundation especially for an organization or system' (Dictionary.com). According to the American Heritage Dictionary of the English Language, the term has been used since 1927 to refer collectively to the roads, bridges, railway lines, and similar public works that are required for the functioning of an industrial economy or its constituent parts. The term is also applied specifically to the permanent military installations necessary for the defence of a country.

In the contemporary political debate, some infrastructures are regarded as 'critical' (in the sense of 'vital', 'crucial', 'essential') by the authorities because their prolonged unavailability would, in all likelihood, result in social instability and major crisis. The etymological origins of infrastructure connote a fixed, unchanging foundation upon which things can be constructed, providing the basis for further development – but without which, conversely, further development and construction are also impossible. Today, these critical infrastructures mostly take the form of interconnected, complex and increasingly virtual systems. The most frequently listed examples of critical infrastructures encompass banking and finance, government services, telecommunication and information and communication technologies, emergency and rescue services, energy and electricity, health services, transportation, logistics and distribution and water supply (Abele-Wigert and Dunn 2006: 386–9). To express just how important they are for the functioning of society, they have been called 'instrumentalities of interstate commerce' (PCCIP 1997: 98) or 'lifelines' (Platt 1995) and have also been metaphorically likened to vital anatomical components such as 'the nervous system', 'the backbone', 'essential arteries' or 'organic essentials' (see, for example, Faber 1997: 219).

Critical infrastructures are seen to be vulnerable to all kinds of threats and risks, ranging from lack of funding, technical error, and natural disasters to malicious attacks of all sorts. Not surprisingly, however, since the terrorist attacks in New York and Washington (2001), Madrid (2004) and London (2005), protecting infrastructures is mainly discussed as a measure against terrorism. Commensurate with the perceived gravity of the threat – the worst-case scenario being the end of society as we know it – a broad range of political and administrative initiatives and efforts are underway both in the US and in Europe in an attempt to better secure these infrastructures, both virtual and physical.

CIP and the zeitgeist of the risk society

The establishment of CIP as one focal point of the current national security debate of Western states can be seen as a confluence of two interlinked and at times mutually reinforcing factors:

1   the perception that modern societies are – by their very nature – exposed to an ever-increasing number of potentially catastrophic vulnerabilities (Beck 1992);
2   the perception of an increasing willingness of dangerous actors to brutally exploit these vulnerabilities (Ackerman *et al.* 2006: x).

It has been noted that in all of the recent cases of Muslim extremism, the perpetrators both exploited and targeted elements of what can be called the civilian infrastructure for the purpose of their attacks. This seems to show a propensity of the 'new' terrorism for targeting the soft underbelly of liberal, open and increasingly networked societies, which are both held together and empowered by their critical infrastructures (Barry 2001: 12ff.) and reciprocally made vulnerable due to dependence on them. As the sophistication of these infrastructures increases, so does the potential risk of sophisticated boomerang effects (Beck 1992: 37) as exemplified by recent terror attacks.

The combination of these two factors has proven to be a key condition for promoting CIP to the forefront of current strategies for providing security. It seems to correspond to the zeitgeist at a time when 'fear of the future has become a significant feature of contemporary political life' (Bigo 2006a) and in which 'the principle of deliberately exploiting the vulnerability of modern civil society replaces the principle of change and accident' (Beck 2006) – while the notion of the 'normal accident' (Perrow 1984) is still lingering in the technological conception of CIP. Narratives about security in connection with CIP are articulated in terms of an ability (or inability) to control the future. Risk is the underlying logic and rationale of CIP, due to its historical development as well as the instruments and tools used for evaluating vulnerabilities. As such, CIP belongs to a set of security issues linked to the emergence of a 'rationale of risk management' in security after the Cold War, a development that is tied in with a discursive shift from threats of identifiable enemies to risks (see also Aradau and van Munster 2006; Castel 1991; Power 2004; Rasmussen 2001, 2004; Dunn Cavelty 2008).

Still, the core ideas of CIP, both as a concept and in practice, are by no means new: in fact, the opposite can be claimed, both for the aspect of vulnerabilities and for the aspect of malicious actors. Long before 11 September 2001, the protection of strategically important installations in the domestic economic and social sphere was an important part of national defence concepts. CIP as a distinct concept for thinking about security linked to the notion of non-deterrable threats has historical roots that can be traced back many decades (see Collier and Lakoff, Chapter 1, this volume). This is no banal observation. There is a tendency, specifically since 2001, to over-endow scholarly texts addressing changes in security concepts and practices with the term 'new'. Such claims of discontinuity are not only used to express a breach with the past, but also to stress the novelty of arguments, and thus also the value of the research. But clearly, the view that these security practices are without precedent and thus in a class of their own prevents us from understanding them in other than superficial ways and this leaves us blind to their historical trajectories. More importantly, calling things 'new' and pointing to a discontinuity also happens to be practiced frequently in the political discourse. Evidence suggests that such 'accounts of the radically new are all too easily transformed into accounts of the radically dangerous' (Bigo 2006a). They are used to mobilise political support and to legitimise exceptional measures, a topic that is also exposed and problematised in this book (see, for example, Chapters 2 and 7, this volume). Newness only makes sense against the backdrop of continuity.

The approach of this book

Thus, rather than claiming to look at something radically new, this volume presents the phenomenon of CIP as a 'specific imbrication of continuity and discontinuity' (Aradau and van Munster 2007: 90), as belonging to a series of events that both preceded and succeeded its birth and evolution, but with distinguishable implications for security. In this understanding, recent developments follow the pathways inscribed by 'old' logics and are the outcome of a trend based on proposals that can be traced back a long way, as a large number of chapters point out (Chapters 1, 2, 4 and 6). By highlighting the continuities and relatively subtle adjustments of CIP as a concept and as a practice, this book helps to play down the 11 September 2001 attacks as a key moment in a narrative 'of an onrushing apocalypse' (Bigo 2006a). Such an approach is all the more warranted because much of the (recent) debate has been driven by politics of near-hysteria on the threat construction side: The CIP discourse is riddled with 'policies based on worst-case scenarios' (Kristensen, Chapter 3, this volume) as epitomised by 'shut-down-the power-grid' stories (Conway, Chapter 5, this volume).

At the same time, we are aware that we are shooting at a moving target: CIP is not a static concept, and it is still evolving. When seen as a 'policy window' (Kingdon 2003), 11 September 2001 made a number of things possible in the realm of CIP, the most obvious of which is the establishment of the DHS and a complete organisational revamp of the previous CIP 'assemblage'. The 2001 attacks thus clearly belong to a series of defining 'moments' for the evolution of the concept – but this volume shows that there were others. For example, as Collier and Lakoff (Chapter 1), Dunn Cavelty (Chapter 2), and Der Derian and Finkelstein (Chapter 4) point out, the shift from a specific emphasis on systems that are essential for military production to a broader concern with the vital systems that are essential for the economic and social well-being of the entire nation was absolutely crucial in the rise of CIP to high prominence, as was the change of emphasis from physical infrastructure to information infrastructures (and lately back again).

A 'constructivist/reflexive' approach (C.A.S.E. Collective 2006: 445) to security allows the contributors to track the transformation and evolution of critical infrastructures (and closely related issues of homeland security) into a security problem and to analyse how practices associated with critical infrastructure protection constitute, and are an expression of, changing notions of security and insecurity. The book also explores the rationalities at play as well as the effects of these security practices, and looks at the implications for our understanding of security and politics today. Explicitly (and at times implicitly) using the techniques provided by Foucault for scrutinising both the practices of language and the creation of objects through institutional practices (Foucault 1994b; Dreyfus and Rabinow 1982: 104), the chapters in this book embed CIP as a concept and CIP as practice in a changing security environment. Situated somewhere between the Copenhagen and the Paris schools of security, the volume looks at aspects of 'securitisation' as well as at practices, audiences and contexts that enable and constrain the production of a specific form of governmentality as exemplified by CIP (C.A.S.E. Collective 2006: 457; cf. Huysmans 2006: 5 and 8). Since critical infrastructures and their protection, as a distinct security concept, are largely constructs of the US government and have lately been reconfigured by the aspiration to fight terrorism abroad and at home at the same time, this book naturally focuses mainly on the US discourse and practice.

CIP: both wide and narrow

This book presents two perspectives on CIP: a narrow one and a broad one. These two conceptions of CIP are the principal ordering principle of the chapters in this volume, which range from the more narrow conception to the broad conception. The narrow perspective on CIP (Part I) is closely associated with how it is represented in the mainstream political discourse. This understanding has a technical character linked to the engineering aspect of infrastructures, and is predominantly the purview of engineers and public policy pundits rather than of political scientists (cf. Radvanovsky 2006; Auerswald *et al.* 2006). From this perspective, CIP programmes focus on mitigating the vulnerabilities of systems to a variety of potentially disruptive events, an approach known as 'all-hazards' approach. CIP is thus not focused on interdicting terrorists, but on making sure that if a terrorist attack (or any other event) should occur, its consequences will not be calamitous. In other words, CIP is not a policing practice, but a *preparedness* practice. In fact, CIP elegantly sidesteps the policing problem. Given that it is difficult to predict, deter or prevent a terrorist attack, one alternative is to develop mitigation measures, by creating systems that are resilient enough to ensure that an attack will not have catastrophic effects. Thus, CIP approaches the threat of terrorism not through surveillance and interdiction, but through a different form of security that is oriented toward ensuring the continuous functioning of critical systems.[1]

The second, broader perspective sees CIP as an important subset of homeland security and counter-terrorism (Part II). In this understanding, CIP is also about technology of control, constituting both a threat and a means of protection, and technological developments within a broader social and political frame, including surveillance. In this view, CIP functions as a framework for the establishment of new degrees and techniques of control over the properties and processes of life. The important point here is the conflation of the human body, of technology and of knowledge in the practice of CIP. This view introduces a double or 'reflexive' aspect of CIP: its focus on technologies shows how some critical infrastructures, most often in the form of information technologies, are used to protect other critical infrastructures and how the information infrastructure is used to protect itself. This view also stresses the danger of the creation of inside/outside spaces or zones of marginalisation through CIP practices, by asking who is protected and who is not; and eliciting who is in fact becoming a potential target of CIP practices. The representation of both viewpoints is of central importance for understanding, on the one hand, how CIP is situated in the wider discourse of homeland security and counter-terrorism (Part II) and, on the other hand, how this wider discourse is affected by the way in which CIP is conceptualised as part of it (Part I). In order to capture this interrelation, the first part of this volume focuses on CIP as a security practice emerging at a specific point in time, clearly linked to what we look at in the second part: the perception of terrorism as the prime threat in today's security environment and how this perception influences security practices in a broader sense.

When focusing on the first view, one key aspect of CIP practices is to create greater resilience, commonly defined as the ability of a system to recover from adversity and either revert to its original state or to assume an adjusted state based on new requirements (McCarthy 2007: 2f.). As previously mentioned, most precautionary and response measures can be employed as protection against unexpected deliberate or natural events, except perhaps for the activities of the intelligence services and certain police and military responsibilities (such as physical protection of facilities), which are all geared toward actor-induced threats. Such practices, even though established and propagated by security professionals, seem to be rather unappealing as topics for security studies scholars, judging from the small amount of publications on them. One reason might be that none of these practices are exceptional. Even though an 'existential threat' (Wæver 1995) is frequently invoked, and the politics of security are often said to depend on the exceptional (Jabri 2006; Dillon 2003; Agamben 2002), much of the actual practice of CIP is very commonplace in character. Another explanation is the clear division between domestic and international scholarship that underpins the discipline, a cleavage that has often prevented the study of concepts situated in both arenas or in between (cf. Abrahamsen and Williams 2006: 45). Clearly, security studies have focused predominantly on discursive and institutional practices 'that rely upon national security and the sphere of the international' (Jabri 2006: 146).

If we look at the threat rhetoric behind CIP and at the measures that are envisaged for protection, we can argue that the history of CIP is littered with failed securitisation moves (cf. Bendrath 2001). But we can also look at CIP from a 'French' point of view. This school of thought perceives security not only as 'exceptional', but also as being concerned with the everyday routines and technologies of security professionals (Bigo 1996, 2002) or as a 'technique of government' (Foucault 1994a). Such an understanding shifts the focus of attention from 'utterances referring to dangerous futures' to the technologies and strategies by means of which security is sought and produced (C.A.S.E. Collective 2006: 469). To see CIP as belonging to the 'politics of protection' (Huysmans *et al.* 2006) helps to let security analysis 'run more flexibly across traditional and less traditional security agencies' and ultimately serves to open up security studies 'to the importance of everyday practices and routines in security practices' (Huysmans 2006: 14). 'Protection is different from security', writes Bigo (Bigo 2006b: 93), and, in this book, we will investigate just how different it is.

This is also the approach taken by Andrew Lakoff and Stephen Collier in Chapter 1. They present CIP as a central example of what is called 'vital systems security' and enquire about the origins of the distinctive concept that views security threats as problems of system vulnerabilities. Using a Foucault-inspired study of problematisations, they track the emergence of CIP as an object of expert reflection in the early 1980s, with ties to far older issues, namely the emergence of strategic bombing after the First World War, and Cold War civil defence programmes. By uncovering a series of important moments, their chapter lays the foundation for understanding many of the later developments. The specific way of providing security by means of vulnerability mapping and other techniques has led to a certain amount of path-dependency or institutional 'lock-in'.

The information revolution as a defining moment...

While tracking the emergence of the CIP apparatus is important for understanding the origins and the current shape of the topic, it is also important to see that current fears exist within a far more complex. technologically dominated polity than the one in which the ideas first emerged. The complex interdependence of liberal (risk) societies and their growing technological sophistication have transnationalised and technologised the types of security problems that they face. We seem to be witnessing scalar changes moving in opposite directions: the power to resist vulnerability moves *outwards* to international markets and international organisations while the power to cause vulnerability moves *inwards*, through classes and groups to the individual. And finally, the information revolution as a defining moment changed the overall scope, aim and shape of CIP when it led to the displacement of the material, in favour of the virtual, as the object of control.

As Myriam Dunn Cavelty shows in Chapter 2, a growing concern with information security in the 1980s and 1990s found a technical vocabulary, a set of analytical tools and practices of intervention in a longstanding mode of thinking about infrastructures as a security problem. By analysing how CIP is expressed by US security policy elites in terms of threat frames (interpretive schemes about what counts as threat or risk, how to respond to this threat, and who or what is responsible for it), the chapter shows how the information revolution is responsible for transforming the issue into a topic of high saliency. With the growth and spreading of computer networks into more and more aspects of life, the object of protection changed. Whereas it had previously consisted of limited government networks, it now encompassed the whole of society. In this environment, the threat image of the cyber-terrorist emerges as the ultimate catastrophic threat, as Maura Conway shows in Chapter 5. Through the globalised media, a threat image combining fear of technology with fear of terrorism is spread *ad absurdum*, leading to what Jean Baudrillard has coined 'hyperreality': a 'reality by proxy' and endless reproductions of fundamentally empty semantic shells and meanings. Fortunately, the exaggerated representation of the catastrophic accident in cyberspace, Conway argues (following François Debrix), means that any real cyber-terrorist attack that might occur is highly unlikely to live up to the simulated scenarios, and will thus not mobilise fear in a substantive way.

For Philippe Bonditti (Chapter 6), the reciprocal relationship between information networks and terrorism, which is also seen as networked, has led to a multilevel transformation of the US agencies of surveillance and control. As Bonditti argues, computer systems are becoming the crucial tool through which the state aims to protect territories and populations from networked terrorist cells. For this reason, cyberspace must be protected first, which establishes a hierarchical relation between the security of 'the homeland' and that of cyberspace, 'the security of the latter becoming the condition of security of the first'. Virtual networks become the ultimate critical infrastructure for securing society.

The information revolution as a defining moment is also addressed by James der Derian and Jesse Finkelstein in Chapter 4. As the information infrastructure emerges as an intermediary between physical assets and physical infrastructure, CIP is being viewed less as a problem of protecting physical resources, and is instead becoming an information problem. In other words, CIP is increasingly about producing and protecting knowledge – and the private sector has become crucial in refashioning the conception of CIP. In Der Derian and Finkelstein's view, the interweaving of the public and private sectors 'marks the difference between biopower in the post-disciplinary society and biopower in the control society'. Likewise, biopolitics have evolved to the point where it is not the body of the state that needs to be secured, 'but the conjoined body of public and private sector networks'. In the conclusion, Julian Reid expands this point even further, focusing on 'the deliberate targeting of the human life that inhabits critical infrastructures with increasingly invasive techniques of governance' that the provision of such infrastructure protection requires.

... and private sector rationale

In many countries, the provision of energy, communication, transport, financial services and healthcare have all been, or are being, privatised as previously protected markets are deregulated (Héretier 2001, 2002). However, while liberalisation has in many cases improved efficiency and productivity, it has also led to concerns regarding the accessibility, equality, reliability and affordability of services. In a non-liberalised economy, the state assumes the responsibility as well as the costs of guaranteeing functioning systems and services. Clearly, assigning responsibility for securing such systems and services is becoming a major issue in a liberalised global economy (Andersson and Malm 2006). In this light, and given the growing importance of information and knowledge that resides within the private sector, how is the state to protect something that, by definition, is beyond its domain of control? The answer is simple: by closely working with the private sector. It comes as no surprise, therefore, that the state seeks to integrate the private owners of critical infrastructure in CIP practices by means of so-called public–private partnerships and information-sharing initiatives (Suter 2007).

Once again, there is nothing new in the perception of the economy as being important for national security. As Collier and Lakoff point out, the complex interdependencies of modern economic systems were seen as their essential weakness as early as the 1930s. One defining moment in the history of CIP was when ACTS theorists came to see the US 'as a collection of critical targets whose destruction would paralyse the economic system'. However, this aspect has been reinforced with the advent of globalisation and information-based economies. More importantly, efforts to involve the private sector in national security measures have transformed the private sector into a security actor that is empowered vis-à-vis the rest of society, but is disciplined by the security policies of the state, as shown by Kristian Søby Kristensen in Chapter 3. He investigates new ways of creating security in an environment of collapsed borders after 11 September 2001 and argues that the traditionally sovereign act of making society secure has moved into the domestic space. 'Moving security into society requires engagement with the civilian and private actors of society', he writes, and shows how the interaction between these two actors is conceptualised. The concept of risk in the CIP discourse 'functions as an opener' that allows the government to engage in security policy based on domestic logic. However, collaboration between the public and the private sectors has never been easy, as Dunn Cavelty's analysis shows: discontent between the private sector and government is deeply rooted in continuing struggles over the definition of 'national security' in the domain of information security. In view of this circumstance, major efforts are undertaken to legitimise 'new' practices of security that seek to distribute responsibility for protecting critical infrastructures.

Breaking down borders, creating new spaces

Through the 'securitization of private actors' (Kristensen), the public/private distinction is effectively broken down (cf. Abrahamsen and Williams 2006; Leander 2006). But in fact, another binary distinction of long standing is demolished – that between inside and outside. In this area, Didier Bigo has published seminal work on the functional and geographical extension of internal security, the export of policing methods and the import of military operations in the national arena (Bigo 1994, 2000). But this distinction is affected in a rather peculiar way by CIP. As Kristensen points out, CIP and homeland security 'rearticulate the relationship between security and territory' by providing a way of providing (national) security *inside* sovereign space. In other words, through CIP, efforts are made to recreate the protective functions of borders inside society. We can therefore observe a double move: at the same time as border policies are exported to the outside, some forms of security policy equally move inside, into the territory of the state.

Elgin Brunner shows in Chapter 7 that the moving of security practices into domestic space is not only done with the help of the concept of 'risk', but also with the help of military language and logic: offensive measures are undertaken in the name of defence. As a consequence of the attacks on New York and Washington in 2001, the dichotomy of the safe 'inside' as opposed to the anarchic and dangerous 'outside' no longer applies: 'home is no longer a safe haven'. By constructing the threat as already being inside US territory, particular strategies for action and rationalities are legitimised. But rather than showing how the state wants to recreate a sense of security for the homeland (as Kristensen does), Brunner shows how the external realm is discursively used in order to push for certain measures at home, so that the homeland security discourse shortly after September 2001 leads to a 'semantic militarization of the domestic space' based on gendered principles. Conway also demonstrates that the active intertwining of home/abroad, safe/unsafe and the breaking down of inside/outside works as a mobilising device, arguing that the continued hyping of 'cyber-terrorism' in the media is also justified by 'separating the inside from the outside, the offline versus online, and the ' "real" or physical from the virtual or imagined'.

But, as seen above, CIP not only breaks down distinctions, it also creates new borders and spaces, such as 'zones of marginalisation'. Bonditti, whose analysis focuses on how security practices 'spatialise' the threat of terrorism by territorialisation, de-territorialisation and technologisation, sees the emergence of 'two different spatio-temporal imaginaries'. The first of these is governed by the geographical territory, in which borders work as lines of demarcation; the other one is governed by fluidity, as exemplified by cyberspace. But he also notices an almost schizophrenic tendency of US security professionals to both territorialise (through the concepts of 'rogue states' and 'terrorism') and de-territorialise ('cyber-terrorism') the threat of terrorism. The first can be called 'spatial fetishism', a tendency to reduce the units of analysis to territorially demarcated national states, a phenomenon that is elsewhere called 'the resilience of the sovereignty frame' (Walker 2006: 154–9). For many, the term 'homeland security' invokes the image of a secluded, delimited and thus ultimately defendable and securable place, where critical infrastructures make up the innermost layer, the core of the US homeland'.

The (im)materiality of CIP

This image of homeland security is painted with the help of CIP. What emerges is a specific kind of materiality, which is both an underlying condition for protection practices, but also reproduced through them. As we have pointed out before, an infrastructure is, in the first instance of its etymology, something that exists, and is also fundamentally on the 'inside'. In other words, we are looking at the practice of protecting physical and inanimate things. Bridges, storage facilities, streets or buildings, for instance, are objects that are easily identifiable (within Euclidian space) and that have a value for society that is usually undisputed. That they should be made safe makes perfect sense to everyone: infrastructure protection is therefore ultimately concerned with protecting property – and it is obviously legitimate for the state to protect its property.

We can even take this argument a step further and argue that cyberspace, too, is grounded in physical reality. Quite obviously, there would be no virtual realm without the physical infrastructures that facilitate its existence. As one observer argues, 'the channelling of information flows ... occurs within the framework of a "real" geography' (Suteanu 2005: 130) made up of servers, cables, computers, satellites, etc. Philosopher and psychoanalyst Slavoj Žizek even suggests that cyberspace realises the oxymoron of being actually virtual – that these technologies materialise virtuality (Žizek 1999). The protection of the critical information infrastructure – like the protection of knowledge – is also concerned with protecting the physical reality of the 'real geography' with the help of electromagnetic-pulse-proof rooms or backup storages in impenetrable mountain reservoirs, but also with the help of better locks on server rooms.

If the (core) rationality of CIP is associated with physical objects that exist in time and space, CIP practices give specific value to the inside, to things that are tangible. More than a metaphysical or legal expression of something that a state has, or is, CI – and CIP – is a concrete instantiation of these properties. CIP identifies, signifies and makes specific the sovereign territory of the state, and is thus a way of re-actualising and re-identifying the state. Seen this way, infrastructure emerges as an alternative to the image of Leviathan as postulated by Hobbes: instead of being made up of its citizens, the state may be regarded as consisting of the things inside its territory that make life there 'good'. Thus, the state consists of assets that are not directly identified with its citizens. Again, CIP, in the first place, sidesteps the traditional set of problems associated with security policy. Most importantly, there are no concerns about freedom/security tradeoffs, and no civil liberty issues are involved, which differentiates CIP from other better-investigated security strategies.

CIP thus seems to slip past Foucauldian bio-politics, and past the *Homo Sacer* of Giorgio Agamben (1999). CIP does not 'depend upon the invocation of a state of emergency' (Dillon 2003: 532), but is 'clean' and unproblematic. However, this ideal-type and utopian view of things is inevitably problematised, because there is no way of avoiding the intermingling with both flows and processes, with the truly virtual, and also with questions related to human subjects and the law. Even if cyberspace is assumed to have a material quality, the objects of protection in CIP include not only static infrastructures, but also various abstract things such as *services*, (information) *flows*, the *role* and *function* of infrastructures for society, and especially the *core values* that are delivered by the infrastructures. The physical pathways through which information is transmitted do matter, but 'the role of the participants in the game, their functional attributes, their position in the virtual context' (Suteanu 2005: 131) matter even more. While technologies may appear to accumulate information objectively and apolitically, the way in which that information is encoded, articulated and interpreted is always political. The protection of 'abstractions', such as 'the population' or 'knowledge' in the security domain becomes problematic rather quickly when considering surveillance programmes, the PATRIOT Act etc.

The implications of security strategies for liberty, citizenship, and the freedom of human subjects has been thoroughly investigated and criticised elsewhere. But CIP emerges as an intermediate entity: even in discussions about virtual aspects or flows and processes, there is always a connection to a place, to a space, to a space of protection. This book shows that homeland security and critical infrastructure protection practices are expressions as well as causes of the breakdown of the central political distinctions between inside/outside, public/private, civil/military and normal/exceptional. It shows that the traditional sovereign act of making society secure has moved into the domestic space, changing the practice of security. In other words, security is privatised while the private is securitised. In transcending the distinction between inside and outside and reconfiguring the conditions for the exercise of sovereign authority, CIP destabilises our relation to space, time and territory. Security is no longer a 'special' and extraordinary issue. This discourse is not primarily about threats and battles against an enemy, the focus of Part II of this volume, but is characterised almost more by an inward-looking narrative about vulnerability (Bigo 2006b: 89). This means that the traditional and normal conditions for day-to-day politics are intermingled with the exceptional dynamics of national security; and new forms of (in)security and protection emerge.

Note

1 We owe this point to Stephen Collier.

References

Abele-Wigert, I. and Dunn, M. (2006) *The International CIIP Handbook 2006: An Inventory of Protection Policies in 20 Countries and 6 International Organizations*, Vol. I, Zurich: Center for Security Studies.

Abrahamsen, R. and Williams, M.C. (2006) 'Privatisation, globalisation, and the politics of protection in South Africa', in Huysmans, J., Dobson, A. and Prokhovnik, R. (eds) *The Politics of Protection: Sites of Insecurity and Political Agency*, London: Routledge, pp. 34–47.

Ackerman, G., Blair, C., Bale, J., Hahn, G., DiLorenzo, E., Vadlamudi, S. and Lunsford, C. (2006) *The Jericho Option: Al-Qa'ida & Attacks On Critical Infrastructure*, San Jose: Lawrence Livermore National Laboratory. Online. Available at: www.llnl.gov/tid/lof/documents/pdf/337776.pdf (accessed 14 October 2007).

Agamben, G. (1999) *Homo Sacer: Sovereign Power and Bare Life*, Stanford: Stanford University Press.

—— (2002) 'Security and terror', *Theory and Event*, 5, 4. Online. Available at: muse.jhu.edu/journals/theory_and_event/v005/5.4agamben.html (accessed 14 October 2007).

Andersson, J.J. and Malm, A. (2006) 'Public–private partnerships and the challenge of critical infrastructure protection', in Dunn, M. and Mauer, V. (eds) *International CIIP Handbook 2006: Analyzing Issues, Challenges, and Prospects*, Vol. II, Zurich: Center for Security Studies, pp. 139–68.

Aradau, C. and van Munster, R. (2007) 'Governing terrorism through risk: taking precautions, (un)knowing the future', *European Journal of International Relations*, 13, 1: 89–115.

Auerswald, P., Branscomb, L.M., La Porte, T.M. and Michel-Kerjan, E. (eds) (2006) *Seeds of Disaster, Roots of Response: How Private Action Can Reduce Public Vulnerability*, Cambridge: Cambridge University Press.

Barry, A. (2001) *Political Machines: Governing a Technological Society*, London: Athlone.

Beck, U. (1992) *Risk Society*, London: Sage Publications.

—— (2002) 'The terrorist threat: world risk society revisited', *Theory, Culture and Society*, 19, 4: 39–55.

—— (2006) 'Living in the world risk society', Hobhouse Memorial Public Lecture delivered on 15 February 2006, London School of Economics. Online. Available at: www.lse.ac.uk/collections/sociology/pdf/Beck-LivingintheWorldRiskSociety-Feb2006.pdf (accessed 14 October 2007).

Bendrath, R. (2001) 'The cyberwar debate: perception and politics in US critical infrastructure protection', *Information & Security: An International Journal*, 7: 80–103.

Bigo, D. (1994) 'The European internal security field: stakes and rivalries in a newly developing area of police intervention', in Anderson, M. and den Boer, M. (eds) *Policing Across National Boundaries*, London: Pinter, pp. 161–73.

—— (1996) *Polices en réseaux. L'expérience européenne*, Paris: Presses de Sciences Po.

—— (2000) 'When two becomes one: internal and external securitisation in Europe', in Kelstrup, M. and Williams, M.C. (eds) *International Relations Theory and the Politics of European Integration: Power, Security and Community*, London: Routledge, pp. 171–205.

—— (2002) 'Security and immigration: toward a critique of the governmentality of unease', *Alternatives*, 27, 1: 63–92.

—— (2006a) 'At the limits of the liberal state: the answers to the terrorist threat', *republic*, 16 November 2006. Online. Available at: www.re-public.gr/en/?p=76 (accessed 14 October 2007).

—— (2006b) 'Protection: security, territory and population', in Huysmans, J., Dobson, A. and Prokhovnik, R. (eds) *The Politics of Protection. Sites of Insecurity and Political Agency*, London: Routledge, pp. 84–100.

C.A.S.E. Collective (2006) 'Critical approaches to security in Europe: a networked manifesto', *Security Dialogue*, 37, 4: 443–88.

Castel, R. (1991) 'From dangerousness to risk', in Burchell, G., Gordon, C. and Miller, P. (eds) *The Foucault Effect: Studies in Governmentality*, Hemel Hempstead: Harvester Wheatsheaf.

Dillon, M. (2003) 'Virtual security: a life science of (dis)order', *Millennium: Journal of International Studies*, 32, 3: 531–58.

Dreyfus, H.L. and Rabinow, P. (1982) *Michel Foucault: Beyond Structuralism and Hermeneutics*, Chicago: The University of Chicago Press.

Dunn Cavelty, M. (2008) *Cyber-Security and Threat Politics: US Efforts to Secure the Information Age*, London: Routledge.

Faber, P.R. (1997) 'Interwar US army aviation and the Air Corps Tactical School: incubators of American airpower', in Meilinger, P.S. (ed.) *The Paths of Heaven: The Evolution of Airpower Theory*, Maxwell Air Force Base: Air University Press, pp. 183–238.

Foucault, M. (1994a) 'Gouvernementalité', in Foucault, M., *Dits et Ecrits*, Vol. 1, Paris: Gallimard, pp. 813–28.

—— (1994b) *The Order of Things: An Archaeology of the Human Sciences*, New York: Vintage Books.

Héretier, A. (2001) 'Market integration and social cohesion: the politics of public services in European integration', *Journal of European Public Policy*, 8, 5: 825–52.

—— (2002) 'Public-interest services revisited', *Journal of European Public Policy*, 9, 6: 995–1019.

Huysmans, J. (2006) 'Agency and the politics of protection: implications for security studies', in Huysmans, J., Dobson, A. and Prokhovnik, R. (eds) *The Politics of Protection. Sites of Insecurity and Political Agency*, London: Routledge, pp. 1–18.

Huysmans, J., Dobson, A. and Prokhovnik, R. (eds) (2006) *The Politics of Protection. Sites of Insecurity and Political Agency*, London: Routledge.

Jabri, V. (2006) 'The limits of agency in times of emergency', in Huysmans, J., Dobson, A. and Prokhovnik, R. (eds) *The Politics of Protection. Sites of Insecurity and Political Agency*, London: Routledge, pp. 136–53.

Kingdon, J.W. (2003) *Agendas, Alternatives, and Public Policies*, 2nd edn, New York: Harper Collins College Publishers.

Leander, A. (2006) 'Privatizing the politics of protection: military companies and the definition of security concerns', in Huysmans, J., Dobson, A. and Prokhovnik, R. (eds) *The Politics of Protection. Sites of Insecurity and Political Agency*, London: Routledge, pp. 19–33.

McCarthy, J.A. (2007) 'Introduction: from protection to resilience: injecting "Moxie" into the infrastructure security continuum', in *Critical Thinking: Moving from Infrastructure Protection to Infrastructure Resilience*, CIP Program Discussion Paper Series, Washington, DC: George Mason University, pp. 1–8. Online. Available at: cipp.gmu.edu/archive/CIPP_Resilience_Series_Monograph.pdf (accessed 12 October 2007).

PCCIP (President's Commission on Critical Infrastructure Protection) (1997) *Critical Foundations: Protecting America's Infrastructures*, Washington, DC: US Government Printing Office.

Perrow, C. (1984) *Normal Accidents: Living with High-Risk Technologies*, New York: Basic Books.

Platt, R.H. (1995) 'Lifelines: an emergency management priority for the United States', *Disasters*, 15: 172–6.

Power, M. (2004) *The Risk Management of Everything: Rethinking the Politics of Uncertainty*, London: Demos.

Radvanovsky, B. (2006) *Critical Infrastructure: Homeland Security and Emergency Preparedness*, London: Taylor and Francis CRC Press.

Rasmussen, M.V. (2001) 'Reflexive security: NATO and international risk society', *Millennium: Journal of International Studies*, 30, 2: 285–309.

—— (2004) ' "It sounds like a riddle": Security Studies, the war on terror and risk', *Millennium: Journal of International Studies*, 33, 2: 381–95.

Suteanu, C. (2005) 'Complexity, science and the public: The geography of a new interpretation', *Theory, Culture & Society*, 22, 5: 113–40.

Suter, M. (2007) 'Improving information security in companies: how to meet the need for threat information', in Dunn Cavelty, M., Mauer, V. and Krishna-Hensel, S.-F. (eds) *Power and Security in the Information Age: Investigating the Role of the State in Cyberspace*, Aldershot: Ashgate, pp. 129–50.

Wæver, O. (1995) 'Securitization and desecuritization', in Lipschutz, R. (ed.) *On Security*, New York: Columbia University Press, pp. 46–86.

Walker, N. (2006) 'Sovereignty, international security and the regulation of armed conflict: the possibilities of political agency', in Huysmans, J., Dobson, A. and Prokhovnik, R. (eds) *The Politics of Protection. Sites of Insecurity and Political Agency*, London: Routledge, pp. 154–74.

Žizek, S. (1999) 'Cyberspace, or the unbearable closure of being', *Cinema and Psychoanalysis*, 6, 1: 96–121.

Part I

Origins, conceptions and the public–private rationale

1 The vulnerability of vital systems

How 'critical infrastructure' became a security problem

Stephen J. Collier and Andrew Lakoff

In recent years, 'critical infrastructure protection' (CIP) has emerged as an increasingly important framework for understanding and mitigating threats to security. Widespread discussion of critical infrastructure protection in the US began in 1996, when President Clinton formed a Commission on Critical Infrastructure Protection. The Commission's 1997 report, *Critical Foundations*, established the central premise of infrastructure protection efforts: that the economic prosperity, military strength, and political vitality of the US all depend on the continuous functioning of the nation's critical infrastructures. As the report stated: 'Reliable and secure infrastructures are ... the foundation for creating the wealth of our nation and our quality of life as a people'. Moreover, the report continued, 'certain of our infrastructures are so vital that their incapacity or destruction would have a debilitating impact on our defense and economic security' (President's Commission on Critical Infrastructure Protection 1997: 3).

In discussions such as these, we find a distinctive approach to identifying, assessing, and managing security threats. The characteristics of this approach include:

1 a concern with the critical systems upon which modern society, economy, and polity are seen to depend;
2 the identification of the vulnerabilities of these systems and of the threats that might exploit these vulnerabilities as matters of national security;
3 the effort to develop techniques to mitigate system vulnerabilities.

In this chapter, we ask: where did this distinctive way of understanding and intervening in security threats come from? How did 'critical infrastructure' come to be regarded as a national security problem? We argue that critical infrastructure protection is best understood as one response to a relatively new *problematization* of security. As Foucault writes, a new problematization occurs when something has 'happened to introduce uncertainty, a loss of familiarity; that loss, that uncertainty is the result of difficulties in our previous way of understanding, acting, relating' (Foucault 1994: 598). As we will show, at pivotal moments in the twentieth century, technological and political developments rendered existing security frameworks inadequate, leading experts to invent new ways of identifying and intervening in security threats. Specifically, what emerged was a way of understanding security threats as problems of *system vulnerability*. The task of protecting national security came to include ensuring the ongoing functioning of a number of vulnerable systems that were seen as vital to collective life.

The chapter follows a series of important moments in the twentieth-century history of system-vulnerability thinking: the interwar articulation of strategic bombing theory in Europe and the US, which focused on the 'vital targets' of an enemy's industrial system; the development of defence mobilization and emergency preparedness in the US during the Cold War as a means of defending the industrial system against a targeted nuclear attack; the emergence of all-hazards planning and 'total preparedness' as paradigms for response to disruptions of vital systems; and the widespread diffusion of formal models for assessing the vulnerability of vital systems (see Table 1).

The account culminates with discussions in the late 1970s and early 1980s among a relatively peripheral group of experts who were thinking about new challenges to national security. These experts had turned their attention to emerging threats – such as energy crises, major technological accidents, and ter-

Table 1 System-vulnerability thinking: 1918–present

	Key events	*Understanding of threat*	*Mitigation measures*
I. Total War and Strategic Bombing	Rise of airpower in the Second World War; Emergence of strategic bombing theory (post-Second World War); ACTS lectures (1930); AWPD-1 (1941)	Air warfare on vital targets/industrial web	Continental defence; early attack on enemy vital centres
II. Civil Defence	Strategic bombing survey; Soviet nuclear test (1949); Civil Defence Act (1950); Korean War	Soviet nuclear attack on critical target	Emergency response; vulnerability mapping; deterrence; second strike capacity
III. All-Hazards and System Vulnerability	1960s–1970s: rise of systems theory; emergency management (up to founding of FEMA in 1979)	All-hazards, nondeterrable, not predictable	Generalized contingency planning; generic system vulnerability analysis
IV. Systems Vulnerability as National Security Problem	Energy crisis and terrorism threat of 1970s through 9/11 and response	Vital systems vulnerability as national security problem	CIP

rorist attacks – that did not fit within the strategic framework of the Cold War. These new threats, they theorized, could not be deterred, and their probability could not be calculated. In this context, they began to draw together techniques and organizational forms developed earlier in the century to define a broad approach to mitigating the perceived vulnerabilities of the nation's critical systems. From their perspective, the ongoing functioning of such systems was a matter of national security. This approach to security problems was identified as central to post-Cold War national security in documents such as *Critical Foundations*, cited above.

In describing the history of how infrastructure became a security problem, our analytic stance proposes neither that security threats are self-evident facts in the world nor that they are simply imagined. Rather, in studying problematizations, we are interested in how a given object – in this case, vulnerable, vital systems – becomes an object of expert reflection and practice. As Foucault writes:

> A problematization does not mean the representation of a pre-existent object nor the creation through discourse of an object that did not exist. It is the ensemble of discursive and non-discursive practices that make something enter into the play of true and false and constitute it as an object of thought (whether in the form of moral reflection, scientific knowledge, political analysis, etc).
>
> (Foucault 1994: 670)

The central figures in this story are mostly unknown planners and technicians in military and civilian bureaucracies who, over the course of the twentieth century, constituted system vulnerability as an object of thought. For the most part, their work has stayed below the surface of political debates about security. But the basic principles and practices they crafted can now be found in initiatives such as CIP. Our goal in tracing this history is to make this increasingly central approach to security problems available for critical scrutiny by analysing its elements and pointing to the contingent historical events and processes that shaped its formation.

Total war, strategic bombing, and the vital target

In this section, we trace the genealogy of system-vulnerability thinking to the rise of total war and the development of strategic bombing theory. The term 'total war' refers to a shift in the very constitution of war. In the nineteenth and early twentieth centuries, wars among major European powers were no longer conceived or conducted as battles between sovereigns. Rather, wars were fought between entire nations and peoples, bringing military and industrial organization into ever closer contact. As Aron (1954: 88) put it in a classic statement, the rise of total war meant that 'The army industrializes itself, industry militarizes itself, the army absorbs the nation; the nation models itself on the army'. In this context, strategists increasingly recognized that military strength depended on the economic and social vitality of the nation, and on the state's capacity to mobilize and direct that vital strength to strategic ends.

The rise of total war meant that the traditional distinction between the military and civilian spheres – at least in wartime – was eroded in a variety of ways. In mobilizing for war, states vastly expanded their interventions in collective life. These interventions included controlling the production and distribution of industrial products critical to the conduct of war, particularly in sectors such as metallurgy and machine building, as well as the construction or regulation of electricity, transportation, and communication systems. These mobilization efforts had their counterpart in a new type of strategic thinking. Military strategists recognized that, just as their own economic facilities were critical to mobilization efforts, the vital nodes of enemy industrial systems could be exploited as vulnerabilities. An attack on these critical nodes could weaken or completely disable the opponent's war effort. Based on this line of reasoning, air power theorists developed a theory of air war – strategic bombing – in which such nodes constituted 'vital targets'.

Strategic bombing: enemy industrial facilities as targets

The Italian air power theorist Giulio Douhet is generally credited with first articulating the theory of strategic bombing. As Meilinger (1997: 8) points out, Douhet's approach was framed by the assumptions of total war. Douhet 'believed that wars were no longer fought between armies but between whole peoples. All the resources of a country – human, material, and psychological – would focus on the war effort'. The rise of total war had an important strategic consequence, according to Douhet: 'the *nation* would have to be exhausted before it would admit defeat'. The difficulty was that 'in an age of industrialization, when factories could produce the implements of war in a seemingly inexhaustible supply', the total defeat of a nation as a whole was an increasingly elusive goal, at least when pursued through conventional means (Meilinger 1997: 8). Douhet's contribution, in this context, was to provide a compelling (if not entirely prescient) vision of strategy in future wars.

Future warfare, Douhet argued, would not resemble the brutal defensive battles of attrition that had characterized the First World War. Rather, it would revolve around offensive actions, and particularly around offensive air power. The first task of strategic operations would be to achieve air dominance by disabling the enemy's air force and air defence. Once command of the air had been achieved, long-range bombers would be deployed to attack the nation itself. Specifically – and for our purposes, this is the crucial concept in Douhet's theory – these bombers would attack 'the most vital, most vulnerable, and least protected points of the enemy's territory' (cited in Meilinger 1997: 4–5). Douhet identified five vital centres of a modern nation that were the key targets of strategic bombing: industry, transportation infrastructure, communication nodes, government buildings, and 'the will of the people' (Meilinger 1997: 11).

Douhet did not substantially develop the theory of targeting beyond his general orientation to attack these vital targets. The most robust development of the theory of strategic bombing in the period between the wars took place in the US. In contrast to Douhet's strategy of using strategic bombing to break the will of an enemy people, the characteristic feature of the US school of strategic bombing was its emphasis on the critical target – the key node in an infrastructural or industrial system that, if destroyed, could bring an entire enemy war effort to a halt.

The most important centre for the development of US strategic bombing theory was the Air Corps Tactical School (ACTS). The ACTS also served as the training grounds for a large portion of the officer corps that applied the theory in developing US plans for air war in the Second World War (Faber 1997). ACTS theorists sought to identify the targets that were vital to a war effort, in particular through the development of the theory of the 'industrial web'. Billy Mitchell, an air power advocate whose ideas prefigured important dimensions of the industrial web theory, had written in 1927 that attacks on a few key nodes would mean that 'within a very short time the nation would have to capitulate or starve to death' (quoted in Greer 1985: 57). The writing and teaching of ACTS theorists echoed this approach. They argued that the complex interdependencies of modern economic systems were their essential weakness. ACTS graduate and, later, instructor Donald Wilson wrote in 1938 that the modern economy was composed of 'interrelated and entirely interdependent elements' (quoted in Faber 1997: 218). By attacking the 'essential arteries', or, in another pregnant metaphor, 'organic essentials' of a modern industrial structure, one could quickly – and economically – paralyse an enemy war effort (quoted in Faber 1997: 219).

One implication of this theory was that strategic bombing depended on detailed knowledge of the economic structure of the enemy nation. As ACTS theorist Muir S. Fairchild argued in 1938:

> Only by a careful analysis – by a painstaking investigation, will it be possible to select the line of action that will most efficiently and effectively accomplish our purpose, and provide the correct employment of the air force during war. It is a study for the economist – the statistician – the technical expert – rather than for the soldier.
>
> (quoted in Clodfelter 1997: 85)

The task of these experts would be to analyse the enemy's industrial systems – steel fabrication, transportation, finance, utilities, raw materials, and food supply – in order to select the 'relatively few objectives whose destruction would paralyze or neutralize' the enemy war effort (Greer 1985: 58).

This theory of strategic bombing profoundly influenced planning for the US air war in Germany and Japan during the Second World War. AWPD-1, the plan for air war against Germany, was based on intensive study of the German industrial system.[1] Beyond that, a clear line can be drawn from the theory of strategic bombing to nuclear targeting strategy after the war (Freedman 1983). But the present discussion follows a different line of development. Just as air power theorists began to conceptualize the vital economic nodes of an enemy nation as a target of attack, they turned their strategic attention to the problem of an attack on the US. Their approach to analysing the vital nodes of an enemy's industrial system, initially developed as an air war strategy, was now transposed to a new understanding of the US as a space of vital and vulnerable targets.

The defence of vital systems: the US as target

For air power theorists, the development of strategic bombing as an offensive theory of attack on enemy vital targets raised the possibility of a similar attack on the US. Air power theorists assumed that the strategic orientation of a possible future enemy would be similar to their own. As a consequence, they began to envision the US – and in particular the critical systems of the US – as a target in a future war.

Continental defence

In the interwar period, military strategists engaged in an intense debate over the nature of air power and its role in a broader military organization. The question was: was air power primarily of tactical importance – to be deployed in support of ground operations? Or was there a separate strategic mission for air power that would justify an independent air force, and the development of long-range bombers? In the US, this dispute unfolded in discussions of continental defence. The long-standing assumption of US strategists had been that the central feature of US continental security was the presence of large oceans separating the US from potential enemies. Thus, traditionally, the Navy was assumed to bear primary responsibility for continental defence. Proponents of air power in the interwar period argued that the advent of long-range aircraft had changed the strategic situation dramatically. As another major ACTS figure, Lt. Kenneth Walker, put it:

> The importance assigned to Air Forces by major European powers, among which may be potential enemies, leaves no doubt our future enemies will unquestionably rely greatly, if not primarily, upon the actions of their Air Forces to bring about the defeat of the United States.
>
> (quoted in Faber 1997: 193)

Against long-range bombing, a model of continental defence based on naval power would be quickly rendered obsolete.

In making their argument for a new, air power-based approach to continental defence, ACTS theorists envisioned an air attack on the US by a coalition of

European and Asian powers to illustrate the problems the military might face in a future war, given its current strategic assumptions and force structure. An ACTS theorist, Captain Robert Olds, laid out a scenario for a future war in testimony before the Federal Aviation Commission in 1935. One message of Olds' scenario (emphatically delivered with italics) concerned the necessity of creating an air force that was independent from other branches of the military. He argued that in a plausible war scenario, the existing air divisions of the US military – all of which were subordinated to the army and the Navy – would be drawn off to army or Navy engagements.

> A coalition of European and Asiatic powers have declared war on the United States. Superior naval forces … seek a decisive naval engagement in the vicinity of the Panama Canal…. Such actions draw the U.S. Navy to Caribbean waters, *with its naval aviation*. Land forces from the Orient, using Alaska as an advanced base, seek … to establish a salient in the area Washington, Oregon, California, and inland to about Salt Lake City, as a land base for further offensive operations in U.S. territory. The concentration of the U.S. Army *with its aviation*, in the western theater of operations would be mandatory to resist the land invasion.
>
> (quoted in Faber 1997: 194)

The implication of this scenario was that, given the existing force structure of the US military, the most vital targets of the US industrial system would be vulnerable to attack by the enemy air force.

> Simultaneously, the mass of the Allied [i.e., enemy] air forces have been flown, or shipped under submarine and patrol boat convoy, from Ireland to Newfoundland and are prepared to launch air attacks, from air bases in eastern Canada, against any targets of their choice in the vital industrial heart of our country.
>
> (quoted in Faber 1997: 194)[2]

The strategists at ACTS assumed that, following their own approach to strategic bombing, an enemy would attack the 'vital industrial heart' of the country. This meant, specifically, 'an industrial triangle extending from Portland, Maine, to the Chesapeake Bay to Chicago'. In this triangle lay '75% of all U.S. factories, almost all the nation's steelworks, most of its coal, and a number of major railroad centers, including New York, Washington, Pittsburgh, and Cleveland' (Faber 1997: 193). Attacks on the triangle would focus on rail lines, refineries, electric power, and water supply (Faber 1997: 194).[3] Following Douhet, the assumption was that an attack on these facilities might well destroy the American population's will to resist.

In anticipating such an attack, and in pressing their vision of the likely pattern of future war, ACTS theorists engaged in what was perhaps the first effort to catalogue the critical infrastructure of the US. In a lecture delivered in

1938 on 'National Economic Structure', Muir S. Fairchild declared that 'the key elements of American production were 11,842 "critical" factories, almost half of which were located in New York, Pennsylvania, and Massachusetts. The factories in those three states were "a concentrated objective which one might not suspect existed in this great continental industrialized nation of ours"'. Their destruction, or that of the transportation or power systems linking them, would 'apply tremendous pressure to our civilian population while at the same time seriously imparing [sic] our ability and capacity to wage war' (Faber 1997: 85).[4] The ACTS theorists, in short, were beginning to see the US as a collection of critical targets whose destruction would paralyse the economic system.

However, little action was taken in preparing the US for attack in the period before the Second World War. It was only during the course of the war, and really in its aftermath, that serious thought and organizational energy was given to the problem of organizing civil defence in the US.

Civil defence: mapping domestic vulnerability

Civil defence efforts in the US after the Second World War were, in a very direct sense, the defensive counterpart to strategic bombing doctrine, as the assumptions behind strategic bombing were transposed into a paradigm for the protection of vital systems against nuclear attack.[5] In the early years of the Cold War, planners developed techniques that made it possible to identify likely targets in the US, to model the effects of nuclear attack, and to anticipate requirements for emergency response.

The United States Strategic Bombing Survey, a massive effort to assess wartime bomb damage in Japan, Germany, and Britain, linked prewar strategic bombing and postwar civil defence.[6] The *Survey* took advantage of a rare opportunity to observe the effects of strategic bombing in practice. In doing so, it also necessarily assessed the civil defence efforts of these countries. One of the *Survey's* major findings was that civil defence had, in many cases, been effective in mitigating the effects of strategic bombing campaigns, and in maintaining an ongoing capacity to wage war in the face of attack. It concluded that a concerted national effort at civil defence was necessary, given the postwar threat the US faced from the Soviet Union. This finding led to a multi-year planning process that culminated in a 1950 report entitled *United States Civil Defense* (National Security Resources Board 1950)[7], which laid the groundwork for civil defence after the Second World War and for many aspects of emergency management in the US.

The approach articulated in *U.S. Civil Defense* was firmly situated in the assumptions of total war and of strategic bombing theory. 'The outcome of two world wars', it noted:

has been decided by the weight of American industrial production in support of a determined fighting force. In any future war, it is probable that an enemy would attempt at the outset to destroy or cripple the production capacity of the US and to carry direct attack against civilian communities to disrupt support of the war effort.

(National Security Resources Board 1950: 8)

U.S. Civil Defense assumed that a potential attacker would plan an attack based on the same principles of strategic bombing that were at the centre of US Air Force doctrine. As the report put it:

The considerations which determine profitable targets are understood by potential enemies as well as our own planners. Such considerations include total population, density of population, concentration of important industries, location of communication and transportation centers, location of critical military facilities, and location of civil governments.

(National Security Resources Board 1950: 8)

A number of questions followed from this argument: what would be the impact of attacks on these 'profitable targets'? What kinds of preparations would be appropriate to meeting this threat? And who should be responsible for organizing them? Elsewhere, we have argued that *U.S. Civil Defense* answered these questions by laying out a conceptual and organizational framework that we call 'distributed preparedness' (Collier and Lakoff 2008). Distributed preparedness delegated responsibility for civil defence functions to different levels of government, and to both public and private agencies, according to their competencies, capacities, and, of course, their spatial relationship to a likely target. Here, we focus on an aspect of distributed preparedness that is significant for the subsequent development of system-vulnerability thinking: a set of techniques we group together under the term 'vulnerability mapping'.

The purpose of vulnerability mapping was to gauge the potential impact of a nuclear attack on specific US cities, to assess how an attack would affect critical facilities, and to develop the capacities necessary to respond to such an attack. Vulnerability mapping enabled planners to understand cities and the systems that composed them as sites of potential future disaster and as complex landscapes of response. The basic technique was to create maps that visually juxtaposed an attack's projected impact against the existing infrastructure of an urban area. Using these maps, planners could assess weaknesses in existing response capacities and determine where resources would have to be directed in order to improve civil defence preparedness.[8]

The techniques used in vulnerability mapping deserve some elaboration. Three steps of the process are of particular relevance here:

1 cataloguing key elements of collective life in a target zone;
2 assessing the vulnerability of these elements to nuclear attack;
3 developing contingency plans that would mitigate these vulnerabilities.

In a first step, planners conducted an 'urban analysis' by creating an inventory of a given city's salient features for the purposes of civil defence. In various ways, these features could prove relevant to vulnerability in the event of an attack. Thus, for example, information about land use could help in estimating possible damage to urban facilities and in mapping the distribution of population – which was crucial to assessing likely casualties from a blast. Industrial plants were significant as possible targets of sabotage or bombing, and as important elements in police and fire-control planning.

The second step was to assess the vulnerability of the various elements in this inventory to a nuclear attack on a vital target. This assessment was conducted by juxtaposing a spatialized map of bomb damage over the existing features of a city. A transparent acetate overlay with regularly spaced concentric circles was placed on top of a map of industrial facilities and population concentrations. Each circle marked a zone in which the impact of a blast would be felt with a common intensity.[9] It was then possible to estimate the damage that a bomb of a given size, hitting a given point, would inflict on the significant features identified in the urban analysis.

The analysis of likely bomb damage made possible a third and final step, which was to use the estimate of the spatial distribution of physical damage and casualties over the existing structure of a city as a basis for emergency response plans. For example, information about damage to streets and highways, or general information about the spatial distribution of casualties, might be provided to engineering departments and 'incorporated in the general civil defense transportation map' (United States Federal Civil Defense Administration 1953: 53). Evacuation routes would thus be planned on the basis of the likely volume of evacuees over certain routes. What emerged from this analysis was a new understanding of cities in a nuclear age: as possible targets and as collections of vulnerable systems that had to be understood in their complex interrelationship.

A generalized approach to system vulnerability

The civil-defence approach to national vulnerability was initially designed for anticipating and organizing response to a Soviet nuclear attack. However, planners soon recognized that many of the assessment techniques and organizational forms developed to prepare for nuclear attack could also be useful in preparing for other types of threats, such as natural disasters. During the 1960s and early 1970s, techniques for analysing the vulnerability of systems and for planning response were generalized. This process was not the result of an overarching, explicit strategy, nor was it a central aspect of US national security thinking at the time. Rather, it took place through a series of autonomous developments that – as we show in the next section – were later brought together in a coherent framework as experts identified new problems of national security in the 1970s.

'Total preparedness' and all-hazards planning

As early as the 1948 Hopley Report, civil defence planners had suggested that the methods of nuclear attack preparedness could be extended to preparedness for other types of emergencies, such as natural disasters (Roberts 2006). In the 1950s and after, federal civil defence agencies were involved in disaster relief. For example, after Hurricane Diana struck the Northeast in 1955, the Federal Civil Defense Agency (FDCA) helped in coordinating assistance to states faced with disastrous flooding (Flemming 1957).

Nonetheless, for much of the Cold War period, preparations for disaster response remained secondary for federal civil defence agencies. Indeed, in the 1960s and early 1970s, federal officials were hesitant to allow state and local emergency management offices to use civil defence funds in preparation for natural disasters (Quarantelli 2000). Gradually, however, federal civil defence agencies began to accept the idea that organizing for nuclear attack and for natural disasters were complementary activities that drew on the same practices of vulnerability assessment and crisis management.

The practice of using civil defence resources for peacetime disasters was institutionalized by a 1976 amendment to the 1950 Federal Civil Defense Act. This shift was further advanced in the Defense Civil Preparedness Agency (DCPA) under President Carter.[10] The director of the DCPA co-authored a May 1977 statement summarizing discussions among federal, state, and local civil defence agencies, which acknowledged the legitimacy of using civil defence funds for natural disaster preparedness and defined a concept of 'total preparedness' that incorporated both civil defence measures and natural disaster preparedness: 'Local and State governments have the responsibility to provide preparedness for enemy attack as well as peacetime disasters. Therefore, DCPA's financial assistance to local and State governments may in the future be used to achieve *total preparedness against any risk*' (Joint Committee on Defense Production 1977: Appendix A, 38). All-hazards planning became official policy at the federal level with the establishment of the Federal Emergency Management Agency (FEMA) in 1979 (for a summary of key organizations in this story, see Figure 1).

The shift to 'total preparedness' can also be observed in the area of defence mobilization. During the Cold War mobilization that began in 1950, a series of governmental agencies had the task of ensuring that a productive and logistical network was in place to support a US war effort. In doing so, these agencies – some of which were part of civil defence programmes, some of which were in military branches – were also concerned about the condition of this production and distribution network after a nuclear attack. The Office of Defense Mobilization in the Executive Office of the President (1950–8) was one site for such preparedness planning.

As in emergency response, the organizations involved in defence mobilization – whose official task was to assure the nation's industrial capacity for war-fighting – were, nearly from their inception, also involved in planning for

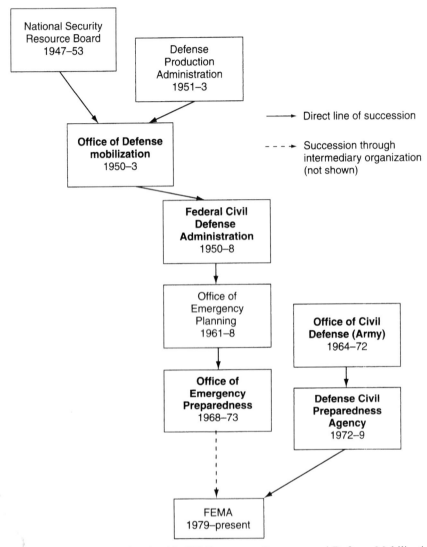

Figure 1 Organizations involved in US Emergency Response and Defense Mobilization (organizations mentioned in text indicated bold face).

other types of threat. For example, in the mid-1950s, the Office of Defense Mobilization explored the possibility of adapting its nuclear attack damage-assessment procedures to natural disasters. A devastating 1955 flood in California provided the occasion for one such experiment. However, as was the case with civilian emergency response in the 1950s, the main emphasis in defence mobilization remained on war readiness. Civil defence planners saw preparedness for natural disasters as an opportunity to test techniques and train personnel for the cataclysmic event of a nuclear war (Flemming 1957).

Over time, defence mobilization officials shifted toward a total preparedness approach. In part, they did so to convince the managers of private sector utilities – who were convinced of the need for natural disaster preparedness, but reluctant to engage in nuclear preparedness – to voluntarily implement safeguards against nuclear attack. For example, a 1970 manual for oil refineries published by the Interior Department and the Army Office of Civil Defense encouraged managers in charge of safety and reliability to plan not only for typical contingencies like fires or accidents, but to simultaneously prepare for a nuclear bomb blast. The argument from the manual was that the two forms of planning were complementary – and essential to national security in a broad sense.

> Since the petroleum industry including natural gas has the responsibility of supplying over 75% of the energy for our economy, the country must have petroleum processing facilities of adequate strength and management ready to cope with *all emergencies be they of natural origin or doings of mankind.*
> (Stephens 1970: v, emphasis added)

Civil defence planners thus developed a generic notion of 'emergency' that would enable them to take advantage both of local government capacities and private sector activities in the service of total preparedness.

System vulnerability and crisis management

The shift to total preparedness involved not only the kinds of institutional changes described above, but also a number of technical developments. Technicians involved in emergency planning used systems analysis to develop formal models of vulnerability. These models did not assess the impact of specific events, but rather analysed the *intrinsic vulnerability of systems* to disruptions of any kind. The use of such methods was part of the broad diffusion of operations research and systems analysis methods across US government bureaucracies during the 1960s (Jardini 2000; Amadae 2003; Light 2003).

An example of such efforts can be found in the sphere of defence mobilization – specifically, electricity sector preparedness. The Defense Electric Power Administration (DEPA) had been formed in the early 1950s as part of the broader remobilization that began with the onset of the Korean War. Like other defence mobilization agencies created at the time, its aims were both to assure adequate development of power resources for defence production and to prepare for dealing with the damage that production and transmission facilities would suffer in the event of a nuclear attack. In the early 1960s, this agency was calculating the likely effects of a nuclear blast largely by employing the techniques developed in early civil defence described above, which involved estimating the impact of a nuclear attack on a critical target. Toward the end of the 1960s, however, DEPA studies began to adopt formal techniques – such as linear programming – that changed the approach to vulnerability assessment. The shift was from the analysis of specific events to generic models of system vulnerability. As a group of experts in the field wrote in a 1975 report to the Defense Civil Preparedness Agency, 'vulnerability evaluations of electric power systems have progressed from detailed, specific analyses of particular systems reacting to a specific nuclear attack to general methods of evaluation using sophisticated modeling techniques' (Lambert and Minor 1973).

These techniques made it possible to assess the impact of a potential disruption not only on electrical production and distribution, but also on 'secondary' systems – industrial enterprises, for example. This progression was consistent with a shift to an all-hazards approach, but added a specific focus on the intrinsic vulnerability of systems, and a methodology for assessing the interdependencies among systems, to the toolkit. What was novel were the methods of technical analysis: whereas prewar 'industrial web' theorists had been concerned with interdependency and the effect of disruptions on interconnected structures, they did not have a quantitative method for analysing these interdependencies.

By the late 1960s, systems analysis was being employed in other areas of civil defence, such as the White House Office of Emergency Preparedness (OEP). The OEP was a successor to the Office of Defense Mobilization, but its purview was broader. Its mission was to ensure that the government would respond effectively to various types of emergency. The OEP was charged with coordinating response to multiple types of crisis over the course of the early 1970s, including the wage-price freeze of 1970, a threatened Penn Central Railway strike, and the Emergency Petroleum Allocation Act of 1973.

A department within OEP, called the Systems Evaluation Division (SED), was devoted to the formal analysis of critical systems – such as transportation, energy, and communication – as part of a broad vision of crisis management. A major figure in SED was Robert H. Kupperman, a specialist in operations research who had come to OEP from the Institute for Defense Analysis (IDA), a civilian think-tank that conducted technical research for the Defense Department. Kupperman would later participate in discussions about the formulation of critical infrastructure protection programmes in the US, such as the expert panel for *Critical Foundations*. In SED, he initially focused on producing a sophisticated mathematical analysis of the strategic implications of anti-ballistic missile systems (Kupperman and Smith 1972; Hiltz and Turoff 1978). In subsequent work, he applied the tools of systems analysis to the problem of system vulnerability. For example, he led a detailed analysis of the role conservation measures could play in averting an anticipated energy crisis – as well as the economic impact of such measures. This work analysed patterns of energy consumption in multiple sectors, including electricity, transportation, and industrial production.[11]

Through his work in SED, Kupperman became interested in the common structure of response to crisis situations. What was crucial across all of them, he argued, was the need to have crisis management techniques in place *before* the advent of the crisis. In this sense, his work was structurally similar to the all-hazards approach in emergency management. In a 1975 article on crisis management and computer-based communication, Kupperman and his co-authors pointed to characteristics shared by diverse types of crisis – including hurricanes, terrorism, and famine. The authors wrote that in order to adequately respond to such events, which were increasing in number and complexity, coherent systems of preparedness planning must already be in place: 'As we begin to recognize the complex problems that threaten every nation with disaster', Kupperman asked, 'can we continue to trust the ad hoc processes of instant reaction to muddle through?' (Kupperman *et al.* 1975).

System vulnerability as a national security problem

Up until the mid-1970s, these various initiatives in emergency management, civil defence, and defence mobilization were not organized around a single national security framework. Part of the reason was organizational dispersion: they were spread out among various agencies engaged in specific activities such as crisis management. It was also due to the peripheral status of civil defence thinking during the Cold War. Throughout most of the Cold War, civil defence was a fairly marginal aspect of national security debates, which were focused on strategies for deterring the Soviet threat. From the vantage of the dominant strategic paradigm – mutually assured destruction – civil defence was dangerously destabilizing, since it presumed that one could fight and win a nuclear war.[12]

Beginning around the mid-1970s, however, some security experts began to re-conceptualize the objects and aims of national security, particularly in response to events such as terrorist attacks and the energy crisis. They argued that these events presented new national security challenges – which could not be adequately approached within the Cold War strategic paradigm. In this context, one subgroup of experts sought to apply practices that had been developed in areas such as emergency management and defence mobilization to a novel set of threats.

Non-deterrable threats

In the 1970s, a subgroup of security thinkers with ties to civil defence – including Kupperman and his colleagues – became concerned with the rise of threats other than the Soviet Union. Events such as the 1972 Munich terrorist attacks, followed soon after by the Arab–Israeli War and the 1973 oil crisis, indicated to these thinkers that the nation's dependence on critical systems was a vulnerability that could be exploited by actors who lacked the military strength to directly challenge the US.

As we have seen, in OEP, Kupperman was concerned with anticipating and managing potential future energy crises. After the events of the early 1970s, he linked this concern to the problem of terrorism. He argued that terrorism was emerging as a strategic tool in low-intensity conflict – and that terrorists were likely to exploit vulnerabilities in the nation's critical systems (Kupperman *et al.* 1982: 463). This emphasis on the conjuncture of terrorism and the vulnerability of energy systems was shared by other civil defence-oriented security thinkers, such as Maynard M. Stephens, the author of the 1970 study on oil refineries cited above. In a 1979 volume on terrorism co-edited by Kupperman, Stephens wrote that 'the uninterrupted flow of natural gas is economically essential to the country' (Stephens 1979: 213). For this reason, he argued, 'segments of major natural-gas transmission lines should therefore stand out as attractive targets to the saboteur' (Stephens 1979: 213).

Such arguments followed the concern, first developed in strategic bombing theory with critical nodes of a production system that, if disrupted, could knock out an entire industrial web. There was a crucial difference, however. The threat now came not from an enemy's military attack, but from non-deterrable threats – terrorism, and 'threats without enemies' such as technological failures and natural disasters. In short, total preparedness was no longer viewed as an adjunct to the problem of confronting the Soviet Union. Rather, it was seen as a national security problem in its own right.

This elevation of systems vulnerability to the level of a national security concern had a certain political salience in the period, given the contemporary concern with problems such as energy and terrorism. For example, in 1977, the Joint Congressional Committee on Defense Production held hearings and published a two-part report on the nation's 'civil preparedness' programmes. The report was highly critical of the condition of the nation's emergency management plans. It recommended the centralization of federal preparedness efforts and a broadening of these efforts to include non-nuclear threats. The first volume of the report articulated, in now-familiar terms, two key aspects of the vital systems security framework: the dependence of contemporary society on complex technological systems, and the vulnerability of citizens to multiple types of threat. 'An increasingly complex, technology-dependent, industrial economy in the United States', the report argued, 'has made citizens more than ever vulnerable to the effects of disasters and emergencies over which they have little or no control and to which they cannot successfully respond as individuals' (Joint Committee on Defense Production 1977: 3). Moreover, the report noted 'increasing demands made on government by citizens' for protection against such threats'.[13]

In July 1977, soon after the Committee's *Civil Preparedness Review* was published, a major blackout occurred in New York City. The blackout, which was accompanied by extensive riots and looting, brought widespread attention to the frailty and vulnerability of the nation's electrical grid and other critical systems. The Defense Production Committee held hearings shortly after the blackout on the implications of the event for federal emergency preparedness. One conclusion was that these systems were vulnerable to a wide array of threats, ranging from technical accidents to natural hazards and terrorist attacks: 'Electric utilities therefore present a relatively compact and especially inviting set of targets for a saboteur, a terrorist or an attacker, as well as a lightning bolt' (Joint Committee on Defense Production 1977: 1f.). The problem of system vulnerability was projected onto the enemy's strategy, in a mirroring process that was similar to early civil defence.

At these hearings, the director of the Defense Logistics Agency testified about military efforts to protect key defence industries from attack. He noted that the scope of his agency's activity was limited to those industries that had a direct impact on defence needs. Considering the widespread impact of the New York City blackout on economic and social life, he suggested the need for a broader programme to secure critical facilities. This would begin with a cataloguing effort:

> It might be well if there were some sort of national list, if you please, of facilities that would be a key to our economic and societal well-being. Then at least, we would know what they are and whether or not the Federal Government would see fit to involve itself in providing for their security or would provide at least some advice on what these facilities could do for themselves.
>
> (Joint Committee on Defense Production 1977: 117)

What is significant in these recommendations is the proposal that the federal government should generalize its efforts to assure critical infrastructure, from a specific emphasis on those systems essential to military production to a broader concern with the vital systems essential to the economic and social well-being of the nation as a whole.

A mature paradigm

In 1984, the Center for Strategic and International Studies (CSIS) at Georgetown published a report, called *America's Hidden Vulnerabilities: Crisis Management in a Society of Networks* (Woolsey *et al.* 1984). The report was based on the work of a 'Panel on Crisis Management' chaired by Kupperman and R. James Woolsey. It can be seen as a fully articulated vision of system-vulnerability thinking as a distinctive approach to national security. Its producers were marginal to governmental policy at the time. However, this vision would come to the centre of policy discussions a decade later in the Clinton administration with the explicit articulation of 'critical infrastructure protection' as a national security problem.

The CSIS document synthesized the basic elements of system-vulnerability thinking whose development we have tracked so far: it identified the protection of vital systems as a question of national security; it argued that these systems were vulnerable to threats that could not be deterred, and whose risk could not be assessed through probabilistic analysis; it proposed a framework of preparedness that included a range of techniques for mitigating vulnerabilities, including ways of understanding systems (cataloguing, vulnerability assessment), measures to secure these systems; and plans for response to their disruption. But it went one step further, proposing that system vulnerability be seen as an autonomous problem of national security in a post-Cold War world, one that was distinct from the threat of foreign enemies. The elements of 'critical infrastructure protection' discussed at the outset of this chapter were now in place.

Security problem: the protection of vulnerable, vital systems

The report argued that the nation had become economically, technologically, and psychologically dependent on a number of 'highly complex service networks' for 'our daily well-being' (Woolsey *et al.* 1984: 4). It emphasized the risk to national security posed by the fragility and interdependency of these systems: 'We live in a civilization at risk, as much from the increasing fragility and brittleness of its technological fabric as from the more visible and apparently urgent threats from abroad'. The report enumerated the qualities of critical systems that made them both an efficient means of distribution and a source of vulnerability: they are made up of multiple nodes and are interconnected by links that facilitate the circulation of goods and information (Woolsey *et al.* 1984: 11). It was not in principle difficult to disrupt the operations of these networks, given their interdependence: 'denial of the essential resources – human, energy, and fiscal – that make networks function will quickly bring their operations to a halt'.

Threats to vital systems as national security problems

The disasters that threaten these systems, the report argued, were not regularly occurring events, such as those mitigated by insurance; nor were they rational enemies that could be managed through strategies such as diplomacy and deterrence. Rather, the threat consisted of low-probability, high-consequence events. These included terrorists or dissidents who had the capacity and intention to do harm. But other kinds of events, such as natural disasters or technological accidents, could also severely disrupt critical systems, according to the report. The potentially catastrophic effects of such events meant that they had to be planned for even if they were rare or improbable: 'This is an explosive combination that serious and responsible national leaders need to address, however low a probability one might reasonably assign to any particular network vulnerability being exploited at any one time' (Woolsey *et al.* 1984: 7).

Techniques for mitigating vulnerabilities: contingency planning, preparedness

Given that such events could not be predicted, or necessarily prevented, the emphasis in the report was on reducing the vulnerabilities of critical systems. Since these networks were interrelated and interdependent, the report argued, a comprehensive programme of protection must be developed. The report introduced a number of measures for ensuring the continued functioning of critical systems in the event of emergency, most of which had evolved over the years in emergency response and defence mobilization programmes: improving system resilience, building in redundancy, stockpiling spare parts, performing risk analysis as a means of prioritizing resource allocation, and running scenario-based exercises in order to test readiness. A final key element in the report's broad 'philosophy of crisis management' was the specification of responsibilities in the event of emergency – who would make preparations, who would declare a state of emergency, and who would be in charge during the actual emergency. While these recommendations were not directly implemented, the CSIS report is significant for our story in that it exemplifies the process through which systems vulnerability as a problem came to the centre of national security strategy.

Conclusion: vital systems security

In this chapter we have described the process through which a new way of defining and intervening in collective security problems emerged over the course of the twentieth century. Through this process, experts began to define a new class of threats to security: events that threatened the vital systems supporting collective life. In conclusion, we consider how this new way of approaching security problems relates to the notion of 'critical infrastructure protection' as it emerged in the last decade.

CIP as a concept and practice was first explicitly articulated in the 1990s. As Myriam Dunn Cavelty argues (Chapter 2, this volume), early CIP policy focused on cyber-infrastructures, responding to a growing concern regarding information security that had developed in the US government during the 1980s. Experts then expanded the concept to include the entire range of critical infrastructures on which economic and political life were seen to depend. After the attacks of September 11, CIP moved to the centre of domestic security doctrine. The story we have told in this chapter suggests that this development is not best understood as a process of the 'securitization' of a civilian sector. Rather, it would be better to say that in the 1980s and 1990s, a growing concern about information security found a technical vocabulary, a set of analytical tools, and practices of intervention in a long-standing mode of thinking about infrastructures as a security problem.

Although it has not been the focus of this chapter, it would certainly be possible to trace the lines of connection between the history we have recounted and the explicit articulation of critical infrastructure protection in the 1990s. Thus, for example, both Kupperman and Woolsey participated in an expert panel as part of a 1997 Institute for Defense Analysis (IDA) report to the President's Commission on Critical Infrastructure Protection (Institute for Defense Analysis 1997). Furthermore, a remarkable proportion of the support staff for the pivotal *Critical Foundations* report were officers in the Air Force (President's Commission on Critical Infrastructure Protection 1997: iv). More broadly, critical infrastructure protection has clear conceptual connections and institutional precursors going all the way back to strategic bombing theory. Seen against the background of the history of system-vulnerability thinking in the twentieth century, the underlying rationality of critical infrastructure protection is entirely familiar.

Notwithstanding these continuities, the emergence of CIP as an explicit area of government initiative does, we argue, mark an important development in the history of system-vulnerability thinking. For most of the twentieth century, the elements of system vulnerability we have described – 'vulnerability analysis', 'contingency planning', and so on – functioned as adjuncts to a paradigm of sovereign state security that was concerned with defence against foreign threats. As we have shown, in the interwar period and the Cold War, the rudiments of system-vulnerability thinking were developed as specific responses to the challenges posed by the threat of air war or Soviet nuclear attack. We might say that in these contexts system-vulnerability thinking – as a way of conceptualizing security problems and intervening in them – was circumscribed and limited by the exigencies of sovereign state security.

This situation began to change as the major existential threat of the postwar period – Soviet nuclear attack – faded, and new threats such as terrorism, technological failure, and energy crises came to be identified as central to national security. The identification of these threats introduced, in Foucault's language, an 'uncertainty' provoked by difficulties in 'previous way[s] of understanding, acting, relating'. It was unclear whether the questions and concepts of sovereign state security could be meaningfully applied to these new risks. In this context, techniques for understanding and managing system vulnerability were disarticulated from the specific demands of sovereign state security. The mitigation of system vulnerability came to be seen as an autonomous aim of security policy. In the process, national security came to be defined, at least in part, in terms of the security of vital systems (Collier and Lakoff 2006).

It is important to bear in mind that this new way of understanding security problems has not, thus far, produced stable organizational forms or modalities of intervention. For the moment, rather, what we observe is a profusion of plans, schemas, techniques, and organizational initiatives that respond to new kinds of perceived threats to collective security. Critical infrastructure protection is only one such response, and one whose actualization in bureaucratic arrangements, resource flows, and established regimes of security is just beginning to emerge.

Notes

1 The wartime bombing effort also led to the development of optimization techniques (in systems analysis and operations research) that, as we see below, were to prove important in formalizing understandings of system vulnerability in the 1960s and 1970s.

2 According to Greer (1985), this scenario of a European coalition combined with an Asian power was the common assumption used in US military planning before the Second World War.

3 This enumeration of likely targets within the 'industrial triangle' was laid out by Captain Harold Lee George, another major figure in ACTS, at the same hearings.

4 Fairchild's words, quoted by Faber (1997: 85), are in single quotation marks. ACTS theorists worked extensively with examples from the US for reasons other than a concern with continental defense. Extensive information about the industrial structure of other countries was not available, and taking examples that assumed bombing of potential future adversaries by the US military was considered provocative.

5 Civil defense was not the only response to this new awareness of the US as a target. A range of policies were taken to reduce the vulnerability of industries that would be

essential to war production, including the promotion of industrial dispersion, discussed in Galison (2001) and Light (2002), and programmes to assure that the US had enough redundant capacity to manage disruptions of industry due to strikes.

6 McMullen (2001) discusses the relationship of the *Strategic Bombing Survey* to the transformation in Air Force doctrine. Key figures from the ACTS, including Muir S. Fairchild, played central roles in the *Survey* (Faber 1997).

7 *U.S. Civil Defense* led to the 1951 Civil Defense Act – which in turn created the Federal Civil Defense Administration. Lee (2001: 60) argues that *U.S. Civil Defense* – referred to as 'The Blue Book' – served 'as the blueprint for structuring the Federal Civil Defense administration'. More broadly, the document laid out a new model that would subsequently be adopted in a range of other contexts for managing 'emergency' situations. For a review of the studies that led up to *USCD*, see Lee's chapter 'Careful studies and indecision'.

8 This discussion draws in particular on a document titled *Civil Defense Urban Analysis* (United States Federal Civil Defense Administration 1953).

9 Damage from the blast in each zone could be estimated using information from a document that had been prepared by the Atomic Energy Commission and the Department of Defense, called *The Effects of Atomic Weapons* (United States Department of Defense, Los Alamos Scientific Laboratory 1950). This document, based on data gathered in Hiroshima and Nagasaki, provided tables indicating blast damage from a nuclear strike at various distances from ground zero.

10 In testimony to the Joint Committee on Defense Production, the director of Civil Preparedness (who had been appointed in April 1977) noted:

> The previous Administration sought to limit civil defense support of State and local government to preparations for nuclear attack only. This position was rejected by the Congress in P.L. 94–361 and by this Administration under my recently announced policy of dual use preparedness.
>
> (Joint Committee on Defense Production 1977: 35)

11 This work is summarized by the head of the Office of Emergency Management, George A. Lincoln (Lincoln 1973).

12 Patrick Roberts writes that in 1970s, 'civil defense advocates tussled with proponents of mutually assured destruction, who believed that civil defense efforts were futile since the whole point of deterrence was to convince both sides that there could be no winner in a nuclear war' (Roberts 2006: 60).

13 The growth in the significance of the word preparedness, although little remarked, has resulted primarily from two factors: (1) the increasing vulnerability of a complex, highly interdependent industrial society, and (2) the increasing demands made on Government by citizens whose lives may be dramatically affected by a range of emergencies they are unable to prevent or control.

> (Joint Committee on Defense Production 1977: 3)

References

Amadae, S.M. (2003) *Rationalizing Capitalist Democracy: The Cold War Origins of Rational Choice Liberalism*, Chicago: University of Chicago Press.

Aron, R. (1954) *The Century of Total War*, Garden City: Doubleday.

Clodfelter, M.A. (1997) 'Molding airpower convictions: Development and legacy of William Mitchell's strategic thought', in Meilinger, P.S. (ed.) *The Paths of Heaven: The Evolution of Airpower Theory*, Maxwell Air Force Base: Air University Press, pp. 79–114.

Collier, S.J. and Lakoff, A. (2006) *Vital Systems Security*, ARC Working Paper no. 2, Berkeley: Anthropology of the Contemporary Research Collaboratory.

Collier, S.J. and Lakoff, A. (2008) 'Distributed preparedness: space, security and citizenship in the United States', *Environment and Planning D: Society and Space*, 26, 1: 7–28.

Faber, P.R. (1997) 'Interwar US army aviation and the Air Corps Tactical School: incubators of American airpower', in Meilinger, P.S. (ed.) *The Paths of Heaven: The Evolution of Airpower Theory*, Maxwell Air Force Base: Air University Press, pp. 183–238.

Flemming, A.S. (1957) 'The impact of disasters on readiness for war', *Annals of the American Academy of Political and Social Science*, 309: 65–70.

Foucault, M. (1994) *Dits et Ecrits, 1954–1988*, Paris: Gallimard.

Freedman, L. (1983) *The Evolution of Nuclear Strategy*, New York: St. Martin's Press.

Galison, P. (2001) 'War against the center', *Grey Room*, 4, Summer: 6–33.

Greer, T.H. (1985) *The Development of Air Doctrine in the Army Air Arm. 1917–1941*, Washington, DC: Office of Air Force History, U.S. Air Force.

Hiltz, S.R. and Turoff, M. (1978) *The Network Nation: Human Communication via Computer*, Reading: Addison-Wesley.

Institute for Defense Analysis (IDA) (1997) *National Strategies and Structures for Infrastructure Protection. Report to the President's Commission on Critical Infrastructure Protection*, Washington, DC: IDA. Online. Available at: permanent.access.gpo.gov/lps19700/NationalStrategiesStructures.pdf (accessed 16 October 2007).

Jardini, D.R. (2000) 'Out of the blue yonder: the transfer of systems thinking from the Pentagon to the great society, 1961–1965', in Hughes, A.C. and Hughes, T.P. (eds) *Systems, Experts, and Computers: The Systems Approach in Management and Engineering, World War II and After*, Cambridge: MIT Press.

Joint Committee on Defense Production (JCDP) (1977) *Civil Preparedness Review. Part I: Emergency Preparedness and Industrial Mobilization*, Washington, DC: US Government Printing Office.

Kupperman, R.H. and Smith, H.A. (1972) 'Strategies of mutual deterrence', *Science*, 176, 4030: 18–23.

Kupperman, R.H., van Opstal, D. and Williamson, D. (1982) 'Terror, the strategic tool: response and control', *Annals of the American Academy of Political and Social Science*, 463: 24–38.

Kupperman, R.H., Wilcox, R.H. and Smith, H.A. (1975) 'Crisis management: some opportunities', *Science*, 187: 229.

Lambert, B.K. and Minor, J.E. (1973) *Vulnerability of Regional Electric Power Systems to Nuclear Weapons Effect*, Washington, DC: Defense Electric Power Administration.

Lee, C.P. (2001) *An Exercise in Utility: Civil Defense from Hiroshima to the Cuban Missile Crisis*, doctoral thesis, St. Louis: St. Louis University.

Light, J.S. (2002) 'Urban security from warfare to welfare', *International Journal of Urban and Regional Research*, 26, 3: 607–13.

Light, J.S. (2003) *From Warfare to Welfare: Defense Intellectuals and Urban Problems in Cold War America*, Baltimore: The Johns Hopkins University Press.

Lincoln, G.A. (1973) 'Energy conservation', *Science*, 180, 4082: 155–62.

McMullen, J.K. (2001) *The United States Strategic Bombing Survey And Air Force Doctrine*, Maxwell Air Force Base: School Of Advanced Airpower Studies.

Meilinger, P.S. (1997) 'Giulio Douhet and the origins of airpower theory', in Meilinger, P.S. (ed.) *The Paths of Heaven: The Evolution of Airpower Theory*, Maxwell Air Force Base: Air University Press.

National Security Resources Board (1950) *United States Civil Defense*, Washington, DC: US Government Printing Office.

President's Commission on Critical Infrastructure Protection (PCCIP) (1997) *Critical Foundations: Protecting America's Infrastructures*, Washington, DC: US Government Printing Office.

Quarantelli, E.L. (2000) *Disaster Planning, Emergency Management and Civil Protection: The Historical Development of Organized Efforts to Plan for and Respond to Disasters*, Preliminary paper 301, Newark: Disaster Research Center, University of Delaware.

Roberts, P.S. (2006) 'FEMA and the prospects for reputation-based autonomy', *Studies in American Political Development*, 20, Spring: 57–87.

Stephens, M.M. (1970) *Minimizing Damage to Refineries from Nuclear Attack, Natural, and Other Disasters. A Handbook Reviewing Potential Hazards that Could Affect Petroleum Refinery Operations in Times of War and Peace*, Washington, DC: Office of Oil and Gas Department of the Interior.

Stephens, M.M. (1979) 'Industries: a potential target of terrorists', in Kupperman, R.H. and Trent, D.M. (eds) *Terrorism: Threat, Reality, Response*, Stanford: Hoover Institution Press Stanford University.

United States Department of Defense, Los Alamos Scientific Laboratory (1950) *The Effects of Atomic Weapons*, Washington, DC: US Government Printing Office.

United States Federal Civil Defense Administration (1953) *Civil Defense Urban Analysis*, Washington, DC: US Government Printing Office.

Woolsey, R.J., Wilcox, R.H. and Garrity, P.J. (1984) *America's Hidden Vulnerabilities: Crisis Management in a Society of Networks. A Report of the Panel on Crisis Management of the CSIS Science and Technology Committee*, Washington, DC: Center for Strategic and International Studies, Georgetown University.

2 Like a phoenix from the ashes

The reinvention of critical infrastructure protection as distributed security

Myriam Dunn Cavelty

Critical infrastructures are usually defined as systems or assets so vital to a country that any extended incapacity or destruction of such systems would have a debilitating impact on security, the economy, national public health or safety, or any combination of the above. For this reason, critical infrastructure protection (CIP) is currently seen as essential part of national security in numerous countries around the world (Abele-Wigert and Dunn 2006). Protection concepts for strategically important infrastructures and objects are nothing new, as Collier and Lakoff aptly show in this volume: these concepts have, in some form or another, been part of national defence planning for decades (Collier and Lakoff, Chapter 1, this volume; see also Moteff *et al.* 2002). For most of the time, however, the possibility of infrastructure discontinuity caused by attacks or other disruptions played a relatively minor role in the security debate vis-à-vis concerns such as deterrence – only to gain new impetus around the mid-1990s, when CIP as a concept and a practice was first explicitly articulated and became the subject of many hearings, policy documents and study groups.

The main reason for the strengthening of concepts for the protection of vital infrastructures, this chapter argues, has been the information revolution. The relatively recent technological development in information processing and communication technologies and the rapid global dispersion of these technologies – most significantly, the ascent of 'the Internet', a global decentralised communication network of computer networks – is seen, by many observers, to cause an ongoing transformation of all aspects of life through saturation with information and communication technologies (Dunn Cavelty and Brunner 2007). But most importantly, it adds a variety of novel aspects to the older debate about vital system security: first of all, the dependency of modern industrialised societies on a wide variety of national and international information infrastructures, characterised by highly interdependent software-based control systems, is characterised as a new development bringing about novel vulnerabilities. Furthermore, the information revolution is seen to empower new malicious actors, including states as well as non-state actors, and to enhance the overall capability of these actors to do harm by inexpensive, ever more sophisticated, rapidly proliferating, easy-to-use tools in cyberspace. In other words, when 'cyber-threats' were discursively interlinked with the older concept of vital system security in the mid-1990s, the specific form of thinking about security and protection in terms of vulnerable systems arose like a phoenix from the ashes and was elevated, under the new name of CIP, to a high status on the security political agenda. The attacks on New York and Washington of 11 September 2001 only further increased the awareness of vulnerabilities and the need to protect critical infrastructures in the context of terrorism. Afterwards, the term 'CIP' as one of the main pillars of the US homeland security efforts almost became a shorthand expression for domestic security in general.

By focusing on the reinvention of vital systems security in connection with the information revolution, this chapter traces the current conceptualisation of CIP back to the 1980s, starting around the time immediately following the period discussed in the conclusion of Lakoff and Collier's contribution. In particular, this chapter looks at the topic of CIP from the perspective of threat frames. Threat frames are interpretive schemas about what counts as threat or risk, how to respond to this threat, and who or what is responsible for it (see also Eriksson and Noreen 2002; Eriksson 2001a, 2001b). Threat frames are, on the one hand, tools used in the struggle for discursive hegemony and, on the other, indicators for how certain security issues are conceptualised and argued in terms of causes, consequences and solutions.

After first discussing the idea of threat framing in relation to discursive hegemony in more detail, this chapter will explore how CIP is expressed by US security policy elites in terms of threat frames and analyse the consequences of this conceptualisation for security practices. The documents used in this chapter are mainly official government publications and reports. They contain distilled threat frames that are filtered and sedimented so as to be indicative of the dominant discourse of the security elite. The analysis follows a chronological order: first, it focuses on how cyber-threats, defined as the malicious use of information and communication technologies either as a target or as a tool by a wide range of malevolent actors, were firmly established as a national security threat in the 1980s to produce a fairly restricted threat frame, mainly concerned with classified information and government networks. Second, it shows how the two issues of cyber-threats and critical infrastructures were interlinked, paying special attention to the role of the US military in the process, and how the issue was thus turned into a topic of society-threatening import. Third, the chapter focuses on the threat frames established in the 1997 Presidential Commission on Critical Infrastructure Protection (PCCIP) report, a clear culmination point in the more recent CIP history, and how the idea of 'distributed security' was solidified. Fourth, it looks at threat frames in the most recent conceptualisation of CIP under the heading of homeland security. In conclusion, this chapter shows how threat frames are used in the political discourse to legitimise 'new' practices of security that seek to distribute responsibility for protecting critical infrastructures. This notion of 'distributed security' closely follows the rationale of risk management and is intended as a response to a changing threat environment in which the government sees itself as being unable to provide the required level of security on its own.

Threat framing and discourse hegemony

Within the state, there are various positions of authority from which security issues can be voiced; this multiplicity of positions leads to struggles between competing discourses, the goal of each group in the game being to establish a dominant discourse pattern (Boekle *et al.* 2000, 2001; Townson 1992). In order to convince others that they are acting appropriately, the participants of the discourse seek to be argumentatively persuasive. The goal is to control the attachment of meaning to specific terms and therefore to control the discourse, in other words, to obtain discourse hegemony through 'linguistic dominance'. Foreign policy research has shown that discourse participants have better prospects of being convincing when they refer to an already existing discourse formation (Joerißen and Stahl 2003). This practice, which is called 'referencing', seeks to establish linkages with existing terms, which have, in a general discourse, positive connotations such as morality, responsibility, and others. In addition, 'naming', that is, establishing new terms in a discourse such as for example the term 'cyber-terrorism', and 'signifying', that is, being able to dominate a particular discourse and to act as an authoritative source for the 'true' meaning of certain terms, assist in the struggle to gain discourse hegemony (Townson 1992: 25–33). The resulting dominant discourse concurs most closely with common experiences and other indicators of 'truth' and will seem legitimate. It creates (and is created by) a 'common sense' with which a large section of the population concurs, and thus reduces the possibility for societal resistance against particular state actions but, at the same time, also imposes limits on state action.

Social contests for the legitimate definition of reality – the struggle for discursive hegemony – are held by way of different categories, expressed in cognitive frames (see, for example, Lakoff and Johnson 1980; Snow and Benford 1988, 1992). Frames are rooted in and constituted by group-based social interaction and can be defined as the 'underlying structures of belief, perception, and appreciation' through which subsequent interpretation is filtered (Rein and Schön 1994: 23). The activity of framing, whether done actively or passively, thus refers to the selection of certain aspects of an issue in order to cue a specific response (Ryan 1991: 59). Competing frames arise out of the political situation and are expressions of ongoing discursive struggles about different conceptualisations of an issue. The frames of the winning discourse create 'conditions of possibility' (Campbell 1998: 13) and successfully institutionalise the practices that are constitutive for the dominant discourse.

The key driving force behind security policy is the identification and designation of issues that threaten 'the nation'. This articulation of threats is a way to establish the difference between the 'self' and the 'other', a fundamental practice in the ever-continuing construction of national identity (Campbell 1998: 9; Weldes *et al.* 1999: 10). Furthermore, as posited by securitisation theory, government officials and experts use certain phrases and also certain types of stories to make their claim for urgency in the security domain (Wæver 1995). If this security speech act follows the 'grammar of security', i.e. if it constructs a plot containing an existential threat and a point of no return (Buzan *et al.* 1998: 32), the issue under discussion has a better chance of being included in the security agenda. Therefore, when it comes to national security issues, reference is made to terms and concepts that have negative connotations and create fear, anxiety and hostile images.

In the following chapters, three types of (interlinked) frames as outlined by Snow and Benford are identified (1988: 199–202) in order to identify what or who is constructed as threat or risk and how the conditions of possibility are created to respond to this threat. The first type of framing is *diagnostic* framing, which is about defining a problem and assigning blame for the problem to an agent or agencies. This amounts to the designation of two parameters known from securitisation theory: the threat subject – that which threatens; and the referent object – that which is threatened (Buzan *et al.* 1998: 32). The second type is *prognostic* framing, which concerns the proposition of solutions, as well as specific strategies, tactics and objectives by which these solutions may be achieved. The third type of framing is *motivational* framing, in order to 'rally the troops behind the cause' or express a 'call for action'.

The foreign intelligence threat and the encryption debate

As the 1970s gave way to the 1980s, the merger of telecommunications with computers – the basis of the current information revolution – meant that everybody with a computer at home became theoretically able to make use of the slowly emerging computer networks. The introduction of the personal computer created a rapid rise in tech-savvy users, many of whom would dial into bulletin board systems with a modem and download or disseminate information on how to tinker with technology. Together with this emerging cyber-counter-culture, the notion of cyber-crime was born. During this period, the amount of attention given to computer and communications security issues grew incrementally in response to highly publicised events such as politically motivated attacks, computer viruses and penetrations of networked computer systems for criminal purposes (cf. Bequai 1986; Parker 1983). Such events served as indicators of truth in the discourse and shaped it by defining legitimate practices and threat frames.

The dominant topic was cyber-crime. But even though it was called *crime*, the issue was by referencing linked to the topic of espionage and thus elevated to the level of urgency required for an issue to become a national security topic. Mainly by referring to a couple of well-publicised incidents, some of which involved data theft by foreign individuals (Stoll 1989), computer intrusions were successfully framed at an early stage as a national security issue. The Reagan administration's major concern in the domain was the prevention of what it viewed as damaging disclosures of classified information as well as the acquisition of 'sensitive but unclassified' information. The discourse was dominated by two closely connected strands: the first one framed the issue as a growing problem of computer crime, which culminated in the Computer Abuse Act of

1984/86, a piece of legislation defining legitimate punitive practices in the field of computer security until the passage of the Uniting and Strengthening America by Providing Appropriate Tools Required to Intercept and Obstruct Terrorism (USA PATRIOT) Act of 2001. The second strand focused on the protection of federal agencies' computer data from espionage, a debate that was interlinked with an ongoing debate on encryption technology. This led to the Computer Security Act of 1987, which spelled out responsibilities in the area of computer security.

Among the policy documents of the time,[1] one of the first threat frames can be found in the National Security Decision Directive Number 145 (NSDD 145) on 'National policy on telecommunications and automated information systems security', issued on 17 September 1984. The document describes the fusion between telecommunications and computers, a development that is seen to bring opportunities as well as dangers. The threat subject ranges from foreign nations to terrorists to criminals, with a clear emphasis on 'foreign exploitation' (Reagan 1984: § 1). As part of motivational framing, it is pointed out that the technology to exploit these electronic systems is *widespread* and is used *extensively*. In addition, this document must be read in the context of new legislation and regulations aimed at increasing government secrecy and tightening government control over the flow of public information. While this move was justified by reference to the hostile (foreign) intelligence threat stemming from the Soviet intelligence services and 'their surrogate services among the Soviet-bloc countries' (Reagan 1985: § 4), it was not justified by the far more widespread problem stemming from domestic hackers and underage youths who made the news because they easily managed to gain access to multimillion-dollar computer systems (Elmer-Dewitt 1983; Covert 1983).

The document then specifically addresses the problem as relating to the US government. The focus is on 'classified national security information', the integrity of which is presented as a national security issue (Reagan 1984: § 2). It is also stated that 'security', understood in this context as information security, is a vital element of the operational effectiveness of the national security activities of the government and of military combat-readiness, thus making the national-security connotation even more explicit. In this diagnostic threat frame, the referent object is limited to government systems and some business systems carrying critical information, as well as classified material more generally, and does not yet encompass society-threatening aspects of cyber-threats. The reason for this is simple: the technological substructure at the time still lacked the quality of a mass phenomenon that it would acquire once computer networks turned into a pivotal element of modern society, so that any such reasoning would have been outside the 'truth horizon' of the time.

Similar diagnostic threat frames can be found in other documents.[2] While the diagnostic threat frame and its wide listing of possible actors with a focus on foreign exploitation was not contested, there was rather a lot of controversy concerning the prognostic threat frame. In fact, NSDD 145 became a culmination point in the raging conflict between the academic and government cryptography communities. At the time, academic research in cryptography had achieved several major breakthroughs, and the National Security Agency (NSA) was starting to lose control over this technology (Diffie and Hellman 1976; Dam and Lin 1996). With NSDD 145, the NSA was authorised to undertake a 'comprehensive and coordinated' approach to 'protect the government's telecommunications and automated information systems' that 'process and communicate classified national security information and other sensitive information concerning the vital interests of the United States' (Reagan 1984). NSDD 145 also permitted the NSA to control the dissemination of government, government-derived, and even non-government information that might adversely affect national security. On 29 October 1986, National Security Adviser John Poindexter expanded the NSA's information security role even further when he signed the document 'National telecommunications and information systems security policy (NTISSP) No. 2' (text in Office of Technology Assessment 1987: Appendix B). In this document, 'sensitive' information was to include not just unclassified information that would 'adversely affect national security' if acquired by hostile nations, but any unclassified information that might affect any 'other Federal Government interests', a definition so broad it could have been applied to almost any kind of information (Knezo 2003).

In this way, the NSA was assigned responsibilities that fell outside of the scope of its traditional foreign eavesdropping and military and diplomatic communications security roles, a practice legitimised by

1 the construction of the foreign intelligence threat as a pressing and urgent national security matter;
2 phrases such as 'information, even if unclassified in isolation, often can reveal highly classified and other sensitive information when taken in aggregate' or 'other sensitive information' (see above), which tried to redefine the boundaries between national security information and non-national security information;
3 attempts to construct cyber-security as an issue concerning both the government and the private sector, depicting 'offering assistance in the protection of certain private sector information' as a key national responsibility (Reagan 1984: § 4).

This development gave rise to considerable concern within the private sector and in Congress as well as academic circles, especially since the NSA quickly began to exercise its newfound authority. In the face of this, the Computer Security Act of 1987 was introduced. The Act and the activity after the revision of NSDD 145 (resulting in NSD 42) progressively restricted the main focus of the NSA's activities to the protection of defence systems, and the NSA was forced to scale back its interaction with commercial organisations (Electronic Privacy Information Center 1998). However, these struggles over 'signifying' and 'naming' terms in the domain of information security have continued over the years, accompanied by efforts to establish the truth about terms such as 'national security systems', information considered 'sensitive but unclassified', and others.

The struggle was (and is) mainly related to the meaning of 'national security' and about the continued securitisation of cryptology. This particular struggle is a textbook case of a securitisation move that was thwarted: the argument that national security and economic security had become one and the same, and that therefore, the protection of economic information also fell under the purview of the national government, was not accepted. Many of the fundamental advances in personal computing and networking during the 1970s and 1980s were made by people influenced by the technological optimism of the new left, best expressed in Marshall McLuhan's predictions that new technology would have an intrinsically empowering effect on individuals (McLuhan 1964). The emergence of the so-called 'Californian Ideology' mirrored their passionate belief in electronic direct democracy, in which everyone would be able to express their opinions without fear of censorship (cf. Barlow 1994, 1996). This was so fundamentally opposed to what the US security establishment wanted to establish as 'truth' that various exponents of this counter-culture began to forcefully react by promoting their own ideas of reality.

In other words, the controversy over cryptology involved two completely different conceptions of security, and the applicability of related initiatives went beyond the close-knit security community to include exponents of the private sector and academia. The debate basically centred on the question of whether 'security' meant the security of US society as a whole, or whether it only referred to the security of individual users or technical systems, and should therefore be handled by authorities other than national security bodies. As such, the issue discussed here is exemplary for the difficulties inherent in the national security community's relationship with the private sector: an issue neither forgotten nor ever solved.

Interlinking cyber-threats and critical infrastructures

In the late 1980s, documents started to appear that made a clear link between cyber-threats and critical infrastructures (cf. Computer Science and Telecommunications Board 1989). The initiative came from the Department of Defense (DoD), which was in a strong position to interlink the two strands. Information technology had been firmly coupled with national security since at least the Second World War, and specifically so in the wake of the more general debate in the Cold War about technological innovation and warfare (Hinsley and Stripp 2001; Hables Gray 1997). Furthermore, concrete ideas of information warfare date back at least to the 1970s, when it was argued that communications and information support networks were sufficiently linked and cross-dependent to be inviting targets (Rona 1976). Also, as Collier and Lakoff point out in Chapter 1, thinking about vulnerabilities and critical targets had become a well-established part of US air power theorists' culture during the Cold War.

At the beginning of the 1990s, the advantages of the use and dissemination of

ICT that had fuelled the revolution in military affairs (Metz 2000; Rattray 2001), were no longer seen only as a great opportunity providing the country with an 'information edge' (Nye and Owens 1996), but were also perceived as constituting an over-proportional vulnerability vis-à-vis a plethora of malicious actors. In clear continuation from vital system thinking, there was a widespread fear that those likely to fail against the American war machine might instead plan to bring the US to its knees by striking vital points at home (Berkowitz 1997) – these points being fundamental to the national security and the essential functioning of industrialised societies as a whole, and not necessarily to the military in particular (Bendrath 2001). Even though this kind of fear was not completely new, it is not surprising that 'asymmetry' and asymmetric tactics – the intention to circumvent an opponent's advantage in capabilities by avoiding his strengths and exploiting his weaknesses (Kolet 2001) – came to dominate the national security debate in the 1990s. It can be seen as part of the DoD's struggle to come to grasp with the post-Cold War security environment and redefine its foes and tasks. Simply put, since the global distribution of power was unbalanced, it followed that asymmetric strategies would be a natural evolution (Blank 2003; Metz and Johnson 2001: 2). The US as the only remaining superpower was pre-destined to become the prime target of asymmetric warfare.

The information revolution helped to shape this perception. In particular, experiences gained during the 1991 Gulf War, when information warfare concepts were first used, made clear the benefits of the 'information differential' provided by the information systems employed (Campen 1992; Eriksson 1999), but it was also the Gulf War that gave rise to fears about the downside of this development, mainly through experiences with the threat of data intrusion as perpetrated by hacker attacks against 34 Department of Defense computer sites during the conflict (Devost 1995; GAO 1996). In the aftermath, global information networks were established, making it much easier to attack the US asymmetrically, as such an attack no longer required big, specialised weapons systems or an army: borders, already porous in many ways in the real world, were non-existent in cyberspace. Subsequently, it was established in various reports and publications that the information revolution had made the US asymmetrically vulnerable, due to the disappearance of borders and the dependence of military forces on vulnerable civilian infrastructures. At a later stage, a number of computer intrusions, such as the 'Rome Lab incident' in 1994 (AFIWC 1995; GAO 1996) or Solar Sunrise and Moonlight Maze in 1998 demonstrated how a small group of hackers could easily and quickly take control of defence networks.[3] Even more significant were exercises such as 'The Day After' in 1996, or 'Eligible Receiver' in 1997 (Molander *et al.* 1996; Anderson and Hearn 1996; Hamre 2003). The exercises were designed to assess the plausibility of information warfare scenarios and to help define key issues to be addressed in this area. Perhaps most importantly, the link between cyber-threats and infrastructures was already built into the exercise scenarios. Therefore, they naturally demonstrated that US critical infrastructure presented a set of attractive strategic targets for opponents possessing information warfare capabilities. The fears already harboured by experts were thus sub-stantiated.

An exemplary threat frame linking cyber-aspects with vital systems can be found in an influential and much cited report published in 1991. The report, with the title 'Computers at risk: safe computing in the information age', was the outcome of a request from the Defense Advanced Research Projects Agency (DARPA) to address the security and trustworthiness of US computing and communications systems as a reaction to the Morris Worm, the first computer worm. It began with the following observation:

> We are at risk. Increasingly, America depends on computers. They control power delivery, communications, aviation, and financial services. They are used to store vital information, from medical records to business plans to criminal records.... The modern thief can steal more with a computer than with a gun. Tomorrow's terrorist may be able to do more damage with a keyboard than with a bomb.
>
> (National Academy of Sciences 1991: 7)

The threat subject in this document encompasses thieves, terrorists and, less explicitly, nation states, as encapsulated in the phrase 'international nature of military and intelligence threats' (National Academy of Sciences 1991: 8). The report states that the 'the concentration of information and economic activity in computer systems makes those systems an attractive target to hostile entities' (National Academy of Sciences 1991: 8). Furthermore, the report very clearly links information technology to society as a whole: as computer systems become more prevalent, sophisticated, embedded in physical processes, and intercon-nected, it argues, society becomes more vulnerable to poor system design, acci-dents that disable systems and attacks on computer systems (National Academy of Sciences 1991: 1). The report speaks of 'potential disasters that can cause economic and even human losses' if nothing is done (National Academy of Sci-ences 1991: 2). The new aspect in this reasoning is the link it makes to other so-called 'infrastructures' (National Academy of Sciences 1991: 2), its focus on complexity and interconnections between elements of the infrastructure, and the establishment of the whole of society as referent object.

Furthermore, we find a strong motivational frame: the trends that the report identifies suggest to the authors that whatever trust may have been justified in the past will not be justified in the future 'unless action is taken now' (National Academy of Sciences 1991: 11). Basically, it is argued that society has reached a 'discontinuity', and that what lies ahead is new terrain that requires new think-ing, and quickly, because in 'this period of rapid change, significant damage can occur if one waits to develop a countermeasure until after an attack is manifest' (National Academy of Sciences 1991: 11). This urgency is also due to the fact that the threat is bigger and growing, due to the proliferation of computer systems into ever more applications, especially applications involving network-ing; the changing nature of the technology base; the increase in computer system expertise among the general public, which increases the potential for system abuse; the increasingly global environment for business and research; and the global reach and interconnection of computer networks, which multiply system vulnerabilities (National Academy of Sciences 1991: 1).

Various other military reports and studies from the early 1990s list the same broad range of adversaries and refer to the whole nation as being endangered due to its dependence on the information infrastructure (Defense Science Board 1994; Defense Science Board 1996). Again, it is not the diagnostic threat frame that is disputed, but the prognostic one. A report called 'Information warfare – defense (IW-D)' can serve as an example for this ongoing struggle for more influence in the domain (Defense Science Board 1996). In trying to carve out a position for the DoD to take on an active role in the civil sector, the report states: 'We should not forget that information warfare is a form of warfare, not a crime or an act of terror' (Defense Science Board 1996: Exhibit 3-1). To defend the DoD and critical non-governmental systems against information warfare activities, the report recommends new legal authorisation that would allow 'DoD, law enforcement, and intelligence agencies to conduct efficient, coordinated monitoring of attacks on the critical civilian information infrastructure' (Defense Science Board 1996: 6-30).

While such military documents were influential in shaping threat perceptions and in bringing the issue of cyber-threats to the attention of a broad audience, they did not establish the winning threat frame. Apart from the distribution of resources – based on the Computer Fraud and Abuse Act of 1986, the FBI had set up a special Computer Crime Squad in the early 1990s and occupied the strongest position within government – legal norms as 'truth indicators' prevented a more important role for the armed forces in the protection of critical infrastructures. As one report notes: 'the Defense Department is legally prohibited from taking action beyond identification of a cyber-attacker on its own initiative, even though the ability of the United States to defend itself against external threats is compromised by attacks on its C4I infrastructure' (Computer Science and Telecommunications Board 1999: 176).

While a substantial role of the military in CIP was not feasible, these documents started a trend of great importance: at this point in time, the rationale of risk management emerges as a significant feature in military documents. One prominent example is a report of the Joint Security Commission called *Redefining Security*. The commission was tasked with developing a new approach to security that would assure cost-effective security measures in times of shrinking defence budgets (Joint Security Commission 1994). This general study on security after the end of the Cold War not only features a strong focus on information systems, but it also argues that 'the new paradigm' brought about by new kinds of threats that are 'diffuse, multifaceted, dynamic' requires 'a risk management approach that considers actual threats, inherent vulnerabilities, and the availability and costs of countermeasures as the underlying basis for making security decisions' (Joint Security Commission 1994: iv). This attitude marks the beginning of the 'managerial security story' (Aradau 2001), a notion that is linked to non-deterrable threats that provide insurmountable challenges for the state. Such threats and their characteristics imply that complete risk avoidance is no longer possible. This necessitates a shift in strategy from retaliation and deterrence to prevention and preparedness. At the heart of this thinking lies the idea of 'distributed security': a kind of security that is provided in cooperation with various stakeholders who are not necessarily considered key actors in the security domain.

Public–private partnerships as instances of distributed security

This kind of reasoning took root in the domain of CIP after the Oklahoma City bombing in April 1995. The attack on the Alfred P. Murrah Federal Building provided a different indicator of truth for the entire discourse: it solidified fears by demonstrating that scenarios that had previously been contemplated had become reality. The attack on a seemingly insignificant federal building was able to set off a chain reaction due to interdependencies, so that a set of processes controlled from that building were also lost (Critical Infrastructure Protection Oral History Project 2005). One direct outcome of the Oklahoma City bombing was Presidential Decision Directive 39 (PDD-39), which directed Attorney General Janet Reno to 'chair a Cabinet Committee to review the vulnerability to terrorism of government facilities in the United States and critical national infrastructure' (Clinton 1995). The review, which was completed in early February 1996, noted that it was necessary 'to address both traditional "physical" attacks (e.g. bombings) and electronic, "cyber" attacks on the infrastructures (e.g., an attack on a computer or communications system)' in light of the breadth of critical infrastructures and the multiplicity of sources and forms of attack (Reno 1996). The report also called for a 'full-time Task Force' to address the issue. Subsequently, President Bill Clinton set up the Presidential Commission on Critical Infrastructure Protection (PCCIP), chaired by Robert T. Marsh, a former air force general, to recommend a national strategy for protecting and assuring the integrity of critical infrastructures from physical and cyber-threats. The PCCIP report, presented in October 1997, established threat frames that were solidified by Presidential Decision Directives 62 and 63 in May 1998 (Clinton 1998a, 1998b) and a more elaborate version of the same document, the *National Plan for Information Systems Protection*, in January 2000 (Clinton 2000).

The PCCIP noted that potential adversaries included a very broad range of actors 'from recreational hackers to terrorists to national teams of information warfare specialists' (PCCIP 1997: 15). On the side of the threat subject, the threat is thus, once again, constructed as stemming from a very broad range of actors. Harmful attacks can be done by anyone with a computer connected to the Internet, and for purposes ranging from juvenile hacking to organised crime to political activism to strategic warfare. Thus, the new enemy can neither be clearly identified nor associated with a particular state, and the image of the enemy is more faceless and less clearly foreign than in earlier documents, paying tribute to the kind of threat image that had become widespread after the Cold War. Even though the report also lists natural disasters, component failures and human negligence among the threats, most of its content focuses on malicious attacks, the 'least predictable threat to the infrastructure' (PCCIP 1997: A-4). This tendency to 'actorise' a threat, even one that is strongly linked to technical and system failure, seems to be a hallmark of security discourse. This practice links threats to actors, even though they originate to an equal degree in structural conditions such as power outages, floods, epidemics and similar phenomena (Sundelius 1983; Eriksson 2001b: 11f.; Buzan *et al.* 1998: 44).

This can be very clearly seen in the case of the Year 2000 problem, which became an issue in US policy circles starting in around 1997. Although the problem arose from the anticipated technical failure in the information infrastructure, the issue was also linked to potentially malicious human agency in congressional hearings: it was believed that because many people, such as the technicians who updated computers to make them 'Y2K-safe', had been given access to programmes as well as the authority to modify them and place them in service, there was a considerable threat from an insider or foreign contractors (cf. PCCIP 1997: 12; Tenet 1999). Apparently, the spectre of failures or accidents did not convey enough urgency, so that the problem was again linked to an 'enemy' problem. Or, as one analyst noticed in 1999: 'If your system goes down, it is a lot more interesting to say it was the work of a foreign government rather than admit it was due to an American teenage "script-kiddy" tinkering with a badly written CGI script' (Ingles-le Noble 1999).

On the referent object side, it was established that 'the nation is so dependent on our infrastructures that we must view them through a national security lens' (PCCIP 1997: vii). Furthermore, critical infrastructures are 'the foundations of our prosperity, enablers of our defense, and the vanguard of our future. They empower every element of our society. There is no more urgent priority than assuring the security, continuity, and availability of our critical infrastructures' (PCCIP 1997: vii). The dependence of society on the information and communication infrastructure on the one hand, and ever-more complex interdependencies between infrastructures on the other, were established as creating a new dimension of vulnerability, 'which, when combined with an emerging constellation of threats, poses unprecedented national risk' (PCCIP 1997: ix).

Again and again, the PCCIP stresses the evaporation of boundaries and the high degree of interdependency between single infrastructure elements, which creates overwhelming complexity, conveying a sense of powerlessness vis-à-vis technology. This powerlessness seems exacerbated by several business trends within the infrastructures: extensive use of information automation; deregulation and restructuring; physical consolidation; globalisation; and adoption of a 'just-in-time' operational tempo (PCCIP 1997: Appendix A). Technological development is depicted as a force out of control, and the combination of technology and complexity conveys a sense of unmanageability. An overall pessimistic perspective concerning accidents and the limited possibilities of preventing them and coping with them resonates in much of the cyber-threats debate (Perrow 1984). Furthermore, the dynamic interaction of complex systems is believed to overtax the human ability to articulate and evaluate the problem. This discourse is built on a general distrust towards computer technology, which feeds on the fear of the unknown. Technology, including information technology, is feared because it is seen as complex, abstract and arcane in its impact on individuals. Because computers do things that used to be done by humans, there is a notion of technology being out of control that is even strengthened by the increase in connectivity that the information revolution brings (see Conway, Chapter 5, this volume; Pollitt 1997).

A sense of great urgency is created through the almost constant allusion to concepts of discontinuity and newness. The headings of the first three chapters read: 'acting now to protect the future', 'the new geography', 'new vulnerabilities, shared threats' (PCCIP 1997: 3, 7, 11). The threat, with a strong focus on the cyber-dimension, is presented as being so 'new' that old defences become utterly useless, and new ways of thinking and new ways of protecting become indispensable. Such a departure from past experiences calls for 'new thinking' (PCCIP 1997: vii, x). The not-so-new thinking that the report presents is a renewed attempt to get the private sector to cooperate. More urgently than before, the report seeks to convince the business community that the interdependent nature of infrastructures creates a shared risk environment and that managing that risk will require close cooperation between the public and the private sector. This is done by an appeal to responsibility: 'Because the infrastructures are mainly privately owned and operated, we concluded that critical infrastructure assurance is a shared responsibility of the public and private sectors' (PCCIP 1997: i). The responsibility must be shared, because the threats are shared: 'the line separating threats that apply only to the private sector from those associated with traditional national security concerns must give way to a concept of shared threats' (PCCIP 1997: 20, especially Figure 4). These shared threats are terrorism, industrial espionage and organised crime. The appeal to the self-interest of owners and operators of critical infrastructures argues that they are on the frontlines of security efforts, as they are the ones most vulnerable to cyber-attacks (PCCIP 1997: 20).

Thus, the distinction between the private and public spheres of action is dissolved. It is implied that national defence is no longer the exclusive preserve of government, and economic security is no longer just about business. The private sector must focus on protecting itself against the tools of disruption, and should be encouraged to perform a periodic 'quantitative risk-assessment process' (PCCIP 1997: 69), a process that corporations are already very familiar with. In addition, the report advocates a strategy of cooperative 'information-sharing'. Mutual win-win situations are to be created by exchanging information that the other party does not have: 'government can help by collecting and disseminating information about all the tools that can do harm. Owners and operators can help by informing government when new tools or techniques are detected' (PCCIP 1997: 20). In other words, the government flags the proprietary information it requires about potentially hostile groups and nation states and which it intends to acquire through its intelligence services, while the private sector is to give up technological knowledge that the public sector does not have. The approach of the PCCIP report is therefore to firmly establish the idea of 'distributed security', an idea that follows the rationale of the risk management paradigm: the problem owner is no longer only the military or the state; responsibility is distributed.

Homeland security and the resurgence of the physical

When George W. Bush came into office in 2001, CIP had lost some of its drive, and the implementation of Clinton's *National Strategy* progressed more slowly than many had expected (GAO 2001). In addition, Congress had withheld funding for many of the initiatives proposed by the Executive Branch to implement elements of Clinton's *National Plan*. Also, it seems that the incoming Bush administration was generally less interested in the topic of cyber-threats than its predecessors. For example, in his first National Security Presidential Decision (NSPD 1), promulgated on 5 March 2001, President Bush also emphasised that national security also depends on America's ability to prosper in the global economy. In sharp contrast to his predecessor, however, who had always equated the information revolution with economic prosperity, the president did not mention cyber-security or the information infrastructure once (Bush 2001c).

The very physical aspect of the 11 September 2001 attacks, combined with an administration that was less interested in matters related to cyberspace, led to a shift in the overall focus of CIP after September 2001 (Moteff 2003: 3). As one staff member of the President's Critical Infrastructure Protection Board expressed in an interview:

> We were very shocked in the federal government that the attack didn't come from cyberspace ... Based on what we knew at the time, the most likely scenario was an attack from cyberspace, not airliners slamming into buildings ... We had spent a lot of time preparing for a cyber attack, not a physical attack.
>
> (Poulsen 2003)

This 'shock' is the product of 'the extent to which present dangers are constructed through the simulation of future fears', as Der Derian and Finkelstein write in this volume (Chapter 4), referring to Baudrillard's notion of hyperreality. Cyber-exercises like the ones mentioned above and general threat projections had produced a very distinct future reality. When reality struck, it turned out to be rather different. Thus, when securing the nation's critical infrastructure became a vital component of a post-9/11 homeland security strategy, it was accompanied by a new focus on strengthening physical aspects in the existing critical infrastructure policy (Bush 2001a, 2001b). Even though cyber-threats remained on the agenda of decision-makers, the phenomenon got less attention as a threat to CIP in the post-9/11 world, causing many critics to voice their disapproval over the degree of attention devoted to the cyber-dimension (cf. Mark 2004; Verton 2004). This change is also plainly visible in the 2002 *National Security Strategy*; while there had been a strong commitment to cyber-threats and information aspects of power in the previous six national security strategies (Kuehl 2000), the 2002 edition does not use the prefix 'cyber-' even once (Bush 2002).

With the establishment of the Department of Homeland Security, the overall organisational framework of CIP in the US was also restructured. This step, praised as a step towards pulling down the artificial walls between institutions that deal with internal and others that deal with external threats, had been previously legitimised by countless arguments to the effect that the boundaries between 'inside' and 'outside' had been dissolved in the 'new threat environment'. CIP became one of six 'critical mission areas' to reduce vulnerability for 'the homeland', and previously established structures and agencies were integrated or abandoned. CIP was thus completely absorbed into a concept representing 'a new triad of prevention, protection, and response' (Hart and Rudman 2001: 5f.; also DHS 2004: 3). In September 2002, the President's Critical Infrastructure Protection Board released a draft version of its *National Strategy to Secure Cyberspace* for public comment, which described a general strategic overview, specific recommendations and policies, and the rationale for these actions. After a public vetting process that signalled that cyberspace security was still viewed as a public–private partnership, the final version appeared in February 2003 (Bush 2003a). It was closely followed by a *National Strategy for the Physical Protection of Critical Infrastructures and Key Assets* (Bush 2003b), once again clearly showing that critical infrastructure protection was no longer shorthand for cyber-security. The cornerstone of both documents, again, is the implementation of a public–private partnership (Bush 2003a: ix; 2003b: 17).

On the surface, the threat frames established by the PCCIP report remained in place after 9/11. However, at least initially, the threat subject was narrowed down to the specific enemy image of Muslim terrorism, while the main focus in public hearings was on the possibility of terrorists using cyber-means for attacks (Bendrath *et al.* 2007; Conway, Chapter 5, this volume). As in so many other areas, this was sufficient legitimisation to usher in some radical changes: the USA PATRIOT Act, which entered into force on 26 October 2001, contains some of the most substantial changes to US federal cyber-crime laws since the last major revisions of 1996 and amended the Computer Fraud and Abuse Act in several controversial areas. The granularity of what was to be understood as part of the referent object also changed. In his Executive Order of 8 October 2001, George W. Bush expanded the sectors included among critical infrastructures to encompass nuclear material, agriculture and 'special events' of 'national significance' (Bush 2001a: sec. e, § 4). This was followed by other documents that added the chemical industry, postal services and shipping to the list (Bush 2002: 31). When the concept of criticality, and accordingly the notion of what is to be secured, is expanded from interconnected physical networks to include everything with emotional significance, almost everything becomes an infrastructure, and everything is potentially critical: even a minor event of little apparent significance can potentially trigger largely unpredictable cascading effects throughout a large number of sectors. This not only creates great challenges for any protection policy, but also an even greater sense of vulnerability and urgency. Like before, the dilemma is resolved by arguing in favour of the idea of distributed security: first, the federal government argues that there is a great and urgent need for securing the critical infrastructure on which everything depends. Second, it argues that it cannot achieve this by itself. Third, it tries to give away responsibility and, as Kristensen shows in this volume (Chapter 3), does so by encouraging the tools and the rationale of risk management.

Despite this, CIP seems never to have been a priority for the Bush administration. For one thing, it has become bogged down in the details of implementing its own twin strategies, and continues to draw criticism for including thousands of assets in the so-called National Asset Database, which, as of January 2006, contained over 77,000 entries (Moteff 2006, 2007: 25), of which it appears that many have more local than national importance. More importantly, however, despite the rhetoric of how important the protection of critical infrastructures is for the nation, the pursuit of security through attacks on foreign enemies seems much preferred over the often 'nitty gritty' details of preparedness and response, so that distributed security seems an even more attractive option. To argue again and again that complete risk avoidance is not possible is a failsafe way to ensure that in case of an incident, blame does not hit the top echelons of decision-making as hard as might otherwise be the case.

Conclusion: (national) security through distributed responsibility

This chapter has approached the topic of critical infrastructure protection by looking at how threat frames – diagnostic, prognostic and motivational ones – are employed in the struggle for discursive hegemony by US security elites, specifically focusing on how these frames are used to create the sense of urgency necessary to establish a topic as a national security issue. This is mainly done by 'referencing', by linking topics to concepts that are already established as national security issues. For example, cyber-crime was interlinked with foreign intrusion and espionage to elevate it to a national security issue. Then, the resulting threat 'package' was linked to critical infrastructures and terrorism. In this way, the old idea of vital system security was firmly hoisted onto the security political agenda in a new form.

Practices such as referencing, but also naming and signifying, are aimed at legitimising the discourse: in the case of CIP, 'cyber-incidents', or the state of the technological substructure more generally, are specific 'truth indicators' that are used as examples for insinuating that something awful is about to happen, but that also limit what is discursively possible. Changing technological features are therefore partly responsible for change in the discourse, since they bring about a change in the 'truth horizon'. For example, technological development and changes in the referent object are closely interlinked: at first, the threatened elements consisted mainly of government networks and the classified information residing in it. Later, critical infrastructures were conceptualised as constituting the heart of society, with a specific focus on the cyber-dimension. That was possible because computer networks had become a pivotal element of modern society. Finally, the attacks of 11 September 2001 highlighted the fact that terrorists could cause enormous damage by attacking critical infrastructures directly and physically, and not just through the cyber-infrastructure. In this way, the truth horizon was transformed, allowing the previously very dominant cyber-dimension to be downscaled.

When focusing on the threat subject in the diagnostic threat frame, it can be seen that from the beginning, cyber-attacks were constructed as stemming from a very broad range of actors. This broadening of the threat frame to encompass a wider range of potential adversaries underscores a perspective of vulnerability, uncertainty and insecurity. A danger is constructed that emanates from an enemy who is located outside of the US, both in geographical and in moral terms. This picture of a dangerous 'other' reinforces the idea of the nation as a collective self. The use of phrases such as 'our computers' or 'our infrastructures' amplifies this effect. Different focal points were used for different purposes: framed as a foreign intelligence threat, the threat subject is used to argue in favour of allocating more responsibility to the NSA. Later, a more faceless 'malicious actor' that has easy access to information networks is used to create the image of the shared threats as shared responsibility. More recently, a focus on terrorists that are able to employ the information infrastructure for their purposes is used to underscore arguments in favour of changing laws.

Motivational framing became a feature of threat frames in the 1990s, when the threat was more clearly attributed to new and poorly understood vulnerabilities. During this period, everything was represented as being new: the actors, the threats, the way society works, the technology, etc. All this newness is used to create a sense of great urgency, because old ways are no longer sufficient to counter the looming threat. Naturally, these new threats demand a new logic of security, which manifests itself in the prognostic threat frame in the shape of new counter-measures. After some intergovernmental turf battles as to who was to be in charge, CIP was established as an issue in the realm of civil defence, emergency management and preparedness.

It is argued that because absolute security is not possible, it is technically and economically impossible to design and protect the infrastructure to withstand any and all disruptions, intrusions or attacks. The logical consequence is that one has to manage the existing risks. Due to the nature of what is to be secured, policies are predicated on the concept of sharing responsibility with private actors – quite a challenge considering that the government and private industry had been at odds for some time with regard to the regulation of computer products, security issues and the use of encryption technologies. Calls for cooperation with the private sector could only be legitimised on the basis of a convincing argument to the effect that the interests of the national security apparatus and the private sector were one and the same. Therefore, many arguments can be found that try to fuse the two realms of economy and security, as well as the private and the public sectors.

Through such threat frames, a security paradigm based on the idea of distributed security through distributed responsibility is argued into existence. The maintenance of 'business continuity' for an individual, corporate or local actor is treated as being essentially equivalent to security efforts in terms of national or even international security in the realm of CIP and homeland security. Suddenly, grey zones of security become possible: security is no longer inherently binary – meaning that either one is secure, or one is not – but the future state of being secure is continually approached through risk management, creating a sense of security that never fully exists, but is always becoming, like the technological substructure on which critical infrastructures rest. This conceptualisation is both highly convenient and highly legitimate. It has contributed to the fact that CIP has risen like phoenix from the ashes, and is likely here to stay as a key concept expressing the insecurity of modern societies, non-deterrable threats, and a world in which government see themselves unable 'to go it alone'.

Notes

1 EO 12356 of 1982, named 'National Security Information', prescribed a uniform system for classifying, declassifying and safeguarding national security information (Reagan 1982). National Security Decision Directives: NSDD 19 on the 'Protection of Classified National Security Council and Intelligence Information', NSDD 196 on 'Counterintelligence/Countermeasure Implementations Task Force', and NSDD 197 on 'Reporting Hostile Contacts and Security Awareness', NSDD 84 on 'Safeguarding National Security Information'.
2 Such as National Security Directive (NSD) 42, entitled 'National Policy for the Security of National Security Telecommunications and Information Systems', Computer Crime and Abuse Act in 1984 and 1986, and others.
3 *1994, Rome Lab incident*: during March and April 1994, more than 150 Internet intrusions were carried out on the computers of the Rome Laboratory, a research centre reporting to the Air Research and Development Command specialising in electronic systems. During the investigations and the observations of the two hackers by Computer Crime Investigators, one of the hackers accessed a system in Korea, obtained all data stored on the Korean Atomic Research Institute system, and deposited it on Rome Lab's system. Subsequently, it was feared that North Korea could view these intrusions conducted via Rome Lab computers as an act of war (during this period, the US was involved in sensitive negotiations with the North Koreans regarding their nuclear weapons programme). The incident was well-documented by the US Department of Defense and seen to be of particular concern because the attack showed how a small (and, as it later turned out, underage) group of hackers could easily and quickly take control of defence networks.
  1998, Solar Sunrise: In February 1998, more than 500 electronic break-ins into computer systems of the US government and the private sector were detected. The hackers gained access to at least 200 different computer systems of the US military, the nuclear weapons laboratories, the Department of Energy and NASA. At precisely the same time, the US forces in the Middle East were being built up because of tensions with

Iraq over UN arms inspections. The fact that some of the intrusions could be traced back to Internet service providers in the Gulf region led to the initial conclusion that the Iraqi government had to be behind the attacks. The incident provided a major impetus for the formation of a Joint Task Force on Computer Network Defense (JTF-CND) later in the year. A closer investigation of the case later exposed the real attackers: two teenagers from Cloverdale in California and another teen from Israel.

1998, Moonlight Maze: in March 1998, US officials accidentally discovered a pattern of probing of computer systems at the Pentagon, NASA, Energy Department, private universities and research labs. The highly classified incident, called 'Moonlight Maze', had apparently been going on for nearly two years before it was discovered. The invaders were systematically marauding through tens of thousands of files – including maps of military installations, troop configurations and military hardware designs. The Defense Department says it traced the trail back to a mainframe computer in the former Soviet Union, but the sponsor of the attacks remains unknown, and the Russian government denied any involvement.

References

Abele-Wigert, I. and Dunn, M. (2006) *The International CIIP Handbook 2006: An Inventory of Protection Policies in 20 Countries and 6 International Organizations*, Vol. I, Zurich: Center for Security Studies.

AFIWC (Air Force Information Warfare Center) (1995) *A Technical Analysis of the Rome Laboratory Attacks*, Kelly Air Force Base: US Government Printing Office.

Anderson, R.H. and Hearn, A.C. (1996) *An Exploration of Cyberspace Security R&D Investment Strategies for DARPA: 'The Day After ... in Cyberspace II'*, Santa Monica: RAND.

Aradau, C. (2001) 'Beyond good and evil: ethics and securitization/desecuritization techniques', *Rubikon*, December 2001.

Barlow, J.P. (1994) 'The economy of ideas: selling wine without bottles on the global net', *Wired Magazine*, 2.03, March 1994. Online. Available at: www.wired.com/wired/archive/2.03/economy.ideas.html (accessed 9 August 2007).

—— (1996) *A Declaration of the Independence of Cyberspace*, Electronic Frontier Foundation Website. Online. Available at: homes.eff.org/~barlow/Declaration-Final.html (accessed 9 August 2007).

Bendrath, R. (2001) 'The cyberwar debate: perception and politics in US critical infrastructure protection', *Information & Security: An International Journal*, 7: 80–103.

Bendrath, R., Eriksson, J. and Giacomello, G. (2007) 'Cyberterrorism to cyberwar, back and forth: how the United States securitized cyberspace', in Eriksson, J. and Giacomello, G. (eds) *International Relations and Security in the Digital Age*, London: Routledge, pp. 57–82.

Bequai, A. (1986) *Technocrimes: The Computerization of Crime and Terrorism*, Lexington: Lexington Books.

Berkowitz, B.D. (1997) 'Warfare in the information age', in Arquilla, J. and Ronfeldt, D. (eds) *In Athena's Camp: Preparing for Conflict in the Information Age*, Santa Monica: RAND, pp. 175–90.

Blank, S.J. (2003) *Rethinking Asymmetric Threats*, Carlisle: Carlisle Strategic Studies Institute.

Boekle, H., Nadoll, J. and Stahl, B. (2000) 'Identität, Diskurs und vergleichende Analyse europäischer Außenpolitiken. Theoretische Grundlegung und methodische Vorgehensweise', PAFE-Arbeitspapier no. 1, University of Trier.

—— (2001) 'Nationale Identität, Diskursanalyse und Außenpolitikforschung: Herausforderungen und Hypothesen', PAFE-Arbeitspapier no. 4, University of Trier.

Bush, G.W. (2001a) *Executive Order 13228: Establishing the Office of Homeland Security and the Homeland Security Council*, Washington, DC, 8 October 2001.

—— (2001b) *Executive Order 13231: Critical Infrastructure Protection in the Information Age*, Washington, DC, 16 October 2001.

—— (2001c) *Organization of the National Security Council System*, National Security Presidential Decision (NSPD 1), Washington, DC, 5 March 2001.

—— (2002) *The National Strategy for Homeland Security*, Washington, DC: US Government Printing Office.

—— (2003a) *The National Strategy for Physical Protection of Critical Infrastructures and Key Assets*, Washington, DC: US Government Printing Office.

—— (2003b) *The National Strategy to Secure Cyberspace*, Washington, DC: US Government Printing Office.

Buzan, B., Wæver, O. and de Wilde, J. (1998) *Security: A New Framework for Analysis*, Boulder: Lynne Rienner.

Campbell, D. (1998) *Writing Security: United States Foreign Policy and the Politics of Identity*, 2nd edn, Manchester: Manchester University Press.

Campen, A.D. (ed.) (1992) *The First Information War: The Story of Communications, Computers and Intelligence Systems in the Persian Gulf War*, Fairfax: AFCEA International Press.

Clinton, W.J. (1995) *US Policy on Counterterrorism*, Presidential Decision Directive 39, Washington, DC, 21 June 1995.

—— (1998a) *Protection Against Unconventional Threats to the Homeland and Americans Overseas*, Presidential Decision Directive 62, Washington, DC, 22 May 1998.

—— (1998b) *Protecting America's Critical Infrastructures: Presidential Decision Directive 63*, Washington, DC, 22 May 1998.

—— (2000) *Defending America's Cyberspace: National Plan for Information Systems Protection. An Invitation to a Dialogue*. Version 1.0, Washington, DC: US Government Printing Office.

Computer Science and Telecommunications Board (1989) *Growing Vulnerability of the Public Switched Network: Implications for National Security Emergency Preparedness*, Washington, DC: National Academy Press.

—— (1999) *Realizing the Potential of C4I, Fundamental Challenges*, Washington, DC: National Academy Press.

Covert, C. (1983) 'Seven curious teenagers wreak havoc via computer', *Detroit Free Press*, 28 August 1983, Section: WWL, 1F.

Critical Infrastructure Protection Oral History Project (2005) 'Historical Outline', School of Law's National Center for Technology & Law and organised by the Center for History & New Media at George Mason University. Online. Available at: echo.gmu.edu/CIPP/essay/ (accessed 9 August 2007).

Dam, K.W. and Lin, H.S. (eds) (1996) *Cryptography's Role in Securing the Information Society*, Washington, DC: National Academy Press.

Defense Science Board (1994) *Report of the Defense Science Board Summer Study Task Force on Information Architecture for the Battlefield*, Washington, DC: Department of Defense.

—— (1996) *Report of the Defense Science Board Task Force on Information Warfare – Defense (IW-D)*, Washington, DC: Department of Defense.

DHS (Department of Homeland Security) (2004) *Securing Our Homeland: US Department of Homeland Security Strategic Plan*, Washington, DC: Department of Homeland

Security. Online. Available at: www.dhs.gov/xlibrary/assets/DHS_StratPlan_FINAL_spread.pdf (accessed 9 August 2007).

Devost, M.G. (1995) *National Security in the Information Age*, unpublished Masters thesis, University of Vermont, Burlington. Online. Available at: www.devost.net/papers/national_security_in_the_information_age.html (accessed 9 August 2007).

Diffie, W. and Hellman, M.E. (1976) 'New directions in cryptography', *IEEE Transactions on Information Theory*, 22, 6: 644–54.

Dunn Cavelty, M. and Brunner, E. (2007) 'Information, power, and security: an outline of debates and implications', in Dunn Cavelty, M., Mauer, V. and Krishna-Hensel, S.-F. (eds) *Power and Security in the Information Age: Investigating the Role of the State in Cyberspace*, Aldershot: Ashgate, pp. 1–18.

Electronic Privacy Information Center (EPIC) (1998) *Critical Infrastructure Protection and the Endangerment of Civil Liberties: An Assessment of the President's Commission on Critical Infrastructure Protection (PCCIP)*, Washington, DC: Electronic Privacy Information Center.

Elmer-Dewitt, P. (1983) 'The 414 gang strikes again', *Time Magazine*, 29 August 1983.

Eriksson, A.E. (1999) 'Information warfare: hype or reality?', *The Non-Proliferation Review*, 6, 3: 57–64.

Eriksson, J. (ed.) (2001a) *Threat Politics: New Perspectives on Security, Risk and Crisis Management*, Ashgate: Aldershot.

—— (2001b) 'Cyberplagues, IT, and security: threat politics in the information age', *Journal of Contingencies and Crisis Management*, 9, 4: 211–22.

Eriksson, J. and Noreen, E. (2002) *Setting the Agenda of Threats: An Explanatory Model*, Uppsala Peace Research Papers, 6. Online. Available at: www.pcr.uu.se/publications/UPRP_pdf/uprp_no_6.pdf (accessed 9 August 2007).

GAO (1996) United States General Accounting Office, *Information Security: Computer Attacks at Department of Defense Pose Increasing Risk*, GAO/AIMD-96–84, Washington, DC: General Accounting Office, 22 May 1996.

—— (2001) United States General Accounting Office, *Critical Infrastructure Protection: Significant Challenges in Developing Analysis, Warning, and Response Capabilities*, GAO-01–323, Washington, DC: General Accounting Office, 25 April 2001.

Hables Gray, C. (1997) *Postmodern War: The New Politics of Conflict*, New York: Guilford Press.

Hamre, J.J. (2003) Frontline Interview with John Hamre, 18 February 2003. Online. Available at: www.pbs.org/wgbh/pages/frontline/shows/cyberwar/interviews/hamre.html (accessed 9 August 2007).

Hart, G. and Rudman, W. (2001) *Road Map for National Security: Imperative for Change: The Phase III Report of the U.S. Commission on National Security/21st Century*, Washington, DC, US Government Printing Office, 15 February 2001. Online. Available at: handle.dtic.mil/100.2/ADA387531 (accessed 9 August 2007).

Hinsley, F.H. and Stripp, A. (2001) *Codebreakers: The Inside Story of Bletchley Park*, Oxford: Oxford University Press.

Ingles-le Nobel, J.J. (1999) 'Cyberterrorism hype', *Jane's Intelligence Review*, 21 October 1999.

Joerißen, B. and Stahl, B. (eds) (2003) *Europäische Außenpolitik und nationale Identität: Vergleichende Diskurs- und Verhaltensstudien zu Dänemark, Deutschland, Frankreich, Griechenland, Italien und den Niederlanden*, Europäische Akademie Otzenhausen, vol. 121, Münster: LIT.

Joint Security Commission (1994) *Redefining Security: A Report to the Secretary of*

Defense and the Director of Central Intelligence, Washington, DC: US Government Printing Office, 28 February 1994.

Knezo, G. (2003) *'Sensitive But Unclassified' and Other Federal Security Controls on Scientific and Technical Information: History and Current Controversy*, Congressional Research Report for Congress, RL31845, Washington, DC: Congressional Research Service, 20 February 2003.

Kolet, K.S. (2001) 'Asymmetric threats to the United States', *Comparative Strategy*, 20, 3: 277–92.

Kuehl, D. (2000) 'The information component of power and the national security strategy', in Campen, A.D. and Dearth, D.H. (eds) *Cyberwar 3.0: Human Factors in Information Operations and Future Conflict*, Fairfax: AFCEA International Press, pp. 275–87.

Lakoff, G. and Johnson, M. (1980) *Metaphors We Live By*, Chicago: University of Chicago Press.

McLuhan, M. (1964) *Understanding Media. The Extensions of Man*, New York: McGraw-Hill.

Mark, R. (2004) 'U.S. cybersecurity chief resigns', *eSecurity Planet*, 1 October 2004. Online. Available at: www.esecurityplanet.com/trends/article.php/3416161 (accessed 12 October 2007).

Metz, S. (2000) 'The next twist of the RMA', *Parameters*, XXX, 3, Autumn 2000: 40–53.

Metz, S. and Johnson, D.V. (2001) *Asymmetry and U.S. Military Strategy: Definition, Background, and Strategic Concepts*, Carlisle: Strategic Studies Institute.

Molander, R.C., Riddle, A.S. and Wilson, P.A. (1996) *Strategic Information Warfare: A New Face of War*, Santa Monica: RAND.

Moteff, J.D. (2003) *Critical Infrastructures: Background, Policy, and Implementation*, Congressional Research Report for Congress, RL30153, Washington, DC: Congressional Research Service, 10 February 2003.

—— (2006) *Critical Infrastructure: The National Asset Database*, Congressional Research Report for Congress, RL33648, Washington, DC: Congressional Research Service, 14 September 2006.

—— (2007) *Critical infrastructures: Background, Policy, and Implementation*, Congressional Research Report for Congress, RL30153, Washington, DC: Congressional Research Service, 13 March 2007.

Moteff, J.D., Copeland, C. and Fischer, J. (2002) *Critical Infrastructures: What Makes an Infrastructure Critical?* Congressional Research Report for Congress, RL31556, Washington, DC: Congressional Research Service, 29 January 2002.

National Academy of Sciences (1991) Computer Science and Telecommunications Board, *Computers at Risk: Safe Computing in the Information Age*, Washington, DC: National Academy Press.

Nye, J.S. Jr. and Owens, W.A. (1996) 'America's information edge', *Foreign Affairs*, 75, 2: 20–36.

Office of Technology Assessment (1987) *Defending Secrets, Sharing Data: New Locks and Keys for Electronic Information*, OTA-CIT-310, Washington, DC: US Government Printing Office.

Parker, D.B. (1983) *Fighting Computer Crime*, New York: Charles Scribner's Sons.

PCCIP (President's Commission on Critical Infrastructure Protection) (1997) *Critical Foundations: Protecting America's Infrastructures*, Washington, DC: US Government Printing Office.

Perrow, C. (1984) *Normal Accidents: Living with High-Risk Technologies*, New York: Basic Books.

Pollitt, M.M. (1997) 'Cyberterrorism – fact or fancy?', *Proceedings of the 20th National Information Systems Security Conference*, 1997: 285–9.

Poulsen, K. (2003) 'Official: cyberterror fears missed real threat', *SecurityFocus.com*, 31 July 2003. Online. Available at: www.securityfocus.com/news/6589 (accessed 9 August 2007).

Rattray, G. (2001) *Strategic Warfare in Cyberspace*, Cambridge: MIT Press.

Reagan, R. (1982) *National Security Information*, Executive Order 1235b, Washington, DC, 2 April 1982.

—— (1984) *National Policy on Telecommunications and Automated Information Systems Security*, National Security Decision Directive NSDD 145, Washington, DC: The White House, 17 September 1984. Online. Available at: www.fas.org/irp/offdocs/nsdd145.htm (accessed 12 October 2007).

—— (1985) *Radio Address to the Nation on Efforts to Prevent Espionage Against the United States*, 30 November 1985. Online. Available at: www.reagan.utexas.edu/archives/speeches/1985/113085a.htm (accessed 9 August 2007).

Rein, M. and Schön, D.A. (1994) *Frame Reflection, Toward the Resolution of Intractable Policy Controversies*, New York: Basic Books.

Reno, J. (1996) 'Memorandum', Washington, DC: Office of the Attorney General, 14 March 1996. Online. Available at: www.fas.org/sgp/othergov/munromem.htm (accessed 9 August 2007).

Rona, T.P. (1976) *Weapon Systems and Information War*, Boeing Aerospace Co. Research Report, Seattle: Boeing.

Ryan, C. (1991) *Prime Time Activism: Media Strategies for Grass Roots Organizing*, Boston: South End Press.

Snow, D.A. and Benford, R.D. (1988) 'Ideology, frame resonance, and participant mobilization', *Social Movement Research*, 1: 197–217.

—— (1992) 'Master frames and cycles of protest', in Morris, A.D. and McClurg Mueller, C. (eds) *Frontiers in Social Movement Theory*, New Haven: Yale University Press, pp. 133–55.

Stoll, C. (1989) *The Cuckoo's Egg: Tracking a Spy through the Maze of Computer Espionage*, New York: Doubleday.

Sundelius, B. (1983) 'Coping with structural security threats', in Höll, O. (ed.) *Small States in Europe and Dependence*, Vienna: Braumüller.

Tenet, G.J. (1999) *Testimony of Director of Central Intelligence George J. Tenet before the Senate Armed Services Committee*, Washington, DC: United States Senate Committee on Armed Services, 2 February 1999.

Townson, M. (1992) *Mother-tongue and Fatherland: Language and Politics in Germany*, Manchester: Manchester University Press.

Verton, D. (2004) 'Nation's cybersecurity chief abruptly quits DHS post: "I'm not a long-term government kind of guy," says Amit Yoran', *Computerworld*, 1 October 2004. Online. Available at: www.computerworld.com/printthis/2004/0,4814,96369,00.html (accessed 9 August 2007).

Wæver, O. (1995) 'Securitization and desecuritization', in Lipschutz, R.D. (ed.) *On Security*, New York: Columbia University Press, pp. 46–86.

Weldes, J., Laffey, M., Gusterson, H. and Duvall, R. (1999) 'Introduction: constructing insecurity', in Weldes, J., Laffey, M., Gusterson, H. and Duvall, R. (eds) *Cultures of Insecurity: States, Communities, and the Production of Danger*, Minneapolis: University of Minnesota Press, pp. 1–34.

3 'The absolute protection of our citizens'

Critical infrastructure protection and the practice of security

Kristian Søby Kristensen

According to US Secretary of Homeland Security Tom Ridge, the goal of the Department of Homeland Security (DHS) is nothing less than 'the absolute protection of our citizens' (Ridge 2004a). This statement, and the fact that it was made in the first place, should, however, draw our attention to the political function of the DHS. The events of 11 September 2001 both reactualized and destabilized the relationship between security, territory and borders. The US, which had hitherto been imagined to be secure and protected by natural borders, was shown to be insecure and vulnerable to threats and enemies who were already inside the domestic space. Ridge's statement – and the Department of Homeland Security itself – can be seen as attempts to reconceptualize the practice of security under conditions considered in political discourse to be fundamentally new.

This goal of 'absolute protection of our citizens' goes to the heart of the concept of sovereignty. From Thomas Hobbes onwards, the core legitimizing function of the state has been assumed to be the provision of physical security to its citizens inside its territory. This is the essential precondition for the existence of society (Hobbes 1996: 84). Therefore, the attacks of 11 September 2001 could easily be integrated into a narrative that showed the US government to be unable to protect its territory and, accordingly, the foundations of its own sovereignty. By this point in time, borders had lost much of their function as symbolic and physical demarcations between the peaceful and secure inside and the anarchical outside. This is not a new development; on the contrary, the functions of borders have arguably been changing for some time (e.g. Andreas and Biersteker 2003; Albert *et al.* 2001). Nevertheless, the narrative of the 11 September 2001 attacks increased the political salience of the problems in the relationship between borders, territory and security. In the words of President Bush: 'The US government has no more important mission than protecting the homeland from future terrorist attacks' (Bush 2002).

The discourse of the US government can be seen as attempts to rearticulate the relationship between security and territory. The territorial vulnerability manifested by the threat from terror has led to an increased focus on various defensive measures. The creation of the DHS in itself shows the political importance of this 'mission' – a mission aimed at re-establishing the relationship between the sovereign and its subjects in a situation where the functionality of borders is being questioned.

In the following, the focus will be on the issue of 'critical infrastructure protection' (CIP), a core task of the DHS, and a central aim of the government in its attempts to recreate a sense of security and reducing vulnerability inside the US, thus assuring 'the absolute protection of our citizens'. The claim made here is that the discourse on critical infrastructure protection provides an excellent approach with which to understand changing or reactualized meanings attached to the concept and practice of security.

In order to explore critical infrastructure protection and the changing forms of security, the chapter first discusses recent literature on the relationship between security, sovereignty and borders, further making the case for focusing on CIP. This sets the stage for the actual analysis of the CIP discourse. The analysis is focused on exploring how policies are argued by the US administration in trying to make security *inside* sovereign space. This analysis consists of three parts: first, the history of CIP is discussed; this is followed by an investigation of how domestic space both limits sovereign power and empowers new private actors. The third part looks at how the US administration tries to combine the concepts of risk and protection in the rationalization of its security strategy in relation to CIP policies. In conclusion, this chapter analyses the struggle for conceptual coherence concerning the concepts of security, and thus, ultimately, sovereignty, as negotiation and probability are incorporated into the security strategies of the state.

Borders, security and sovereignty

The border is the ultimate place of sovereign control demarcating inside from outside. It has a central symbolic function as the external face of the state. It is supposed to be impregnable and controlled by the state. 'Citizen' and 'non-citizen', 'illegal' and 'legal' entry, 'legitimate trade' and 'smuggling' – all these labels are used to characterize the subjects crossing the border into the territorial space of the state. Borders play an essential function in the production of state sovereignty, security and territorial integrity. The border is the symbolic beginning and end, as well as the primary point of control and surveillance of the state (Bigo 2001: 101). Inside, the social contract applies; outside, there are no such guarantees. This concept of borders and sovereignty has, of course, always been an idealized theoretical description – no such thing as a secure border has ever existed. However, the ideal is an exact description of a pure form, and this pure form of border and security is the conceptual ideal on which the modern nation state is founded (e.g. Hertz 1957; Hinsley 1967; Morgenthau 1948; Kratochwil 1986). This ideal has lived side by side with a sedimented practice that has stabilized inconsistencies between practice and theory, and has reproduced the symbolic value of borders in delimiting sovereign space as well as their practical function as points of control and passage into the inside (Lapid 2001: 8). Borders create places where sovereign power is legitimated – they establish the spatial beginning of the Hobbesian contract.

This practice of state sovereignty at the territorial border has, however, for some time been challenged. Global flows of trade, investment, migration and commerce, it is argued, put the sovereign state under functional pressure. This pressure changes the character and function of borders as barriers to movement, and as points of sovereign control. Globalization favours freedom and the creation of a 'space of flows' decoupled from territorial constraints (Castells 2000; Anderson *et al.* 2002; Sassen 1996). The functions of borders are in the process of changing from 'being boundaries that are heavily protected and militarized to [being] more porous, permitting cross border social and economic integration' (Hertzog 1996: 84). Thus, the state and the 'world of states' (Blatter 2001: 175) are changing as a consequence of changed border practices. The effects of globalization also manifest themselves in relation to security. Society, it is argued, is threatened by these new trans-border flows. For the Western societies, the threat from this new condition of porous borders has been politically conceptualized as being closely entwined with immigration (e.g. Bigo 2000; Wæver *et al.* 1993), as well as terror and organized crime (Andreas 2003; Guild 2003). The state is caught in a dilemma; on the one hand, it has to allow the economically essential flows of globalization. On the other hand, flows of people and things cannot be controlled as in the Westphalian ideal, leaving both state and society vulnerable (Biersteker 2003: 157–61; Rudolph 2005). This leads to new border policies blurring the distinction between inside and outside (Walker 1993; Beck 2003), thus also blurring the distinction between external and internal security (Bigo 2000; Lutterbeck 2005). The border is deterritorialized or debordered (Andreas 2003: 98; Blatter 2001: 176f.). These developments move the sovereign task of providing security away from the border and change its character.

Much of the literature that is based on this assumption of a blurring of the distinction between inside and outside focuses on how internal security dynamics are pushed outwards (Bigo 2000: 171ff.). This is especially true for the way in which the state manages the outsider (asylum seekers, immigrants etc.) and how this subject, in state practices, is associated with terror (Bigo 2000: 174; Bonditti, Chapter 6, this volume; Huysmans 2004). A number of studies have empirically investigated this debordering of the border both in Europe and in America. For instance, developments in Europe displace border controls from the territory of individual states to the EU's external borders as well as to the territory of third countries (Boswell 2003; Huysmans 2000). Similarly, US policy towards Mexico has consisted of pushing its anti-immigration efforts as well as counter-terrorism policies into Mexican territory, while still strengthening controls at the border (Andreas 2003; Serrano 2003). Similarly, the US 'war on drugs' can be seen as an outward displacement of practices traditionally carried out at the border (Andreas 2000). Thus, a widespread and well investigated (and criticized) change in border policies is taking place. States are extending their border policies from the state boundary in order to secure their own societies. However, this change is not a solitary trend occurring in isolation. It coincides with a reverse movement; at the same time, various forms of security policy are moving inside, into the territory of the state.

The sense of security provided by borders – especially in the US – was seriously impaired by the 11 September 2001 attacks. The idealized and traditional conception of borders was destabilized, because 'insecurity is now seen as something "in here" as well as "out there"' (Salter 2004: 71). The attacks of 11 September 2001 constituted yet another attack on the state's ability to maintain the ideal of a secure inside delimited from the outside by its borders. In the words of Secretary Ridge: 'it would be a horrible mistake to conclude that there aren't some Al Qaeda operatives within this country' (Ridge 2002). From this perspective, the events of 11 September 2001 introduced insecurity, and thus a potential state of nature, inside the state. This explains the vehement US response to 11 September 2001. Major efforts have to be undertaken to rearticulate the distinction between the 'secure homeland' and the still dangerous outside. As noted above, a lot of investigative work has been undertaken to analyse how security policies are moved to the outside. CIP, on the other hand, shows how security policy is equally moved into the inside. Basically, providing security through traditional border policies is increasingly rendered difficult and insufficient. The sense of security lost as a consequence of 11 September 2001 entails increased efforts to recreate security by moving it 'inside' into the sovereign territory and thus into society.

This chapter will empirically explore these efforts by analysing the US government's discourse on CIP and relate the findings to how security practices are changing, thus complementing the studies focusing on the move to the outside. Fundamentally the function of discourse is to create conditions of possibility. Thus, when Secretary Ridge makes the statement that he cannot conclude that there are no al-Qaida operatives on US territory, the performative function of the statement is to open up new conditions – or to change the existing conditions – for making security (Wæver 1995). By making this particular statement, by constructing the threat as being already present inside US territory, particular strategies for action and particular rationalities are legitimized; insecurity on the inside requires security strategies on the inside as well. Taken together, this and other statements by US officials form a discourse on CIP that construct certain conditions of possibility for what security is, how it is conceptualized, and what security strategies can and cannot be applied. It follows from this that the answers to questions such as what infrastructure is, what criticality means, and what who does in order to secure it are not given, but constructed in political discourse. By answering these questions, the following analysis shows how the rules guiding security policies are changed as these policies move inside society, and contribute to questioning conceptions of security and sovereignty. In parallel with the questions posed above, the analysis is subdivided into three parts. First, this chapter provides an account of how CIP has developed into what it is today, providing the basis for its present conceptualization in government discourse. This is followed by an investigation of the principal actors and their relationship. Finally, the central strategies and concepts of the US administration are analysed.

A short history of critical infrastructure protection

The basis of the current conception of CIP originated in the post-Cold War discourse on new threats in an unpredictable environment (e.g. Tenet 1997; Studeman 1995; Hart and Rudman 2001). The threats to critical infrastructure were, then as now, primarily constructed as consisting of terrorism, a wide range of cyber-threats, or a combination of these in the concept of cyber-terrorism; but the salience of such threats has increased since 11 September 2001 (compare Clinton 1998: 1 with Bush 2003a: 7).

What is it exactly being threatened and accordingly in need of protection from these threats? The President's Commission on Critical Infrastructure Protection in 1997 defined infrastructure as 'the framework of interdependent networks and systems ... that provide a reliable flow of products and services essential to the defense and the economic security of the United States, the smooth functioning of government of all levels, and society as a whole' (US President's Commission on Critical Infrastructure 1997: 142). Not all infrastructures are equally critical; therefore, Executive Order 13010 identified the most critical of these 'networks and systems'. The list was still comprehensive. Telecommunications, electrical power systems, gas and oil storage and transportation, banking and finance, transportation, water supply systems, emergency services, and continuity of government (PCCIP 1997): all of these are critical infrastructures, considered to be at risk from terrorist attacks, both conventional and virtual. The central element in this definition is the focus on infrastructure owned and run by private actors (Moteff and Parfomak 2004: 4). In fact, 85 per cent of all critical infrastructures are owned or operated by private actors. In the following years, cyber-terrorism was the main focus of both government action and the public debate. A number of commentators pointed to the real and immanent threat of a 'virtual Pearl Harbour', arguing that the offensive potential of virtual – and thus deterritorialized – information technologies left the US just as open, vulnerable and unprepared as it had been in 1941 (e.g. Arquilla *et al.* 1999: 39–84; Robinson *et al.* 1998: 62; Lewis 2003: 34, for a critique, see Conway, Chapter 5, this volume).

Accordingly, infrastructure had by the end of the 1990s attained a set meaning (for the history of CIP, see Dunn Cavelty, Chapter 2, this volume; Collier and Lakoff, Chapter 1, this volume; Lopez 2006). Infrastructure consists, on the one hand, of both individual physical sites and the networks of such sites, which collectively constitute the essential underpinnings of society. On the other hand, the definition also includes virtual data networks that are central to society, both in their own right – as facilitating elements of private and commercial use of the Internet – and as means of controlling the networks of physical sites. Because these networks are both interdependent and interconnected, the distinction between physical and virtual is often blurred, and system failures in one sector can often have cascading effects, thus magnifying the vulnerability of any one network, as well as the entirety of networks (Robinson *et al.* 1998). These systems of networks are increasingly framed throughout the late 1990s as vulnerable and in need of policies to ensure their protection. This task is not easily accomplished, however. First of all, the sheer quantity of sites, systems and sectors is overwhelming. For example, the US transportation infrastructure consists of four million miles of paved roads, 600,000 bridges, more than 300,000 miles of railroads and 500 commercial airports (Moteff *et al.* 2003: 8). Not all bridges are equally critical to the security of 'society as a whole', of course. Nonetheless, defining criticality is a difficult endeavour. By defining the security of 'society as a whole' as the ultimate object to be protected through CIP, there is the obvious risk of casting an overly broad net in defining criticality.

The events of 11 September 2001 – which were easily integrated into a narrative reaching back to the Japanese attack on Pearl Harbor – brought with it a renewed focus on CIP, both physical and virtual, and a number of legislative initiatives in its immediate aftermath focused on infrastructure protection. Already on 8 October 2001, George W. Bush issued an Executive Order establishing the Office of Homeland Security, and directing its functions as related to CIP (Bush 2001). This document expands the sectors included in CIP to encompass nuclear material, agriculture, and 'special events' of 'national significance' (Bush 2001). This is followed by a number of other documents. The USA PATRIOT Act, the Homeland Security Act and the *National Strategy for Homeland Security* all discuss what constitutes critical infrastructure. These documents add the chemical industry, postal services and shipping to the list (Bush 2002: 31). Furthermore, in addition to critical infrastructure, the Homeland Security Act mentions 'key resources', defined as 'publicly or privately controlled resources essential to the minimal operations of the economy and government' (US Congress 2002: 10). Another new term coming to the fore after 11 September 2001 is that of 'key assets'. These are defined in the *National Strategy for the Physical Protection of Critical Infrastructures and Key Assets* as 'individual targets whose attack … could result in not only large-scale human casualties and property destruction, but also profound damage to our national prestige, morale, and confidence' (Bush 2003a: vii). Key assets include, for instance, nuclear power plants and dams, but also sites that are 'symbolically equated with traditional American values and institutions or US political and economic power', that function to 'preserve history, honor achievements, and represent the natural grandeur of our country'. These key assets are especially vulnerable at 'high profile events and celebratory activities that bring together significant numbers of people' (Bush 2003a: vii). Thus, instead of defining criticality only in relation to the physical security of society, public confidence is now also introduced as a measurement of the criticality of any given infrastructure (Bush 2003a: 2).

In sum, while retaining basically the same meaning, CIP has expanded during the last ten years. First, sectors containing critical infrastructure in need of government action have been broadened, and consequently more and more private actors have to take account of the criticality of their businesses from a security perspective. Second, the interdependency and interconnectedness that are essential characteristics of CIP underline the dual character of the object. On the one hand, CIP is the protection of physically existing objects, and on the other hand, CIP is aimed at securing the flows and processes – both physical and virtual – that are deemed central to the continued function of society. Third, the lesson from 11 September 2001 is that not only are critical infrastructures at risk, society itself is threatened by the 'dual-use' character of these infrastructures. Fourth, by including events and sites of importance to the public confidence and morale, both a temporal and psychological dimension are imparted to criticality as well as to infrastructure itself.

The expanding definition of CIP in the discourse changes the politics as well. CIP becomes more intangible and, accordingly, the assessment of risk, threat, criticality and adequate protection becomes less clear-cut. 'A fluid definition of what constitutes a critical infrastructure could complicate policy making', and 'rationally balancing the costs and benefits of increased security' becomes increasingly difficult (Moteff *et al.* 2003: 13). These expansions of the concept in both time and space, as well as its increasingly fluid definition, make critical infrastructure protection difficult. What is to be protected, and how? As the definition of CIP broadens, so does the range of sectors of society that are touched by government action. More critical infrastructure means more government action inside society. This reflects a change away from the classic conception of security at the border towards the completely different concept of creating security on the inside. Moving security into society requires engagement with the civilian and private actors of society. How these inside actors and their relationship with government are conceptualized in the CIP discourse has important consequences for the elaboration of security strategies. Accordingly, relations between the central actors – both in government and in the private sector – are discussed in the following.

Sovereign prerogative or normal market-driven politics

One important aspect of critical infrastructure is that about 85 per cent are owned and operated by private actors. The challenge for CIP policies is thus to create security in an environment not controlled by the state. Inside society, other considerations have to be taken into account. However, the final aim of government politics is still to make society secure. This leaves the government with a fundamental dilemma in its CIP policies – a dilemma that is only made more explicit by the expanding definition of what critical infrastructure is.

On the one hand 'The United States government has no more important mission than protecting the homeland from future terrorist attacks' (Bush 2002: unnumbered preface). The quote frames the politics of homeland security in terms normally associated with the national security discourse. If homeland protection is the most important mission of government, then one could expect swift, ubiquitous, and decisive action to regulate the various sectors containing critical infrastructure, thus ensuring their safety and protecting the homeland. This line of action and reasoning fits perfectly with classical Hobbesian security, and would re-establish things as they 'should be'.

This has not been the case, however, because on the other hand, 'Homeland security ... in the context of CIP and key asset protection is a shared responsibility that cannot be accomplished by the federal government alone' (Bush 2003a: vii). The government cannot 'alone protect this nation's expansive and widely distributed national infrastructures' (Liscouski 2004). On the contrary, homeland security 'requires coordinated and focused effort from our entire society' (DHS 2004: 9). A large part of the responsibility for this 'important mission' of government is thus moved away from the Hobbesian state and placed on the shoulders of society, and – concerning the protection of critical infrastructure – on the shoulders of private owners and operators. This results in changes both in the role of government and in the strategies pursued to secure the homeland; creating security inside society is not the same as doing so on the outside. The private actors involved with critical infrastructure are now integrated into the security strategies of government; these private owners and operators become central actors in the discourse on CIP.

Two aspects are useful for understanding this change. First, by defining both criticality and infrastructure broadly, the task of securing them has an equally broad range. Second, the policies of homeland security and CIP are blurred by domestic considerations. The management of infrastructure should not be the prerogative of government, because it is privately owned; instead, it should be based on the market, limiting government intervention. The economic considerations of society collide with the security concerns of the state when infrastructure – governed by the market – is framed as an object that is both threatened and itself a threat to society. Accordingly, the discourse has to tread carefully between these two priorities: 'We face a two-pronged challenge: Safeguard our homeland, but at the same time ensure that the free flow of people, goods and commerce is not disrupted' (Ridge 2003). In sum, how can governments allow the economically critical 'space of flows' of globalization to persist while securing their citizens?

The central challenge is to square the circle by somehow merging these two priorities. One way is to redefine the roles and identity of the actors participating in CIP. First, homeland security in general is argued as a task that only can be accomplished by an 'effort from our entire society' (DHS 2004: 9). As stated in the *National Strategy for Homeland Security*: 'Private firms bear primary and substantial responsibility for addressing the public safety risks posed by their industries' (Bush 2002: 33). Again, the responsibility of private actors is underlined. However, the 11 September 2001 attacks made it clear that the ordinary safety measures undertaken by business in the past to secure their assets are not enough to secure society in the present 'threat environment' (Bush 2003a: x). Government action is required as well. How the interaction between these two actors is conceptualized becomes a central aspect of how to create security on the inside. The role of government is to 'enable, not inhibit, the private sector's ability to carry out its protection responsibilities. The Nation's infrastructure protection effort must harness the capabilities of the private sector to achieve a prudent level of security' (Bush 2002: 33). Consequently, it is still the private sector that is responsible for security. Its ability to meet this responsibility is, however, to be facilitated by the government, which must 'use all available policy instruments to raise the security of America's critical infrastructures and key assets to a prudent level, *relying to the maximum possible extent on the market* to provide appropriate levels of security' (Bush 2002: 33, italics added).

Government involvement is conceptualized as somewhat limited. Instead of participating directly, the role of government is to 'help sectors organize themselves' and to function only in an 'active partnership' (Liscouski 2004: 3). Government action is described in terms such as 'coordination', 'exploring', 'facilitating', 'encouraging', 'supporting' and 'seeding' (Bush 2003a: 16; Bush 2003b: 6). The argument of the discourse is that if government fosters cooperation and if the distribution of best practices is achieved, then business will be able to live up to their responsibility and secure their assets on their own. It is as if the natural way of things would be to have maximum security driven by market forces. This has not been the case in government discourse, partly because of lack of attention from the private sector. The role of government becomes more that of a midwife than of a sovereign state. By facilitating cooperation and information-sharing, the state can make the private industry secure critical infrastructures without compromising the basic economic logic that dictates non-interference from the state. The state plays an auxiliary role as a 'force multiplier' building on existing incentives, while the efforts made by the private sector are conceptualized as based on calculated self-interest only. The market seems to be given priority.

Nonetheless, the cooperative, but market-driven relationship between the actors is only part of the government discourse on how to integrate business; it is reinforced with elements of patriotism. Homeland security is 'about the integration of a nation' (Ridge 2004b). This means, again, that responsibility not only rests with the federal government. On the contrary, homeland security is about 'local governments, communities, business, organizations and citizens, all coming together around a shared goal of keeping our country safe' (Ridge 2004b). The market is not the only important concept in government discourse. As the quote shows, private enterprise apparently has other goals than profit. Keeping the country safe, it is argued, is just as much of an obligation for private businesses. Once one has accepted this dual conceptualization of private operators of infrastructure, participating in government programmes makes sense, as it is both 'practical and patriotic' (Liscouski 2004: 9). Participating in CIP policies will help achieve the necessary level of security – which private actors should be encouraged to strive for primarily through market incentives. Additionally, businesses can by 'voluntarily sharing such critical information ... demonstrate responsiveness to government need and public good'. The corporate sector is expected to voluntarily participate in – and acknowledge the goal of – the 'integration of the nation', thereby showing 'good corporate citizenship' (Liscouski 2004: 9). Companies are expected to express the national virtue that the struggle against terror and 'the shared goal of keeping our country safe' will require. Arguing along this discursive structure, Secretary Ridge can state that:

The citizens of this country rely on you ... to strengthen the security of your facilities with your dollars and with your determination. It is what we must ask of everyone – to make the fullest protection of this nation, the highest charge of all.

(Ridge 2004c)

According to the government discourse, there are thus two concepts that drive the actions of the private sector: profit and corporate citizenship. By conceptualizing private actors in this way, it is discursively possible for the government to achieve the ultimate aim – which it cannot achieve alone – of making society safe. The relationship between the subjects participating in CIP is conceptualized as being both normal and internal. Both 'the market' and 'corporate citizenship' are labels that legitimately engage private actors and thus legitimize government action inside society. However, the discourse simultaneously points in another, somewhat different direction.

Information-sharing is argued as one of the key activities in engaging private actors, and cooperation on this issue is seen as essential for achieving the necessary protection (Bush 2003a). Information-sharing, however, presents problems, as it runs counter to the competitive nature of the market. Sharing information between private actors on how their business is run and organized goes against the normal conception of the market, and, accordingly, also against the regulative framework. Companies engaged in government CIP programmes have voiced concern that by participating, business will run the risk of violating antitrust regulations and potentially face liability lawsuits from their shareholders (Malcolm 2002: 2). A second problem is how to treat the shared information generated in these partnerships. Normally, the US government is bound by the Freedom of Information Act stating that agency records must be made available to the general public (Stohs 2002). This fact has been pointed out by private businesses as a major impediment to information-sharing, as the information could potentially be used in civil litigation. In this respect, government actions have departed from normality. Instead of subjugating CIP to the normal regulations that apply to private business and government transparency, the strategy has consisted of making exemptions. Basically, information-sharing is portrayed as being essential to achieving 'the absolute protection of our citizens', and, when push comes to shove, national security discourse mingles with the discourse of the domestic inside. The government response has been to make exemptions to the Freedom of Information Act for information provided by owners and operators of critical infrastructure (US Congress 2002: 41). The same approach is being considered in relation to liability issues (Chertoff 2005a). The sovereign power shows itself not in the regulation of private actors, but in the granting of exemptions from other 'normal' domestic regulations.

In sum, while securing society is the core task of government, this is simultaneously impossible for a government to achieve by itself. This dilemma explains why government discourse states that CIP is both the responsibility of government and simultaneously the responsibility of private-sector infrastructure owners. From this comes the overall duality in the discourse. We find both the domestic concepts of market and corporate citizenship and, somewhat in the background, the exemptions normally associated with national security. In this relationship, characterized by shared responsibility and partnership, security becomes domesticated and subjugated to economic considerations. Simultaneously, however, economic policy is influenced by security considerations. The discourse makes security an inherent part of doing business in the US (see also Petersen 2008). The result is that these private actors – as far as they follow the dictates in government discourse on 'partnership' and 'responsibility' – are empowered in comparison with other parts of society. Businesses both 'bear a part of the security burden as well as become part of the security solution' (Chertoff 2005b). They thus become acting subjects in the CIP discourse. Their existence as essential partners in government CIP strategies both creates and limits the conditions of possibility for government action. The position of these actors both allows them to participate in negotiating how to make security and limits or changes the role of the state as an actor in its own right.

This process of securitizing private actors – by exempting them from normal domestic rules – is, however, not devoid of disagreements: 'Although private- and public-sector stakeholders share similar objectives, they have different perspectives on what constitutes acceptable risks and how to achieve security and reliability'. Therefore, establishing what President Bush calls a 'sustainable security threshold' is not always a straightforward exercise (Bush 2003a: 48f.). Definitions of critical infrastructure, as well as the relation of government to private actors, are factors that have direct implications for the determination of which strategies are viable and rational in government discourse, and for what can and what cannot be done. The following section focuses on how the concepts of risk and protection collide in the overall security strategies associated with CIP.

Homeland protection or homeland risk?

Until now, the analysis has focused on the characteristics of infrastructure, and on the ways in which different actors and their relationship are articulated in CIP discourse. In the following, focus is on how a sustainable 'security threshold' can be established. This is obviously a core question in any strategy – including that of critical infrastructure protection. Again, the creation of security inside society is characterized by a fundamental dualism.

On the one hand, the stated goal is 'the absolute protection of our citizens' (Ridge 2004a). Furthermore, when President Bush states that the US government 'has no more important mission than protecting the homeland from terrorist attacks' (Bush 2002: preface), the importance of the task is underlined, and critical infrastructure protection is again conceptualized in line with the traditional national security discourse. In explaining the strong government commitment to this task, reference is even made to the constitutional obligation of the government to defend society, clearly referring to the traditional contractual

Hobbesian relationship between the state and society (Bush 2003a: 16). In short, physically securing the citizen body and the territorial homeland of the US is the core task of the government. This line of argumentation again invokes the out-of-the-ordinary dynamics of security policy. When the security of every citizen is at play in conjunction with what is in fact the survival of the constitutionally legitimate government, the goal of securing both obviously takes precedence, and protective measures naturally spread to include more and more issues and sectors of society. This all-inclusive strategy runs through much of CIP discourse, and the expansion of the concept in particular can be understood as a consequence of this discursive function. When the security of the nation and every citizen as well as the legitimacy of the government are defined as being at stake, then everything that could possibly have an effect immediately becomes critical, and thus a potential object for securitization. The strategies in the CIP discourse relate directly to potentiality and securitization, as they attempt to answer questions concerning the potential impacts of certain developments. The emphasis on networks, interdependency and interconnectedness in the conceptualization of CIP has to be seen from this perspective. Even a discrete event of little apparent significance could entail largely unpredictable cascading effects throughout a large number of sectors. These factors, combined with the high stakes involved, give rise to a natural impulse to protect everything. Furthermore, the expansion of the concept to include both a psychological perspective and public trust in government is also an illustration of the above dynamic of eliciting possible outcomes. For example, a terror attack on a local school (Bush 2002: 42) does not in itself threaten the continued functioning of US society. However, the psychological effect of such an attack on the public might very well have 'cascading' consequences for both the continued functioning of society and indeed for public trust in government. The concept of criticality, and accordingly what is to be secured, is thus expanded from interconnected physical networks to include everything with an emotional attachment ranging from schools to national monuments. In the words of President Bush: 'every terrorist attack has a potential national impact' (Bush 2003a: ix). In principle, everything has to be protected. But this follows not from an assessment of the particular threat, but from an a priori definition of terrorist attacks as constituting critical threats. From the argument that any terrorist attack is a potential threat to the nation, it automatically follows that everything that can be targeted is a critical infrastructure. Therefore, everything has to be secured; the constitutional legitimacy of government depends upon it. This is in line with the traditional conception of security inside the sovereign space. Every citizen everywhere inside sovereign space should be able to demand absolute protection. The universal character of the discourse leads to policies based on worst-case scenarios.

But protecting everything is impossible. It is not in the power of the sovereign to absolutely secure the homeland, because 'we must accept some level of terrorist risk as a persistent condition of our daily life' (Bush 2003a: 13). The threat is already inside: '[T]errorism is insidious. Terrorists seek to infiltrate our society, scope out targets and wage war in our streets and cities' (Ridge 2003).

The consequences for the provision of security are considerable. As we have seen, inside sovereign space, sovereign power is paradoxically limited, and the almost natural tendency of the state to protect everything is equally and necessarily limited. Inside society, the state faces other political imperatives than that of security. Absolute protection can only be achieved by imposing severe restrictions on activities inside society; by going against the economic prerogative of private actors. As stated by Secretary Chertoff: 'I can guarantee you perfect security at a port, for example, if I shut the port down' (Chertoff 2005c: 8). Instead, to avoid these consequences, the aim is 'to create a security environment that works with the grain of commerce' (Chertoff 2005a). Consequently, how does the state secure the homeland and carry out its constitutional obligations, while still bearing in mind that absolute protection is impossible because on the inside state action is limited. That is the project of the DHS – to create a security environment that on the one hand protects society, but on the other hand 'works with the grain' of society. Again, the issue is how to balance the differences between security and the market, and between state and society. This is to be achieved through the concept of risk.

The concept of risk functions in a twofold way in government discourse. First, it serves to bridge the gap between government and private security strategies. Second, the concept of risk promises to provide – without shutting down society – a new or different form of a society-wide state of security. We have shown above how, in government discourse, the market and cooperate citizenship were conceptualized as driving private actors for the initial focus on CIP, thus making them security actors. Parallel to this, the government argues that risk is essentially a private logic: 'Customarily, private sector firms prudently engage in risk management planning and invest in security as a necessary function of business operations and customer confidence' (Bush 2003a: x). Dealing with risk is accordingly part of the 'normal' actions of private actors. The concept thus functions as an opener, allowing the government to engage in security policy based on domestic logics. By arguing in the terminology of risk, government and private-sector actions are brought in line with each other. Secretary Ridge can thus combine the two and argue that 'if you look at homeland security from a business perspective, we are in a diverse risk-management business' (Ridge 2004a).

Arguing CIP by means of the concept of risk indicates that government must 'carefully weigh the benefit of each homeland security endeavor and only allocate resources where the benefit of reducing risk is worth the amount of additional cost' (Bush 2002: 64). Risk becomes the baseline for government action. This argument puts government strategy in line with that of private actors, and government can thus justifiably argue that:

> The private sector should conduct risk assessments on their holdings and invest in systems to protect key assets. The internalization of these costs is not only a matter of sound corporate governance ... but also an essential safeguard of economic assets for shareholders, employees, *and the Nation*.
>
> (Bush 2002: 12, italics added)

Recourse to the government's conceptualization of private actors as both economic and patriotic subjects, as well as to the concept of risk, ensures that the
strategies of the two actors are compatible, as the rationalities and not least the
goals are in fact argued as being essentially the same. Security is thus not
exclusively defined as absolute and unconditional protection. Now a fundamentally economic logic is introduced to the government discourse. Securing critical
infrastructure is conditioned on whether it is worth the additional cost. The
concept of 'risk' is argued as a new basis for providing security inside sovereign
space. It works 'with the grain' of society. The traditional conceptualization of
security, on the other hand, limits and hinders the processes necessary for the
continued function of society; it creates boundaries. Conversely, risk strategies
apparently fit in, enable and facilitate the flows of society, as they are already
part of society. Accordingly, risk becomes a central concept in the discourse on
how to provide CIP. According to Secretary Chertoff, the term is the basis for a
whole new 'philosophy' applied to security (Chertoff 2005d). Security becomes
guided by the concept of risk.

What does 'risk' mean in this context? It is not easy to find a clear-cut definition of what exactly a risk-based approach will achieve, apart from providing a
new solution to what is seen as a new problem, which, at the same time, will
'provide a baseline for investment decisions' (Bush 2003a: 34). Risk is argued
as a new way of thinking about how to manage threats and constitutes 'a general
model for assessing risk and deciding on the protective measures we undertake
(Chertoff 2005b). The central point is how risk assessment is done. In the words
of Secretary Chertoff: '[W]henever we make a risk analysis, we have to also
make a cost-benefit analysis' (Chertoff 2005c). This is clearly an expression of
government action rationalized by an essentially economic discourse, which
differs from the traditional worst-case discourse of security. However, the conceptualization of risk is not in sync with that of private actors. In the context of
risk, talking the talk is easier than walking the walk, because government strategies inevitably become entwined with traditional worst-case security scenarios.
When it is stated that in the present 'threat environment ... private sector owners
and operators should reassess and adjust their planning, assurance, and investment programs to better accommodate the increased risk presented by deliberate
acts of violence' (Bush 2003a: x), it is clear that although the rationale guiding
government and private actors may be the same, the assessment of what is
necessary is not. The costs and benefits associated with risk-based critical infrastructure protection do not add up in the same way. Although government discourse might be changing, the ultimate goal is not. The function of 'risk-based
analytical tools' is to bring government 'in a position to anticipate the national
security, economic, and public safety implications of terrorist attacks' (DHS
2004: 11). On the face of it, this leaves the impression that government action –
on the basis of risk assessments – aims at discriminating between various terror
attacks and their effects. It thus follows that there are some terrorist attacks that
have only insignificant implications for national security, or maybe even none at
all. Terror is made relative by the concept of risk.

This view is diametrically opposed to the conception outlined earlier. If, as stated by President Bush, every terrorist attack has a national impact (Bush 2003a: ix), then every terrorist attack is important. This effectively annuls the discriminating function of risk. There are two simultaneous CIP rationalities at work in government strategies, with two opposing goals. On the one hand, the goal of absolute protection inevitably expands the meaning of critical infrastructure protection, and security concerns cover more and more parts of society and thus necessarily integrate an increasing number of private actors. On the other hand, the concept of risk makes anti-terror strategies relative, dependent on other goals besides absolute protection. There is a fundamental conceptual instability in the discourse on how to protect critical infrastructure and secure society. Risk introduces probability as the basis for action, which makes sense from the economic-risk perspective of business. Taking action based on calculated risk is a normal and legitimate business practice. However, that is not the way things usually work when national security is at stake. In the national security context, action is usually justified by the precautionary principle of 'better safe than sorry' (on the precautionary principle as security strategy, see Rasmussen 2006: 123–9; Aradau and van Munster 2007). Risk analysis depends on how important the object of analysis is deemed to be, and on how the consequences of putting it at risk are assessed; ultimately, it depends on a cost–benefit analysis. Furthermore, when protection from terror has already been defined as the most important activity of the state, the costs of a terrorist attack are always already analysed as being too high; the risk of incurring such an attack would always be catastrophic. Applying a risk perspective will not fundamentally change this, and thus the goal of securing the homeland is still conceived as consisting of 'absolute protection'. The two opposing conceptualizations, which are not easily made compatible, both live on in the discourse.

Paradoxically, applying both probability and security to critical infrastructure protection are not without political effects in the government's discourse. First, working with the concept of risk opens the door to domestic space. The traditional tools of security are neither applicable nor legitimate in the long run when applied inside society, as mentioned above; to shut down a port completely is not a viable strategy. Risk functions as a means of legitimizing state interventions in domestic space. By arguing security through risk as a 'normal' activity routinely carried out by private actors in making their own security policies, the focus of which is by definition domestic, the government can create security inside its sovereign space by applying the same concept. The concept of risk, in addition to opening domestic policy fields to direct government action, also opens up discursive space for engaging private actors. By arguing government strategies as being based on risk, the policies and goals of government are brought into agreement with, and argued in the same language as, private business. The concept of risk helps to discipline private actors and to ensure that they work towards government goals, without applying the traditional disciplinary means of sovereign power. Second, the conceptual differences between risk and absolute protection introduce two temporalities with two different rationales. Risk functions as a means of managing the present, and the goal of providing absolute protection is pushed into the future. The state can thus claim to fulfill its constitutional commitments by continuously arguing that it is minimizing risk in the present. This gives the government the conceptual means to construct the reality of CIP as a constant 'work in progress'. Taken together, the concepts of present risk management and future absolute protection allow the government to argue that it is working towards an end-state when protection will be simultaneously absolute, all-inclusive, and devoid of the drawbacks of traditional security policy. The goal of the discourse then consists of effectively combining the two in a future when 'security measures are a comfortable, convenient part of our routine' (Chertoff 2005d).

Conclusions: critical infrastructure and the changing practice of security

The attacks on New York and Washington on 11 September 2001 revealed the vulnerability of the continental US, and made clear that the protective functions of traditional border practices are not sufficient to secure the territory and population of the US. But providing security and territorial integrity is still a central conception of state sovereignty; it is argued as a constitutional commitment. 'Homeland security' consists of protecting the sacred territory from the dangerous outside (Lipschutz 2001: 75). In order to do so, the security strategies of the state are decoupled from the physical borders of the nation; border control practices are moved to the outside. Simultaneously, efforts are made to recreate the protective functions of borders inside society. Accordingly, political discourse on critical infrastructure protection can be seen as part of an effort aimed at maintaining state sovereignty under conditions seen as new and dangerous. This development can be seen as an empirical manifestation of the state's attempts to come to terms with how to make security in an era of debordered borders. This chapter has attempted to break down the discourse and open it up for analysis by splitting it up into three parts: the definitions of CIP, the relationship between the actors, and finally the concepts and strategies of the discourse. In this way, new conditions of possibility for security were illustrated.

Due to the very broad conception of the objects of CIP, which makes them almost synonymous with society in general, integrating private actors in the practice of security becomes a central aim for the state. To this end, private actors are given a privileged position. Together, these two aspects – how private actors and critical infrastructure are conceptualized – are of great importance for the strategies that governments can pursue. These changes create new conditions of possibility for the provision of security that diverge from traditional security practice. As security changes – in accordance with what is considered new conditions – maintaining the meaning of sovereignty is made difficult. Security is changed as the practice moves into society. On the one hand, the task of securing society is privatized by sharing responsibility with owners and operators of critical infrastructure. Government discourse declares them to be security actors, and this empowers them vis-à-vis the rest of society. Simultaneously, sovereign power is limited by this domestication. The state has to subjugate itself to the domestic logic of the market in order to act inside domestic space and to negotiate security strategies with private actors, which is achieved largely by employing the concept of risk. On the other hand, the goal is still 'absolute protection', which implies a spillover of the traditional dynamics of security into society. Security is domesticated and privatized, while the private is securitized. The outside and inside faces of the state are conflated when the state attempts to make security on the inside. The traditional conception of state practice is changed by this conflation, and the discursive formation on which this practice rests is destabilized.

Employing the concept of risk is a strategy that in itself further destabilizes the discourse. Security is traditionally a binary concept. You are either secure or you are not; the concept is an existential one aiming at finality, and at 'the absolute protection of our citizens'. As such, it is opposed to risk, which is a probabilistic concept aimed at managing an ongoing process. Risk is essentially linked to the notion of being insecure. The discourse of the current US administration is paradoxically applying both, by using risk management as a strategy to achieve a secure end-state. This central duality runs through the discourse on CIP. This has been the case both in the way in which the sovereign prerogative of providing security clashed with market-based politics, and in how the goal of absolute protection clashed with risk management strategies. This duality lives on in the discourse, and will be a constant source of conceptual instability in debates over how to provide security inside society; the security strategies of the state will inevitably find themselves strung out between the absolute rationalities of the sovereign state and the diversified concerns of society. The duality leaves the state in an almost schizophrenic position.

Consequently, instead of creating finality, merging these concepts leads to conceptual instability and a continuing sense of insecurity. The threat is argued as an existential one, but by simultaneously employing risk strategies, it is conceded that the threat can only be managed, not overcome. The combination of these two factors implies that the condition of security inside society and thus also US sovereignty will constantly be questioned. CIP and other homeland security initiatives cannot ensure public confidence in the government. They can only, as Bush states in the *National Strategy for Homeland Protection*, '*reassure* the public and *reinforce* its confidence in our institutions' (Bush 2002: 11, italics added). Security requires constant reassurance and reinforcement, and there is thus a tendency for the state to spread security – in the form of CIP or other practices – to cover more and more parts of society. But as illustrated, this is not feasible from the perspective of a liberal state. The state is caught in a dilemma between expansion and retreat. The conceptual conflict between absolute security and the flows of (global) society lives on in practice.

References

Albert, M., Jacobson, D. and Lapid, Y. (eds) (2001) *Identities, Borders, Orders: Rethinking International Relations Theory*, Minneapolis: University of Minnesota Press.

Anderson, J., O'Dowd, L. and Wilson, T.M. (2002) 'Why study borders now?', *Regional and Federal Studies*, 12, 4: 1–12.

Andreas, P. (2000) *Border Games: Policing the US-Mexico Divide*, Ithaca: Cornell University Press.

—— (2003) 'Redrawing the line: borders and security in the twenty-first century', *International Security*, 28, 2: 78–111.

Andreas, P. and Biersteker, T. (eds) (2003) *The Rebordering of North America: Integration and Exclusion in a New Security Context*, New York: Routledge.

Aradau, C. and van Munster, R. (2007) 'Governing terrorism through risk: taking precautions, (un)knowing the future', *European Journal of International Relations*, 13, 1: 89–115.

Arquilla, J., Ronfeldt, D. and Zanini, M. (1999) 'Networks, netwar and information age terrorism', in Lesser, I.O., Hoffman, B., Arquilla, J., Ronfeldt, D. and Zanini, M. (eds) *Countering the New Terrorism*, Santa Monica: RAND.

Beck, U. (2003) 'The silence of words: on terror and war', *Security Dialogue*, 34, 3: 255–67.

Biersteker, T. (2003) 'The rebordering of North America? Implications for conceptualizing borders after September 11', in Andreas, P. and Biersteker, T. (eds) *The Rebordering of North America: Integration and Exclusion in a New Security Context*, New York: Routledge, pp. 153–66.

Bigo, D. (2000) 'When two become one: internal and external securitizations in Europe', in Kelstrup, M. and Williams, M. (eds) *International Relations Theory and the Politics of European Integration*, London: Routledge, pp. 171–204.

—— (2001) 'The Möbius ribbon of internal and external security(ies)', in Albert, M., Jacobson, D. and Lapid, Y. (eds) *Identities, Borders, Orders: Rethinking International Relations Theory*, Minneapolis: University of Minnesota Press, pp. 91–117.

Blatter, J. (2001) 'Debordering the world of states: towards a multi-level system in Europe and a multi-polity system in North America? Insights from border regions', *European Journal of International Relations*, 7, 2: 175–209.

Boswell, C. (2003) 'The 'external dimension' of EU immigration and asylum policy', *International Affairs*, 79, 3: 619–38.

Bush, G.W. (2001) *Executive Order Establishing Office of Homeland Security*, Washington, DC, 8 October 2001. Online. Available at: www.whitehouse.gov/news/releases/2001/10/20011008–2.html (accessed 23 October 2007).

—— (2002) 'Preface' to *The National Strategy for Homeland Security*, Washington, DC: Office of Homeland Security. Online. Available at: www.whitehouse.gov/homeland/book/ (accessed 23 October 2007).

—— (2003a) *The National Strategy for the Physical Protection of Critical Infrastructures and Key Assets*, Washington, DC: The White House. Online. Available at: www.whitehouse.gov/pcipb/physical_strategy.pdf (accessed 23 October 2007).

—— (2003b) *Homeland Security Presidential Directive/HSPD-7*, Washington, DC, 17 December 2003. Online. Available at: www.whitehouse.gov/news/releases/2003/12/20031217–5.html (accessed 23 October 2007).

Castells, M. (2000) *The Rise of the Network Society*, 2nd edn, Oxford: Blackwell Publishers.

Chertoff, M. (2005a) *Transcript of Secretary of Homeland Security Michael Chertoff at the U.S. Chamber of Commerce*, Washington, DC: US Chamber of Commerce, 29 April 2005. Online. Available at: www.dhs.gov/xnews/speeches/speech_0250.shtm (accessed 23 October 2007).

—— (2005b) *Remarks for Secretary Michael Chertoff U.S. Department of Homeland Security George Washington University Homeland Security Policy Institute*, Washington, DC: George Washington University, Homeland Security Policy Institute, 16 March 2005. Online. Available at: www.dhs.gov/xnews/speeches/speech_0245.shtm (accessed 23 October 2007).

—— (2005c) *Testimony by Secretary Michael Chertoff Before the House Homeland Security Committee*, Washington, DC, 13 April 2005. Online. Available at: www.dhs.gov/xnews/testimony/testimony_0034.shtm (accessed 23 October 2007).

—— (2005d) *Transcript of Secretary of Homeland Security Michael Chertoff at the Center for Strategic and International Studies*, Washington, DC; Center for Strategic and International Studies, 19 May 2005. Online. Available at: www.dhs.gov/xnews/speeches/speech_0252.shtm (accessed 23 October 2007).

Clinton, W. (1996) 'Executive Order 13010: critical infrastructure protection', *Federal Register*, 61, 138: 37347–50.

—— (1998) *The Clinton Administration's Policy on Critical Infrastructure Protection: Presidential Decision Directive 63*, Washington, DC, 22 May 1998. Online. Available at: www.fas.org/irp/offdocs/paper598.htm (accessed 23 October 2007).

DHS (Department of Homeland Security) (2004) *Securing Our Homeland: US Department of Homeland Security Strategic Plan*, Washington, DC: US Department of Homeland Security. Online. Available at: www.dhs.gov/xlibrary/assets/DHS_Strat-Plan_FINAL_spread.pdf (accessed 23 October 2007).

Guild, E. (2003) 'International terrorism and EU immigration, asylum and borders policy: the unexpected victims of 11 September 2001', *European Foreign Affairs Review*, 8, 3: 331–46.

Hart, G. and Rudman, W. (2001) *U.S. Commission on National Security/21st Century*. Online. Available at: www.au.af.mil/au/awc/awcgate/nssg/ (accessed 23 October 2007).

Hertz, J. (1957) 'Rise and demise of the territorial state', *World Politics*, 9: 473–93.

Hertzog, L. quoted in Albert, M. and Brock, L. (1996) 'Debordering the world of states: new spaces in International Relations', *New Political Science*, 35, Spring: 69–106.

Hinsley, F. (1967) 'The concept of sovereignty and the relations between states', *Journal of International Affairs*, 21, 2: 242–52.

Hobbes, T. (1996) [1651] *Leviathan*, Oxford: Oxford University Press.

Huysmans, J. (2000) 'The European Union and the securitization of immigration', *Journal of Common Market Studies*, 38, 5: 751–77.

—— (2004) 'A Foucaultian view on spill-over: freedom and security in the EU', *Journal of International Relations and Development*, 7, 3: 294–318.

Kratochwil, F. (1986) 'Of systems, boundaries, and territoriality', *World Politics*, 39: 27–52.

Lapid, Y. (2001) 'Introduction. Identities, borders, orders: nudging International Relations theory in a new direction', in Albert, M., Jacobson, D. and Lapid, Y. (eds) *Identities, Borders, Orders: Rethinking International Relations Theory*, Minneapolis: University of Minnesota Press, pp. 1–20.

Lewis, J. (2003) 'Cyber terror: missing in action', *Knowledge, Technology & Policy*, 16, 2: 34–41.

Lipschutz, R. (2001) '(B)orders and (dis)orders: the role of moral authority in global poli-
tics', in Albert, M., Jacobson, D. and Lapid, Y. (eds) *Identities, Borders, Orders:
Rethinking International Relations Theory*, Minneapolis: University of Minnesota
Press, pp. 73–91.

Liscouski, R. (2004) *Statement by Robert Liscouski, Assistant Secretary for Infrastructure Protection, US Department of Homeland Security, Before the House Homeland
Select Subcommittee on Infrastructure and Border Security and Subcommittee on
Cybersecurity, Science, and Research & Development*, Washington, DC, 21 April
2004. Online. Available at: www.iwar.org.uk/cip/resources/hsc-apr-21–04/Liscouski.
doc (accessed 12 November 2007)

Lopez, B. (2006) 'Critical infrastructure protection in the United States since 1993', in
Auerswald, P., Branscomb, L.M., LaPorte, T.M. and Michel-Herjan, E. (eds) *Seeds of
Disaster, Roots of Response: How Private Action can Reduce Public Vulnerability*,
Cambridge: Cambridge University Press, pp. 37–50.

Lutterbeck, D. (2005) 'Blurring the dividing line: the convergence of internal and external security in Western Europe', *European Security*, 14, 2: 231–53.

Malcolm, J. (2002) *Statement of John G. Malcolm, Deputy Assistant Attorney General,
Before the Committee on Governmental Affairs, US Senate*, Washington, DC: US
Senate, 8 May 2002. Online. Available at: www.senate.gov/~gov_affairs/
050802malcolm.htm (accessed 23 October 2007).

Morgenthau, H. (1948) *Politics Among Nations*, New York: Knopf.

Moteff, J. and Parfomak, P. (2004) *Critical Infrastructure and Key Assets: Definition and
Identification*, CRS Report to Congress, Washington, DC: Congressional Research
Service and Library of Congress.

Moteff, J., Copeland, C. and Fischer, J. (2003) *Critical Infrastructures: What Makes an
Infrastructure Critical?* CRS Report to Congress, Washington, DC: Congressional
Research Service and Library of Congress.

PCCIP (President's Commission on Critical Infrastructure Protection) (1997) *Critical
Foundations: Protecting America's Infrastructures*, Washington, DC: US Government
Printing Office.

Petersen, K. (forthcoming, 2008) 'Terrorism: when risk meets security', *Alternatives*,
special issue.

Rasmussen, M. (2006) *The Risk Society at War: Terror, Technology and Strategy in the
Twenty-First Century*, Cambridge: Cambridge University Press.

Ridge, T. (2002) quoted in *The New York Times*, 6 September 2002, p. 14.

—— (2003) *Statement of Secretary Tom Ridge, Department of Homeland Security,
Before the Senate Committee on Commerce, Science and Transportation*, Washington,
DC: Senate Committee on Commerce, Science and Transportation, 9 April 2003.
Online. Available at: www.globalsecurity.org/security/library/congress/2003_h/
030409-ridge.htm (accessed 23 October 2007).

—— (2004a) *Secretary Ridge's Remarks at Harvard Business School's Leadership and
Values Forum*, Boston, 11 February 2004. Online. Available at: www.dhs.gov/xnews/
speeches/speech_0154.shtm (accessed 12 November 2007).

—— (2004b) *Remarks by Secretary of Homeland Security Tom Ridge at the
Public/Private Sector Program on Emergency Preparedness*, Phoenix, 28 September
2004. Online. Available at: www.dhs.gov/xnews/speeches/speech_0217.shtm
(accessed 12 November 2007).

—— (2004c) *Secretary Tom Ridge on the One-Year Anniversary of the Department of
Homeland Security*, speech at the George Washington University, Homeland Security

Policy Institute, Washington, DC, 23 February 2004. Online. Available at: www.dhs.gov/xnews/speeches/speech_0155.shtm (accessed 12 November 2007).

Robinson, P., Woodard, J.B. and Varnado, S.G. (1998) 'Critical infrastructure: interlinked and vulnerable', *Issues in Science and Technology*, 15, 1: 61–7.

Rudolph, C. (2005) 'Sovereignty and territorial borders in a global age', *International Studies Review*, 7, 1: 1–20.

Salter, M. (2004) 'Passports, mobility, and security: how smart can the border be?' *International Studies Perspectives*, 5, 1: 71–91.

Serrano, M. (2003) 'Bordering on the impossible: US-Mexico security relations after 9–11', in Andreas, P. and Biersteker, T. (eds) *The Rebordering of North America: Integration and Exclusion in a New Security Context*, New York: Routledge.

Sassen, S. (1996) *Losing Control? State Sovereignty in an Age of Globalization*, New York: Columbia University Press.

Stohs, B. (2002) 'Protecting the homeland by exemption: why the Critical Infrastructure Information Act of 2002 will degrade the Freedom of Information Act', *Duke Law & Technology Review*, 18. Online. Available at: www.law.duke.edu/journals/dltr/articles/2002dltr0018.html (accessed 23 October 2007).

Studeman, W. (1995) *Testimony of Acting Director of Central Intelligence William O. Studeman*, ADCI Testimony 4/6/95, Washington, DC: US House Judiciary Committee, 6 April 1995. Online. Available at: www.fas.org/irp//congress/1995_hr/h950406s.htm (accessed 23 October 2007).

Tenet, G. (1997) *Statement by Acting Director of Central Intelligence George J. Tenet Before the Senate Select Committee on Intelligence, Hearing on Current and Projected National Security Threats to the United States*, Washington, DC, 5 February 1997. Online. Available at: www.fas.org/irp/cia/product/dci_testimony_020597.html (accessed 23 October 2007).

US Congress (2002) Homeland Security Act of 2002, HR 5005 EAS, Washington, DC. Online. Available at: news.findlaw.com/hdocs/docs/terrorism/hsa2002.pdf (accessed 23 October 2007).

US President's Commission on Critical Infrastructure (1997) *Critical Foundations: Protecting America's Infrastructures: The Report of the President's Commission on Critical Infrastructure Protection*, Washington, DC: US Government Printing Office.

Walker, R. (1993) *Inside/Outside: International Relations as Political Theory*, Cambridge: Cambridge University Press.

Wæver, O. (1995) 'Securitization and desecuritization', in Lipschutz, R. (ed.) *On Security*, New York: Columbia University Press, pp. 46–86.

Wæver, O., Buzan, B., Kelstrup, M. and Lemaitre, P. (eds) (1993) *Identity, Migration and the New Security Agenda in Europe*, London: Pinter Publishers.

4 Critical infrastructures and network pathologies

The semiotics and biopolitics of heteropolarity

James Der Derian and Jesse Finkelstein

60 years ago a moth flew into a Mark II computer in a Harvard lab crashing it and the term computer 'bug' was born.

And although the planning was not complete, a lot of work had been done. But there were two problems here. First of all, it's as if someone took that plan and dropped an atomic bomb simply to make it more difficult. We didn't merely have the overflow, we actually had the break in the wall. And I will tell you that, really, that perfect storm of combination of catastrophes exceeded the foresight of the planners, and maybe anybody's foresight ... I think we have discovered over the last few days that with all the tremendous effort using the existing resources and the traditional frameworks of the National Guard, the unusual set of challenges of conducting a massive evacuation in the context of a still dangerous flood requires us to basically break the traditional model and create a new model – one for what you might call kind of an ultra-catastrophe.

> (Secretary of Department of Homeland Security Michael Chertoff,
> 3 September 2005 [CNN 2005a])

At a news conference, Mr. Chertoff called the hurricane and subsequent flooding, an 'ultra-catastrophe' that exceeded the foresight of planners. Asked what the government's response signified about the nation's preparedness for a potential terrorist attack, Mr. Chertoff said, 'If an ultra-catastrophe occurs, there's going to be some harmful fallout'.

> (McFadden 2005)

When our security mandarins so badly mix disasters as well as metaphors and so baldly duck responsibility by coining terms like 'ultra-catastrophe', it is probably time to run for the hills. Under the Bush administration, the hype of the 'global war on terror', the fiasco of Iraq, and the debacle of New Orleans converged to produce a rising tide of 'toxic soup', as the residue of Hurricane Katrina became charmingly known. Numerous investigations were launched into immediate causes and consequences. A common feature of all these developments was a failure of intelligence, of the technical kind that relies on satellites, spies and analysts but also of critical intelligence, the kind that searches out unasked questions and alternative solutions rather than hide behind linguistic gymnastics, bureaucratic excuses, and political apologia. Unsurprisingly, this failure also plagues the latest growth industry of the national security state: critical infrastructure protection (CIP).

This chapter aims to disturb conventional definitions, interrogate general assumptions and challenge the very validity of 'critical infrastructure protection'. In order to do so, it raises some fundamental questions: what makes an infrastructure 'critical' and in need of protection? Who says so, and by what authority? How have new actors redefined the security discourse? We seek answers to these questions by undertaking a *semiotic* investigation of a new *heteropolarity*, in which networked private actors challenge the exclusive prerogatives and capacities of the public sector to define and protect its citizens, creating a new *biopolitics* that trumps the traditional security concerns of the body politic.

The evolution of critical infrastructure protection: the physical, the virtual and the network

The spread of hybrid networks combining public and private sectors means that the ultimate guarantor of infrastructure security, the sovereign state, is in a bind. The most powerful networks are now global in nature, and, by definition, they resist state control. As a result, the legitimacy and efficacy of the traditional institutions of the international system, like balance of power, diplomacy and international law, have been greatly attenuated. International order can no longer be sustained by uni-, bi-, or multipolar configurations of power: the new global order is *heteropolar*, in the sense of a wide range of different actors, not only states, capable of producing profound global effects through interconnectivity. Varying in identity, interests and strength, new global actors gain advantage through the broad bandwidth of information technology; networked IT provides new global actors with the means to traverse political, economic, religious and cultural boundaries, changing, for instance, not only how war is fought and peace is made, but making it ever more difficult to maintain the very distinction of war and peace.

The 'West' might currently enjoy an advantage in the new heteropolar order, with its domination of surveillance, media and military networks; but the 'Rest', including fundamentalist terrorist groups, non-governmental organizations, and anti-globalization activists, have fully tapped the political potential of networked technologies of information collection, transmission and storage. In the recent past networked information technologies have traditionally signified the superiority of Western civilization over barbarian others; the perpetrators of the 11 September 2001 attacks were referred to as 'cave dwellers'. But a less culturally biased and more semiotically sensitive examination challenges this artificial distinction, one which is rhetorically perpetuated at our peril. Networks now produce (not always intentionally) shifting zones of inferiority and superiority, each with contingent advantages and disadvantages that are often based on the leveraging of power asymmetries. For instance, Bin Laden's appeal as well as longevity is a study of strategic choices of when best to be off the grid (and in the cave) or on the Internet (and promoting jihad).

Of course, the national security state, eminently powerful and intermittently pathological, is still very much with us, and will remain so, as *the* black box within a grid of networks. The challenge for the investigator is to get inside the operational box while staying outside the semiotic box of security discourse. To understand how the essential features of critical infrastructure – the powerful nodes, hubs and flows of networks – have transformed global politics, one must navigate between state secrecy and corporate opacity as well as between meta-theoretical debates and conventional levels of analysis.

Our response is to adopt a supra-state and extra-disciplinary approach for understanding what makes an infrastructure critical. We begin with Kevin Kelly's definition of a network, as 'organic behavior in a technological matrix' (Kelly 1999: 31). It might not be the most transparent definition, but it does capture a dual aspect of networks, linking the technical structure and effects of networks to innate features of human agency and complex vulnerabilities. The linkages become obvious when one considers the dual nature of globalized human networks (for instance, greater economic opportunity, but also more human trafficking), or digital interconnectivity (increased information flows, but a higher likelihood of computer virus attacks), or media convergence (broader coverage, but also increased likelihood of cascading dissimulations).

The primacy of the virtual: CIP as an information problem

Semiotics, or the study of signs, is not an approach endorsed by mainstream International Relations. Yet its origins, in the art of military signalling, was central to the security of the sovereign state. The same is true of 'infrastructure', which originally referred to physical installations that formed the basis or target for any military operations. From these shared origins we can surmise how the formation and potential destruction of the state and its capital city – or centre of gravity – first gave rise to a science of studying the fundamental facilities and systems of a physically specified territory, like transportation and communication systems, power plants and schools. Semiotics also provides us with clues for understanding how the modifier 'critical', added a new element to the assessment of vital interests. Just as 'national security' came to displace 'national interest' as stronger concept for appreciating the dangers of the nuclear age, so too has 'critical infrastructure' come to represent both physical structures *and* virtual systems in an information age.

The coining of 'critical infrastructure' is more than a single semantic shift: it represents an historical evolution in the determination of what is to be deemed critical. In recent years, the tag of 'critical infrastructure' gives primacy to infor-mational networks over physical assets. In Executive Order 13231 of 16 October

2001 *Critical Infrastructure Protection in the Information Age*, infrastructure is understood largely in the context of information:

> The information technology revolution has changed the way business is transacted, government operates, and national defense is conducted. Those three functions now depend on an interdependent network of critical information infrastructures. The protection program authorized by this order shall consist of continuous efforts to secure information systems for critical infrastructure, including emergency preparedness communications, and the physical assets that support such systems. Protection of these systems is essential to the telecommunications, energy, financial services, manufacturing, water, transportation, health care, and emergency services sectors.
>
> (Bush 2001)

President George W. Bush's Order is telling because it describes the complex hierarchy of infrastructural systems, both informational and physical. The goal of the Order is to 'secure information systems', where physical infrastructure is understood as 'supporting such systems'. Concomitantly, 'informational assets' support a more diverse array of systems, like financial services and energy. Here, informational infrastructure provides the structure that relates physical infrastructure to primary assets. This emphasis on the informational content of CIP is important definitionally, but also critically, as we will see later on, in determining the effectiveness and risks of CIP.

We can identify three stages to the semantical evolution of 'infrastructure'. It begins as a description of physical systems in a military space, and then expands to designate physical systems that sustain a territory. With the Internet boom and the emergence of cyberspace a new distinction is added to the meaning of infrastructure, between the virtual and the physical. Then, after 11 September 2001 and the creation of the Department of Homeland Security, we arrive at a more complicated picture where physical infrastructure is subsumed by the realm of virtual systems.

Within this general etymology, we can identify divergences and contradictions. As we mentioned previously, the international system increasingly resembles a heteropolar matrix with competing and collaborating actors, each with their own comprehension of CIP. In Global Security Matrix, our web-based visualization of these ideas (www.globalsecuritymatrix.org), we have organized these interpretations according to the levels of analysis provided by different infrastructures: Human, State, System, Network and Global. Human security is defined by two core negative rights of the individual: to be free of fear (safety) and free of want (well-being). Similarly, the definition of state security is negative, in that the state is charged with averting the extreme dangers of anarchy and tyranny. System security refers to those institutions and organizations that play a role in formalizing and institutionalizing norms and relations between states and non-state actors. Network security can be defined as the integrity of those webs of interconnectivity that allow various organizations of people to communicate, transfer and process information free from infringement and subversion. Global security refers to the prevention of events that present a danger beyond statehood or the individual, like nuclear holocaust or global warming. Each of these levels anticipates a different sense of what it means to be critical and what is referred to as infrastructure.

Our discussion of CIP touches on all of these levels, but for the time being, we will return to the most salient ones: the state, the network and the system. It is these levels of analysis that the President's Order directly refers to when discussing CIP. These levels also represent those sectors that are in the powerful position to frame the discussion of CIP. The state and the system are two of the most powerful, contending and collaborating levels of analysis that have gone the greatest lengths to define CIP. The term 'state' refers here to the federal and local levels of government, and 'system' refers to organizations such as think-tanks, corporations and NGOs that have made CIP their business. Throughout this chapter, we will more generally refer to these levels as the 'public' and 'private sectors', respectively.

When we previously discussed the evolving definition of infrastructure, we pointed out a major turning point that occurred after 11 September 2001, whereby CIP, which previously referred to two distinct terrains of infrastructure, was redefined. CIP became an information problem, in such a way that 'physical' and 'human assets' became terms in a virtual system. We would like to argue that this shift is primarily the result of the growing importance of the private sector in reframing CIP as a commodity both to drive corporate growth and to structure corporate responsibility.

The private sector's understanding of CIP

The private sector has a different appreciation for CIP than the public sector. Firms are not primarily interested in the peace and well-being of the nation – their main concern is the bottom line, which is their financial welfare – though this may require peace. One may argue that if a firm can continue to operate regardless of an attack or insure itself against risks to its 'body', then the motivation to invest proactively in CIP is minimal. Certainly, a peaceful environment is necessary for some companies to operate, but their ultimate goal is not peace, but wealth.

Another consideration for the private sector is the role of the US government in standardizing protocols for CIP. Since 11 September 2001, CIP has increasingly become a top priority of 'homeland security', i.e. the need to pre-empt, mitigate and recover from terrorist attacks. The DHS has understandably taken the lead in this effort, instituting the National Infrastructure Protection Plan (NIPP) to unify and integrate efforts towards CIP within a national programme. Companies are not required by law to implement CIP procedures, but the development of the NIPP is a strong indication that the US government may, in the near future, attempt to legislate for this standardization. In fact, since 2001, the general public's concern over security has driven many companies to invest in areas like CIP. This move seems primarily a public relations one – firms want to improve their public image by showing a deep commitment to the overall safety agenda of the US. With anticipated future attacks against the US and its allies, security investment will likely become an increasingly powerful tool to enhance a firm's reputation.

But what firms disregard in terms of physical assets they prize in virtual assets. In a brutal sense, any individual person in a firm is replaceable, and loss of employees is covered by insurance. If a company's building is destroyed or if an employee is killed, a new building can be purchased, a new employee can be hired. But theft, leaks or loss of information can mean the end of a corporation's livelihood. There is not just the danger of information disappearing or being leaked; the continuity and flow of that information is of equal importance, especially for many companies for whom time is a crucial factor in determining gains.

The most significant private-sector forces driving CIP, therefore, are cyber-crime and intellectual property theft. As we mentioned earlier, international relations has become a heteropolar matrix, and this fact is clearly evident in the threats against the private sector's knowledge resources. At almost every level of analysis, there is a potential risk to a company's IT infrastructure: from hackers looking to profit from stolen information, to 'cyber-terrorists' looking to compromise important resources. Entire nations have been identified as alleged perpetrators in the struggle against corporate IT espionage. In 2005, FBI Assistant Director for Counterintelligence David Szady cited Russia, Iran, Cuba, North Korea and China among countries allegedly engaging in espionage against the US (CNN 2005b).

While the 11 September 2001 attacks may have revealed the vulnerability of US physical assets, the private sector understood the attacks as foreshadowing the dangers posed to their information networks. In this way, the discourse and technology of CIP has moved increasingly towards the security of virtual assets. According to French Caldwell, an employee of Gartner, a leading technology analyst group, 'in a real-time economy, the physical and electronic systems are becoming more interdependent. In that real-time world, the Internet is the most critical infrastructure of all – without information and data, the real-time world grinds to a halt' (Caldwell 2003).

Whether this concern over the vulnerability of the virtual is legitimate, that is how CIP is being sold to the public sector. As will be shown in the following chapter, CIP is moving away from being seen as strictly a problem of protecting key physical resources, and is increasingly being regarded as an information problem. Moreover, this information problem is not simply a matter of protecting knowledge, but involves harnessing information to predict and protect infrastructures. Clearly, CIP cannot be reduced to hardware: again, networked technology not only exhibits organic, human behaviour, but in its more complex forms, to invoke Arthur C. Clarke, 'sufficiently advanced technology is indistinguishable from magic' (Clarke 1961). The greatest challenge is when negative synergy and cascading effects in dense networks produce *super-human* effects.

CIP technology trends for public and private crisis situations

As others have noted, CIP is fundamentally a human issue. This is true in many ways. Most notable is the way in which CIP technologies are articulated around the individual. For instance, knowledge management tools aim to codify human knowledge into the institutional workings of public and private-sector organizations. Organizations continually struggle with high turnover rates, as people switch jobs routinely. Knowledge management technologies help companies capture, manage and retain existing data so that an up-to-date knowledge base is available in real time across the organization. The intersection of knowledge management and CIP is clearly demonstrated by the fallout of 11 September 2001. The destruction of the World Trade Center greatly undermined the US economy. This was partly a consequence of the loss of information that was crucial to the performance and integrity of the firms residing in the Twin Towers. While the impact of human and technology 'inputs' cannot be determined with a safe margin of predictability, it is apparent that the loss of human knowledge presents a loss to a corporation's resources. Knowledge management tools are crucial for CIP, because they help retain important information despite massive catastrophes or risks. As one company has explained, in an era of increased uncertainty, in which companies are broadening their geographic reach, protection against loss of information and routine preservation of knowledge become crucial for the continued performance and effectiveness of the private and public sectors.

It is crucial that we interrogate this conflation of humanity, technology and CIP in order to reveal other human implications of CIP. In the following, we offer four depictions for the dual application of CIP technology in both national security and private corporate crisis situations. Knowledge management tools understand people as living networks – repositories of knowledge and data exchange. The role of knowledge management technology is to draw out this information and reinscribe it into the larger networks of public and private organizations. What is determined critical, then, is not the human 'incubator' of this knowledge, but the knowledge itself. Technology indeed becomes indistinguishable from magic when it can be used for extracting human thought from an individual, or possibly this is what makes it super-human.

This point brings us to the first human implication of CIP, which is, once again, the question 'what is critical'? According to the private sector, information networks appear to be the most crucial asset worthy of protection. As indicated above, 'the Internet is the most critical infrastructure of all'. The public sector may take a different approach to this question. One would hope that governments consider human life to be their most critical asset, yet states have an unfortunate history of attaching more importance to some people than to others. We shall remain sceptical for a moment and say that like corporations, governments value the persistence of their own information networks above the protection of their citizens. As we will show below, the 'information problem' that was previously the responsibility of corporations is now being handed over to governments. In other words, for the public sector, CIP is an information problem that can be managed using the same predictive and analytical technologies that many firms use to determine buying patterns. Now governments can purchase technologies that purportedly forecast criminal activity.

While the juridical implications of these technologies are daunting, many countries have been quick to mobilize this software to maintain the integrity of their networks. Which introduces us to the second human implication and question we shall engage with: who is CIP protecting? And, more importantly, who is CIP *not* protecting? Any introduction, by the public or private sector, of resources and technology that is intended to maintain the security of critical assets raises explicit political and juridical questions. For whose benefit these assets are protected, and how this protection is achieved, speaks directly to the condition of those outside the safety zone, and it is often these people whose critical assets are in the greatest need of protection. Always bearing in mind these all-too-human elements, we shall consider four situations, each of which refers to the main technological drivers behind CIP.

Scenario one: radio frequency identification (RFID)

RFID, or radio frequency identification, is a system for tracking and identifying items through a combination of tags placed on the items to be tracked and readers that interrogate those tags (via radio waves) at appropriate points in a distribution chain. RFID tags contain small integrated circuits that have tiny antennae for communicating with the RFID readers as well as the ability to store identification information. For the past two-and-a-half years, Wal-Mart has been working with the Auto-ID Center, a non-profit research organization based at the Massachusetts Institute of Technology, to develop and test RFID technology that will allow companies to track goods using a universal Electronic Product Code (EPC). The Auto-ID Center's long-term vision is for companies to use smart shelves to monitor how many items are on each shelf. When the inventory is low, the software would notify a store manager that more items need to be brought from the storeroom. Subsequently, readers in the storeroom would monitor the inventory and alert the distribution centre when more products are needed, and so on back through the supply chain. Ultimately, RFID is intended to help retailers refine supply orders and product placement.

A related development is the broader application of supply chain score-carding. Supply chain score-carding aligns operations with an organization's supply chain management strategy. By quantifying goals and objectives using shared criteria and metrics, a firm benefits from understanding how day-to-day operating decisions influence supply chain capability and performance. Top performers are rewarded while firms reduce dependency on sluggish trading partners. By monitoring and analysing data received from RFID chips, companies are better equipped to develop these metric indicators. Terrorist attacks, political instability in the developing world, and supply chain complexity have awakened managers to supply chain risks, some of which had been introduced or heightened by the very actions companies had taken to reduce costs in their supply chains. RFID allows companies to track the movement and stock of goods, so that, for example, if Indonesia should experience a civil war, Wal-Mart would be able to contact vendors in other countries to make up for supply shortfalls in the company's lumber products.

RFID is now being used to sustain the complex logistics of the occupation of Iraq. In the past ten years, the DOD has invested US$100 million in the implementation of active RFID chips. Active RFID tags have a battery, which allows them to emit a signal that increases the read range of the tag, while increasing the amount of data that the tag can store. Currently, the Department of Defense (DoD) is collaborating with Wal-Mart to advance passive RFID technology, which does not require manual scanning, but updates data automatically. One of RFID's chief advocates from the military is Vice Admiral (ret) Arthur Cebrowski, the father of 'network-centric warfare', who went on to head the DoD's Office of Force Transformation, and whose mantra is that the US should wage war like it conducts business – with Wal-Mart as his prime example. According to Alan Estev, Supply Chain Chief of the DoD:

> In Operation Iraqi Freedom – and in Operation Desert Storm, for that matter – logistics did not cause battlefield deaths. But your ability to operate and your ability to move about the battlefield are constrained by your ability to support the logistics, and RFID is a tool that will enable us to better support that force in a dynamic environment.
>
> (quoted in Gilbert 2004)

The role of RFID in security is not limited to overseas military activity. The Department of Homeland Security (DHS) is investing heavily in RFID technology, or what the DHS is referring to euphemistically as 'contactless chips'. Like passive RFID technology, contactless chips do not require manual scanning; instead, they emit a frequency which is automatically read by handheld or stationary scanners. In 2005, the DHS began issuing RFID-tagged employee ID cards (which include fingerprint records) to tens of thousands of its employees. The employee ID card used by the DHS has 'contactless' technology to give workers faster access to secure areas. The DHS is also evaluating technology pitches from several RFID tag manufacturers for an RFID-tagged passport containing biometric data. The government's plan will earn billions of dollars for the RFID suppliers while helping security officials track individuals more effectively by detecting their ID documents' radio signals in airport terminals, or wherever reader devices are present.

This use of RFID represents an important feature of CIP technology, because it demonstrates the desire on the part of the public sector to organize the system of networks that pervade and cross a nation's borders. However, this desire is nothing new. Since the first cities, fortifications were constructed to regulate movement and contact amongst neighbours. CIP distinguishes itself from these rudimentary efforts because the technology is not concerned with the physical space. As the recent efforts by the DHS indicate, CIP technology now converges on the virtual and biological. Paul Virilio points out in *Pure War* that technology has made the world smaller; the last fields of exploration and control will take place in the microcosm of the body and the elusive channels of the virtual (Virilio and Lotringer 1998). And, crucially, it is these two spaces, the virtual and the biological, that CIP technology conflates. Our biology becomes indistinct from the processor chips and memory cards that we use to compute information.

Scenario two: grid computing

Best known through the SETI programme, the concerted computer effort to detect intelligent life in the universe (*not* supported by the White House), grid computing has the potential to provide seamless and scalable access to widely distributed resources. Computational grids enable the sharing, selection and aggregation of a wide variety of geographically distributed computational resources (such as supercomputers, compute clusters, storage systems, data sources, instruments and people) and presents them as a single, unified resource for running large-scale, data-intensive computing applications.

The problem that underlies the grid concept is the difficulty of coordinating resource-sharing and problem-solving across multi-institutional virtual organizations. For instance, an industrial consortium formed to develop a feasibility study for a programme that would spatially model bio-terrorist attacks and natural pandemics undertakes a multidisciplinary simulation of such an event. This simulation integrates proprietary software components developed by different participants, with each component operating on that participant's computers and having access to the appropriate design databases and other data made available to the consortium by its members. Enabling these many virtual organizations to communicate and share information is the goal of grid computational architecture. Here, the establishment, management and exploitation of dynamic, cross-organizational firms sharing relationships require grid architecture, because the technology identifies the fundamental system components, specifies the purpose and function of these components, and indicates how these components interact with one another.

The operation of virtual organizations requires sharing relationships amongst *any* potential participants. Interoperability is thus the central issue to be addressed. In a networked environment, interoperability means common protocols. Grid architecture is first and foremost a protocol architecture, with protocols defining the basic mechanisms by which users and resources negotiate, establish, manage and exploit sharing relationships.

Another CIP-related example would be an internal crisis management team of a large chemical company responding to a chemical spill by using local weather and soil models to estimate the spread of the spill, determining the impact based on population location as well as geographic features such as rivers and water supplies, creating a short-term mitigation plan (perhaps based on chemical reaction models), and tasking emergency response personnel by planning and coordinating evacuation, notifying hospitals and so forth. The technology enabling this crisis management team to negotiate and manage the variety of information is the same technology that allowed the consortium of the previous scenario to develop the feasibility study. Grid architecture, in this latter case, allows the crisis management team to collect and evaluate a large amount of data from various resources to model the damage of the chemical spill.

Scenario three: network security and Trusted Information Sharing (TIS)

Just as a system is more than the sum of its parts, there is more to a network than nodes, hubs and connections (see Kelly's definition of networks). Since 11 September 2001, we have witnessed the emergence of competing sources of power in the shape of heteropolar networks, where different actors are able to produce profound global effects through interconnectivity. Trusted information-sharing and network security technologies help to prevent intrusion, whether from terrorists, competitors or state actors. Consider again the example of an industrial consortium developing a feasibility study on the spatial modelling program for bio-terrorist attacks and pandemics. Not only must this multidisciplinary and multi-firm effort integrate various independent technologies and elements of proprietary software, the consortium must also share important information to help model the incident. For instance, one firm, which specializes in tracking past disaster relief programmes, wants to contribute disaster relief models used in previous scenarios, but this firm wants only to share those models that are specific to the incidents measured by the consortium. Trusted information-sharing technology allows that firm to give the other members of the consortium access to data that the firm deems appropriate. For companies whose primary commodity is knowledge, trusted information-sharing is crucial, because the mediated distribution of information allows these companies to transfer knowledge efficiently without exposing the entirety of their data.

The introduction of trusted information-sharing technology in the preceding example is different than in the more infamous cases of hacked systems. In 2005, 40 million credit card accounts were jeopardized when computer data at an Arizona company was stolen, and nearly four million customers of the Citigroup financial services company were put at risk when UPS lost data tapes with personal information (Fountain 2005). More recently, hackers have stolen credit card accounts and other personal information from AT&T (Morphy 2006). In these instances, trusted information investment is not really a means of protecting data, but gives the impression or appearance of protection, which is, in many ways, more important. For AT&T, Citigroup or UPS, the loss of personal information does not really affect their operations. Those companies are far more concerned with protecting information that may yield future monetary gains, like patented applications or analytic programmes. Consumer faith in the integrity of such companies is an issue of public relations. If a company invests heavily in the protection of consumer data, that investment is worthless if it is not publicized. Alternatively, if a company's database containing consumer information is hacked, the hack will not affect the company's value if it is not publicized. The distinction in the type of implementation of TIS is significant, because in our discussion of CIP, determining what is actually 'critical' illuminates the most powerful use of technology.

Scenario four: Maximum Availability Architectures (MAAs)

Maximum Availability Architectures (MAAs) are ways of configuring computers so that even if one or more servers should crash, data and functionality are preserved. All hardware components of a storage array must be fully redundant, from physical interfaces to physical disks, including redundant power supplies and connectivity to the array itself. The complete storage is replicated at the secondary site for adequate data protection. A highly available network infrastructure may include redundant devices, such as DNS servers, to allow routing between primary and secondary sites, load balancers for routing to any available application servers, load balancers for routing to any available database node in the cluster, and physical layer switches.

In August of 2003, a power outage in the US reportedly affected more than 50 million people, including in the New York, Detroit and Cleveland metropolitan areas. Because New York City is a global financial centre, concern immediately arose about potential economic impacts of the outage. The power went out just after the stock markets closed Thursday, and the New York Stock Exchange quickly moved to assure investors it would be open for business as usual on Friday morning. While the attacks of 11 September 2001 brought disaster recovery and the need for redundancy to the forefront for many enterprises, other companies have beefed up their ability to withstand outages for business reasons. Despite the massive blackout in 2003, the Internet had enough redundancy and resilience to withstand most problems. Nonetheless, eBay recently signed a deal to outsource some of its web hosting to Intel in a bid to disperse its servers and prevent the kind of downtime that had plagued the company in the previous year, likely causing millions of US dollars in lost sales. The redundancy protocols that allowed the Internet and the World Wide Web to continue to perform also enabled companies and information resources, like CNN, to maintain their own individual services. The MAA implications for government are evident, as energy sources, such as electric grids, are frequently pinpointed as potential terrorist attack sites. In order to sustain operations in case of an attack, the public sector needs to be able to shift virtual resources quickly and flexibly from one location to another. In this way, MAA lends to the further virtualization of information, detaching data from any specific physical site, and transporting it to the ether of the information network.

The desert of the real

Before pushing these technological trends further and trying to realize the true potential of CIP technologies in the conflation of public and private sectors' efforts to monitor and routinize behaviour, we want to turn our attention back to the question of vulnerability and agency in networks. An early foray into this critical aspect of networks was made by sociologist Charles Perrow. In his now-classic book, *Normal Accidents: Living with High Risk Technologies*, he deploys the seemingly oxymoronic concept of the 'normal accident' to make sense of how catastrophes are inherent features of complex technologies, like nuclear power, petrochemical plants, the Space Shuttle and advanced weapon systems (Perrow 1984). He is particularly interested in how non-linear, tightly-coupled systems can produce a 'negative synergy' built upon a false mimicry of human decision-making. Perrow presents in detail how particular incidents escalate into systemic disasters when contrived 'solutions' interact to produce a negative synergy of increasingly complex problems. Might a similar effect be in operation when multiple networks – media, military and terrorist – become densely interconnected under the imperative of national security? In other words, is the national security state, in its very effort to prepare against catastrophic risks, actually increasing the probability of what could be called 'planned disasters'?

Scenario-making, modelling and gaming might differ in terms of the degree of abstraction and quantification involved, but what they have in common is a belief in the power of simulation to reduce the contingencies of reality. This faith might just be more dangerous than the dangers that simulations seek to anticipate and pre-empt. Do these technologies of representation actually contribute to outcomes that they are supposedly only attempting to predict? Are present dangers being constructed through the modelling of future threats? Channelling Jean Louis Borges (and in turn inspiring Morpheus' soliloquy in the movie *The Matrix*), Jean Baudrillard suggests that the simulation precedes and engenders the reality it purports only to model:

> Today abstraction is no longer that of the map, the double, the mirror, or the concept. Simulation is no longer that of a territory, a referential being, or a substance. It is the generation by models of a real without origin or reality: a hyperreal. The territory no longer precedes the map, nor does it survive it. It is nevertheless the map that precedes the territory – *precession of simulacra* – that engenders the territory, and if one must return to the fable, today it is the territory whose shreds slowly rot across the extent of the map. It is the real, and not the map, whose vestiges persist here and there in the deserts and that are not longer those of the Empire, but ours. *The desert of the real itself.*
>
> (Baudrillard 1994: 1)

This is not to deny that there are 'real' threats out there, including hostile actors and dangerous weather patterns. Rather, we aim to expose the extent to which present dangers are constructed through the simulation of future fears. This fear-induced syncretism of simulation and reality bubbles to the surface with every 'ultra-catastrophe', from 9/11 to Katrina to most recently the California wildfires – to which FEMA notoriously responded with a simulated press conference presented as the real thing (Lipton 2007).

A cautionary tale: CIA Sim/Stim 1

At the cusp of the twenty-first century, in the year 2000, the CIA's National Intelligence Council organized a crystal-ball exercise called Global Trends 2015, which can serve as an example of threat-constructing simulations. Organized around a year-long series of workshops at think-tanks, war colleges and universities, GT-2015 was designed to be a 'dialogue about the future among non-governmental experts'. The last event, 'Alternative Global Futures: 2000–2015', was co-sponsored by the Department of State's Bureau of Intelligence, and although it took place inside the Washington beltway, it was very much 'out of the box' based on the character of the participants.

After a series of pedagogical warm-up exercises, the participants were divided into break-out groups and asked to develop their own alternative future scenarios. As one might suspect, no one came back with simultaneous aerial terrorist attacks on the World Trade Center and the Pentagon. However, displaying less reluctance than others to mix fiction and fact, one of the authors of this chapter, James Der Derian (JDD) was selected to present the resulting scenario to the re-convened group. Here is what JDD presented to the assembled group:

> An electrical power grid goes down, and a black-out quickly spreads throughout the East Coast. President Warren Beatty publicly responds as if it is a catastrophic accident; but he is convinced by his National Security Council that a terrorist cyber-attack is actually to blame. Retaliatory strikes are ordered against suspected training camps in the Middle East; however, a plane is shot down by Stinger missiles (accidental blowback from an earlier struggle against the Soviet Union), a rescue mission is botched, and the situation quickly escalates into a shooting war. The kicker? It turns out after the fact that the originating cause of the electrical failure was neither intentional or accidental, but the result of a local electrical company mistaking a simulation training exercise of a terrorist attack as the real thing, leading to a series of cascading network effects that quickly run out of human control, transforming a local accident into a global event.

If Arnold Schwarzenegger rather than Warren Beatty had been cast as the acting president, perhaps the scenario would have made it into the final report. However, a few years later JDD was 'spooked' – in both senses of the word – after the November 2003 massive electrical power failure in the Northeast (set off by a falling branch in Ohio and spread through a series of cascading power surges), and which was bracketed – though this was not reported widely in the

US media – by significant electrical grid failures in Spain and Italy (two of the most prominent coalition partners of the US in Iraq).

Apart from making us wonder once again about technologies of representation and how they might actually contribute to outcomes that they are only predicting, there are four lessons that might be learned from the GT-2015 scenario and JDD's foray into world of scenarios: first, the networked nature of critical infrastructures – from the Internet to the electrical grid to the jihadist cell – will make it increasingly difficult to determine whether effects are the result of attack, accident – or some quantum blurring of the two. This not only makes it more difficult to map, game or simulate, but also to prevent, pre-empt and effectively manage future critical infrastructure events. Second, every new critical infrastructure has hard-wired into it the potential for an accident as well as a vulnerability to attack. Like the Titanic, Chernobyl, the Challenger shuttle and Wall Street, all new technologies produce disasters that can act as diagnoses for improvement – or grounds for termination. Third, the densely networked nature of critical infrastructures, even when taking into account redundancy and resiliency, makes it increasingly difficult to isolate or contain a future failure or attack. Fourth, facing critical infrastructure failure and being unable to deliver on its traditional promissory notes of safety, security and well-being, the sovereign state, even the US exercising state-of-emergency exceptions to reaffirm its hegemonic status, must increasingly turn to regional, international or private institutions to protect itself against and manage eventual attacks and failures.

This takes us into the apocalyptic – but suddenly more realistic – realm that Paul Virilio refers to as the 'integral accident' (Virilio 2007). Traversing and transgressing multiple boundaries (territorial, demographic, ideological and, most fundamentally, epistemological), triggering even more disastrous auto-immune reactions through preventive measures and punitive attacks, offering states the means to deny their diminished significance as well as to evade their public responsibility, the networked integral accident elevates the 11 September 2001 attacks on New York and Washington and the 7 July 2005 attack in London, as well as the US military debacle in Iraq and the mishandling of the Hurricane Katrina catastrophe, from singular episodes to an escalating continuum of disasters. Or, as Virilio once put it: 'The full-scale accident is now the prolongation of total war by other means'.

CIA Sim/Stim 2 and 'The Cycle of Fear'

There is a flip side to Virilio's conjecture that we have entered the age of accidents. The full-scale accident is not just one of catastrophe or trauma, but of *non*-accident. In 2003, the CIA followed up on its 2001 project with an updated version of its future scenarios. The published document, *Mapping the Global Future: Report of The NIC's 2020 Project*, described four different futures for the year 2020: *Davos World*, *Pax Americana*, *A New Caliphate* and *A Cycle of Fear* (National Intelligence Council 2004). While the CIA's dramatic flair makes each simulation interesting in of itself, the most relevant appears to be *A*

Cycle of Fear. A Cycle of Fear imagines a world in which 'fear begets fear' – nuclear proliferation runs rampant, and the 'draconian measures implemented by governments to stem proliferation and guard against terrorism' have put the fear of life into everyone. The text-message exchange between a 'terrorist' and an 'arms-dealer' provides the context for this scenario. The two protagonists have to evade technology that screens their communication; maintain the suspicion that the other person on the line might be a mole; and elude the monitoring chip that is embedded in people as a result of new post-PATRIOT Act laws.

Let's push this scenario further by combining it with the CIP technology trends identified above. Unlike the previous scenarios, there is no single event to contextualize this scenario. The US and its allies experience a few minor terrorist attacks, but nothing so radical occurs that puts the nation in jeopardy. Instead, things appear to be steadily moving along in a peaceable manner. All individuals are implanted at birth with a passive RFID chip that alerts authorities to their whereabouts, ethnicity, address, criminal history, health history, marital status and income. Imagine a continuously operable census that communicates with the government at all times. Then there are the analytic programmes which process this information through advanced equations to determine life expectancy and future criminal activity. In this way, authorities can pre-empt future crimes, and monitor individuals and areas that 'mathematically' hold a greater disposition towards violence or risk. These analytic programmes are enabled by the grid computing systems set up amongst various corporate sponsors: one develops the equations to determine individual risk, one spatially maps violent activity, one provides surveillance, and the last communicates with the police about individuals at risk. The public sector would not be able to introduce this RFID technology without help from the private sector, so the government leases out some of this personal data to corporations. Now, when customers enter a Wal-Mart, the RFID chip alerts the store to their buying patterns and other personal information, which allows the employees to better service their needs and anticipate their requirements.

In addition to functioning as an information-gathering device, the RFID chip also works with trusted information-sharing technology to assign virtual and physical access rights. In order to gain access to some communities, housing complexes or stores, one must have the appropriate access rights. This goes the same for Internet activity. Since all interaction with computer systems requires Internet dashboards, the moment one signs on, the computer communicates with the RFID chip, and customizes the dashboard with rights appropriate to the user. Children will automatically be directed to 'safe sites'; violent individuals will be restricted from contributing to and accessing inflammatory sites; sexual deviants will be unable to access various pornography sites. Trusted information-sharing technology is no longer the domain of corporations protecting knowledge, but now that it is conflated with CIP, TIS becomes a matter of conditioning the human mind.

Juridical and biopolitical implications of CIP technology

The above scenarios illustrate the juridical and biopolitical repercussions of CIP technology. We may return to the questions first asked in this paper concerning the human implications of CIP: what is deemed critical? Who/what is being protected? And who is not being protected? To answer these questions, let us first return to our discussion on the pathology of networks and relations of power.

There is something retrograde about CIP technologies. The diffusion of surveillance technology and RFID chips recalls the panopticism that Michel Foucault wrote was characteristic of the eighteenth century. From the time that the first factories, schools, prisons, barracks and hospitals were constructed, surveillance served to maintain the integrity, security and organization of social networks. However, not all modern spaces were under surveillance – as RFID technology has the potential to achieve. Modernity, according to Foucault, involved the construction of a private subjectivity engendered by these panoptic institutions. This private subjectivity was then reproduced in the public sphere. Individuals would become normalized by submitting themselves to observation and discipline and, in that sense, prevent their own crimes before they might happen. The penitentiary and panopticon produced the normal individual by also producing its twin – the criminal or abnormal:

> Prison and police form a twin mechanism; together they assure in the whole field of illegalities the differentiation, isolation and use of delinquency. In the illegalities, the police-prison system segments a manipulable delinquency. This delinquency, with its specificity, is a result of the system; but it also becomes a part and an instrument of it. So that one should speak of an ensemble whose three terms (police-prison-delinquency) support one another and form a circuit that is never interrupted. Police surveillance provides the prison with offenders, which the prison transforms into delinquents, the targets and auxiliaries of police supervisions, which regularly send back a certain number of them to prison ... Judges are the scarcely resisting employees of this apparatus. They assist as far as they can in the constitution of this delinquency, that is to say, in the differentiation of illegalities, in the supervision, colonization and use of certain of these illegalities by the illegality of the dominant class.
>
> (Foucault 1995: 282)

The same institutional techniques that disciplined the individual through surveillance also allowed for self-discipline by producing an Other by which 'normal' individuals could measure their success and articulate their limitations. In other words, a minority of delinquents was always necessary to re-encode the normal, 'law-abiding' individual when those disciplinary institutions failed to do so.

While CIP technology may resonate with this eighteenth-century network of power relations, Foucault and, more prolifically, Gilles Deleuze argue that the institutions of modernity (factories, schools, prisons, hospitals and barracks) are, in fact, in a state of obsolescence. The moment of disciplinary power, though its effects are still felt today, is long past. What Deleuze, following Foucault and Virilio, named 'the societies of control', are now replacing the disciplinary societies.

In an observation that is significant for our purposes, Deleuze traces the discontinuities in the transition from sovereign societies to disciplinary societies, and from disciplinary societies to control societies, by considering the evolution of technology and the machine (see also Bonditti, Chapter 6, this volume):

> It's easy to set up a correspondence between any society and some kind of machine, which isn't to say that machines determine different kinds of society, but that machines express the social forms capable of producing them and making use of them. The old sovereign societies worked with simple machines, levers, pulleys, clocks; but recent disciplinary societies were equipped with thermodynamic machines presenting the passive danger of entropy and the active danger of sabotage; control societies function with a third generation of machines, with information and technology and computers, where the passive danger is noise, and the active danger is piracy and viral contamination. This technological development is more deeply rooted in a mutation of capitalism.
>
> (Deleuze 1997: 181)

A number of crucial points follow: first, CIP is representative of this third generation of machines. As we discussed previously, the discussion of what is deemed critical in the public sphere is increasingly predicated on the private sector's interests. This discourse is partly shaped by the reselling of private-sector technologies to the public sector in the form of CIP, so that interpretations of protection and criticality are transferred along with the exchange of funds. As a result, the private sector takes on greater power in its relations with the public. Deleuze describes this mutation in capitalism as a shift from stricter, often government- and police-based forms of confinement and discipline of the social body to more flexible forms of control based in the corporation:

> The mutation has been widely recognized and can be summarized as follows: nineteenth-century capitalism was concentrative, directed toward production, and proprietorial. Thus it made the factory into a site of confinement ... But capitalism in its present form is no longer directed toward production, which is often transferred to remote parts of the Third World, even in the case of complex operations like textile plants, steelworks, and oil refineries. It's directed toward metaproduction ... It's a capitalism no longer directed toward production but toward products, that is, toward sales or markets ... Family, school, army, and factory are no longer so many analogous but different sites converging in an owner, whether the state or some private power, but transmutable or transformable coded configurations of a single business where the only people left are administrators.
>
> (Deleuze 1997: 182)

The new corporate methods of control are anticipated by such technologies like RFID, but there are contemporary examples such as the analytics used by Internet sites to track customer buying habits. Perhaps, RFID is the Internet taken out into the actual streets rather than merely existing in virtual space. However, what Deleuze may not have anticipated is this odd admixture of corporate control and discipline. This appears to be the most unnerving aspect of CIP technologies: the increasing conflation of public and private-sector interests, which obscures the usefulness of technology for individual humans. And in some way, this conflation obscures the relationship between the virtual and the physical, where humans are only viewed as so many gigabytes within a larger store of data.

This brings us to our second point, which is the biopolitical implication of this third generation of machines. During the latter half of the nineteenth century, Foucault describes a new technology of power which succeeds disciplinary power: 'the new nondisciplinary power is applied not to man-as-body but to the living man, to the man-as-living-being; ultimately, if you like, to man-as-species' (Foucault 2003: 242). The new technology addresses a multiplicity of humans, the 'biopolitics' of the human race:

> Biopolitics deals with the population, with the population as a political problem, as a problem that is at once scientific and political, as a biological problem and as power's problem ... In a word, security mechanisms have to be installed around the random element inherent in a population of living beings so as to optimize a state of life ... it is, in a word, a matter of taking control of life and the biological processes of man-as-species and of ensuring that they are not disciplined, but regularized.
>
> (Foucault 2003: 247)

Biopolitics anticipates Virilio's integral accident, but implicates humans, not technology, as the culprit behind the fallout. Therefore, human behaviour must not simply be disciplined, but kept apace with technology to prevent the accident. When we recall Deleuze's discussion of the third generation of machines, he mentions the active threat of viral contamination, which lends these virtual networks the quality of something biological. In our discussion of CIP, it is not humans that must be protected, but rather the network and the human as a node in the network that must be secured. Foucault understood biopolitics as illustrative of a form state power identified with nationalism, but what CIP technologies indicate is that biopolitics has evolved to a system of power where it is the health of the network – 'organic behavior in a technological matrix' – that becomes critical. It is not the body of the state that we must secure, but the conjoined body of public and private-sector networks.

This interweaving of the public and private sectors marks the difference between biopower in the post-disciplinary society and biopower in the control society. Foucault refers to biopower in conjunction with the rise of ethno-nationalism and specifically National Socialism. In this way, biopower becomes linked with racism, so that the state intervenes at this point by introducing a biological continuum of the human race, fragmenting the field of biological controls. Racism is:

> in short, a way of establishing a biological-type caesura within a population that appears to be a biological domain. This will allow power to treat that population as a mixture of races, or to be more accurate, to treat the species, to subdivide the species it controls, into the subspecies known, precisely, as races.
>
> (Foucault 2003: 255)

In this way, the continuity and the livelihood of the state are threatened by the invasion of inferior races – war is reintroduced or maintained in the political. Racism establishes a relationship, a war set in biological terms: 'the death of the other, the death of the bad race, of the inferior race (or the degenerate, or abnormal) is something that will make life in general healthier: healthier and purer' (Foucault 2003: 255). A good example is the recent evidence that the US census bureau reported Japanese Americans to US security agencies during the Second World War.

Unlike the strict hierarchy of the state, the power of the network resides partly in its ability to manage its perpetuation horizontally. Unlike the binary of 'inferior race' and 'übermensch', networks allow for greater flexibility in regulating controls and responsibilities – any one person can inhabit different roles in different situations. For instance, while various minorities in the US may receive the short end of the stick in terms of job opportunities, governmental support and political representation, those same minorities may occupy a more empowered position while consuming and shopping. In this way, the state does not annihilate and is not compelled to annihilate 'inferior races', since those groups are economically useful as consumers. It is this networked form of social organization that allows for these more mutable identities.

But the flexibility of networks does not mean that they are immune to racism, and herein lies the greatest misconception about CIP technologies. Information is never depoliticized, and while technologies like RFID may appear to accumulate information objectively and apolitically, how that information is encoded, articulated and interpreted is always political. It is important to remember that the Nazis were among the first to employ IBM listing technology in order to compute census data and to survey social threats. While CIP technology may provide some potential good, we cannot disconnect it from the systems of control and power that produced it.

Conclusion

If simulations and scenarios exacerbate rather than cure the pathology of networks, how are we to anticipate the next threat and protect our critical infrastructures? No one understood this conundrum better than Jorge Luis Borges, the great Argentinean writer on labyrinths and language. He once remarked 'that everything touches everything' – and it does so through the ubiquity of signs. Consider, then, that the modern systematic study of signs, or semiotics, first emerged in the sixteenth century, strangely connecting the arts of war *and* medicine. Semiotics referred not just to new methods of military manoeuvre based on a system of visual signalling, but also to new medical techniques for identifying symptoms of disease in humans. From the start, semiotics served to kill as well as to cure. Just as information is 'any difference that makes a difference' (Bateson 1979: 242), networks differentiate the living (organic) from the dead (inorganic). In the twenty-first century, in an age that is designated as the 'age of information' one day and the 'age of terror' the next, labels that both rely on interconnectivity, we need to recognize, to learn how to read the new semiotics of networks. We need to imagine the global politics of networks, as it rapidly cycles from Ground Zero to Zeros and Ones and back again, not as impending threat, but as ubiquitous code whose meaning can never be 'cracked' by a single source. The heterodox nature of this language can appear as a threat – or as an invitation to negotiate under conditions of heteropolarity differences of meaning with those who most radically differ from us. Otherwise, we will continue to treat the most powerful effects as well as the most morbid symptoms of networks with utopian schemes and morality plays, rather than reaching a common understanding of the power and the pathology of complex networks that become critical infrastructures.

References

Bateson, G. (1979) *Mind and Nature – A Necessary Unity*, New York: E.P. Dutton.

Baudrillard, J. (1994) *Simulacra and Simulation*, Ann Arbor: University of Michigan Press.

Bush, G.W. (2001) *Executive Order 13231: Critical Infrastructure Protection in the Information Age*, Washington, DC, 16 October 2001.

Caldwell, F. (2003) *What's Critical in Critical Infrastructure Protection*. Online. Available at: www.gartner.com/DisplayDocument?id=390753 (accessed 30 October 2007).

Clarke, A.C. (1961) *Profiles of the Future: An Inquiry into the Limits of the Possible*, New York: Harper & Row.

CNN (2005a) 'Chertoff: Katrina scenario did not exist. However, experts for years had warned of threat to New Orleans', *CNN Online*, 5 September 2005. Online. Available at: edition.cnn.com/2005/US/09/03/katrina.chertoff/ (accessed 30 October 2007).

—— (2005b) 'FBI spy chief asks private sector for help: Szady highlights threat of Chinese espionage', *CNN Online*, 11 February 2005. Online. Available at: edition.cnn.com/2005/US/02/10/fbi.espionage/index.html (accessed 30 October 2007).

Deleuze, G. (1997) *Negotiations 1972–1990*, trans. Martin Joughin, New York: Columbia University Press.

Foucault, M. (1995) *Discipline and Punish: The Birth of the Prison*, trans. Alan Sheridan, New York: Knopf Publishing Group.

—— (2003) *Society Must Be Defended*, trans. David Macey, New York: Picador USA.

Fountain, H. (2005) 'Worry. But don't stress out', *New York Times*, 26 June 2005.

Online.   Available   at: www.nytimes.com/2005/06/26/weekinreview/26fount.html (accessed 30 October 2007).

Gilbert, A. (2004) 'RFID goes to war', *CNET News.com*, 22 March 2004. Online. Available at: www.news.com/RFID-goes-to-war/2008–1006_3–5176246.html (accessed 30 October 2007).

Kelly, K. (1999) *New Rules for the New Economy*, London: Fourth Estate.

Lipton, E. (2007) 'FEMA fake news conference about wildfires', *New York Times*, 30 October 2007. Online. Available HTTP: www.nytimes.com/2007/10/30/washington/30fema.html?_r=1&ref=us&oref=slogin (accessed 30 October 2007).

McFadden, R.D. (2005) 'Bush pledges more troops as evacuation grows', *New York Times*, 4 September 2005. Online. Available at: www.nytimes.com/2005/09/04/national/nationalspecial/04storm.html (accessed 30 October 2007).

Morphy, E. (2006) 'Hackers steal AT&T customers' credit card data', *TechNewsWorld*, 30 August 2006. Online. Available at: www.technewsworld.com/story/52729.html (accessed 30 October 2007).

National Intelligence Council (2004) *Mapping the Global Future: Report of The NIC's 2020 Project*, Washington, DC, December 2004.

Perrow, C. (1984) *Normal Accidents: Living with High-Risk Technologies*, Princeton: Princeton University Press.

Virilio, P. (2007) *Original Accident*, Cambridge: Polity Press.

Virilio, P. and Lotringer, S. (1998) *Pure War*, New York: Semiotext.

Part II

Terrorism and the politics of protecting the homeland

5 Media, fear and the hyperreal

The construction of cyberterrorism as the ultimate threat to critical infrastructures

Maura Conway

[Cyberterrorism] isn't so much a threat to national security as a threat to civilization.

(Paul Vixie, quoted in Adams and Guterl 2003)[1]

More cyberterroristic than the cyberterrorists themselves, the cyberterror-inducing media have the information world at their mercy.

(Debrix 2001)

A central element of the post-11 September 2001 efforts to beef up US 'homeland security' has been an almost paranoid emphasis on the potentially catastrophic threats posed by cyberterrorism. A vast array of political, military, business, academic and media commentators have appeared on television and been quoted in newspapers predicting deadly attacks by terrorists on (and with the help of) the computerized infrastructures that now constitute the critical underpinnings of everyday urban life in the US. This depiction of computerized systems as a super-critical infrastructure and thus the Achilles' heel of advanced industrial societies, has been further fuelled by the use of everyday urban infrastructures as both weapons and targets of mass murder in the physical attacks of 2001 (Graham 2004).

Following the collapse of the USSR, a number of developments highlighted the growing influence of information technology in the realms of both national and international security. Examples include the high level of IT capability displayed by US troops in the first Gulf War (1990–1) and the increasingly global nature of media coverage, as demonstrated in the Somali (1993) and Balkan conflicts (1992–9). More recently, increased systems failures resulting from the activities of hackers, as evidenced by the cyber-attack(s) targeting Estonia in May 2007 and the growing use of the Internet for 'infowar' purposes by al-Qaida and a plethora of other sub-state political violence groups, have garnered substantial attention. The growing dependence of states, particularly of the US, on information technology was highlighted by these and other events, prompting fears of a radically new security threat: the possibility of information systems serving as both weapons and targets of attack.

This cyber-threat became the object of increased attention from the US federal government in the 1990s, in close connection with the more general critical infrastructure protection debate (see Dunn Cavelty, Chapter 2, this volume). A particular concern was that enemies of the US, unable to defeat US forces on the conventional battlefield, would pursue alternative approaches to inflicting damage on the sole remaining superpower (Pollard 2004: 43). The events of 11 September 2001 were therefore doubly shocking for many US government officials: not only were the attacks appalling in themselves, but the conventional (though asymmetric) nature of the attacks was also completely unexpected. Far from reducing the fear of cyber-attack however, for many, the 2001 attacks only served to increase the credibility of the cyber-threat.

According to a study released in June 2001, 75 per cent of Internet users worldwide believe in the existence of cyberterrorism. The survey conducted in 19 major cities around the world found that 45 per cent of respondents agreed completely that 'computer terrorism will be a growing problem', while 35 per cent of respondents agreed somewhat with the same statement (Poulsen 2001). In a July 2002 survey conducted by the American Business Software Alliance, 82 per cent of information technology professionals were said to believe that US businesses were ill-equipped to deal with cyberterrorism (King 2002), while a survey carried out by *Federal Computer Week* and the Pew Internet and American Life Project in 2003 found that about half of US citizens fear terrorists will launch cyber-attacks on those critical infrastructures that operate the banking, electrical, transportation and water systems, disrupting everyday life and crippling economic activity (Pew Internet and American Life Project 2003).[2] What these statistics show is that fear of cyberterror is in the zeitgeist. This chapter seeks to show how this threat image took root there and eventually came to be viewed as the ultimate threat to critical infrastructures.

The chapter's core argument is that US media outlets have been significant contributors not just to the dissemination, but to the actual discursive construction of the contemporary cyberterrorist threat and, further, that it is their emphasis on the (imagined) fatal connectivity between virtual networks and physical infrastructures that makes the concept of cyberterror so powerful. The chapter is divided into four sections. The first section explores the chapter's theoretical underpinnings, particularly the important role of the mass media in framing the threat and thus in agenda-setting. The second section focuses on how fears associated with terrorism and technology are linked in so-called 'shutdown-the-power-grid scenarios' to hype the threat to critical infrastructures from cyberterrorists. In the third section, two popular analogies associated with the cyberterror threat discourse are investigated: the possibility of an 'electronic Pearl Harbor' and the equation of cyber-attack tools, so-called 'weapons of mass disruption', with the threat from 'weapons of mass destruction' (WMD). The identification of specific antagonistic actors is crucial to successful threat construction; the shift in media focus from terrorist hackers to hacker terrorists is therefore at the centre of the fourth section. Finally, the conclusion looks at the consequences the cyberterror threat image has for the critical infrastructure debate, particularly the effects of cyberterror's 'hyperreal' character as displayed in the media and the interplay between threat construction, apocalyptic expectations and actual occurrences.

Theoretical underpinnings: threat politics

Traditional security studies views threat images as relatively unproblematic and assumes that real-world threats are directly reflected in security policy. In the last decade or so, practitioners of so-called 'new security' approaches have argued, on the contrary, that there is no natural or self-evident correlation between the substance of a threat image and whether it has an impact on the political agenda (see Buzan 1991; Buzan *et al.* 1998). They argue instead that the formation of agendas depends on power and politics, particularly on the ability of an actor or actors to 'speak' a threat into existence. Threat is first constructed in the individual consciousness; individuals view something as a threat. The next step is for an actor or actors in the threatened society to give form to the threat by talking or writing about it in public fora. That is, the threat assumes the trappings of language and is transformed into a topic of public debate. Very often, this happens through the dissemination of newspaper stories, magazine articles, television documentaries and, eventually, mass-market books and movies.

In the context of mass media, this process of formulating problems, finding scapegoats and coming up with solutions has been labelled 'framing'. For Robert Entman, '[t]o frame is to select some aspects of a perceived reality and make them more salient in a communicating text, in such a way as to promote a particular problem definition, causal interpretation, moral evaluation, and/or treatment recommendation for the item described' (1993: 52). Framing is a verbal expression of thought. Individuals perceive and interpret events; events are never simply given. Perception and interpretation are usually followed by verbalization: that is to say, actors give verbal form to their conceptions of threats and risks. The movement is thus from thought to speech and from the individual to the collective level of analysis. Generally, the choice of 'speech costume' has a major impact on whether an issue makes it onto the political agenda (Eriksson and Noreen 2002: 10).

One of the most significant forms of 'threat framing' or 'costuming' is to identify something as a 'security' threat. In the literature, this behaviour has come to be called 'securitization'. Security policy is often regarded as having precedence over all other policy fields, while national security policy is invariably viewed as the foundation of all security policy (Wæver 1995: 49). The upshot of this is that security policy and associated threat images are extremely loaded issues (Deibert 2002: 115). Exploitation of the politically loaded concepts of security and threat may, therefore, make it easier to insert an issue into the political agenda.

Agenda-setting

The agenda-setting model of the media posits that the mass media have an influence on what the public recognizes as important issues, and the theory has been supported by a wealth of empirical studies. There are two main approaches in this area: one focuses on elites, and the other is pluralist-based. The elite approach focuses on formal political power and highly-placed decision-makers, the second approach broadens the concept of the 'political agenda' to include such factors as the agenda(s) of the media. The contention here is that the US news media act as the main source of political information for mass publics – both within the US, but increasingly, due to the spread of satellite television and the Internet, also abroad – and as the primary 'transmission belt' communicating public fears and desires to political elites and government actors. The 'media establishment' has been described as a 'major power broker' which exerts 'unprecedented power over the dissemination of news' (West 2001: viii). In fact, Timothy Cook identifies the news media as a political institution in itself because it 'engages, along with other political institutions, in the authoritative allocation of values in American society' (1998: 85f.). Not only does it act as an intermediary between the mass public and the government, but also within and among branches of government. Gronke and Cook go even further when they posit that:

> in a system of declining rates of affiliation with political parties and falling levels of participation in community, civic, and other political organizations, it is not unreasonable to suggest that the news media is *the* dominant intermediary organization in American democracy.
>
> (2002: 1)

As a purveyor of threat frames, therefore, the mass media is unparalleled.

Fear of technology, fear of terrorism

Frequently, it is our basic perceptions that determine how we conceive of an issue, which is filtered through our prism of preconceived notions. A large amount of social psychological research has found that the uncertain and the unknown generally produce fear and anxiety. This is the psychological basis of the classic ghost story: the fear is greatest when you suspect something, but you're not certain what it is (Eriksson and Noreen 2002: 8). The term 'cyberterrorism' unites two significant modern fears: fear of technology and fear of terrorism. Both of these fears are evidenced in this quote from Walter Laqueur, one of the most well known scholars of terrorism: 'The electronic age has now made cyberterrorism possible. A onetime mainstay of science fiction, the doomsday machine, looms as a real danger. The conjunction of technology and terrorism make for an uncertain and frightening future' (Laqueur 1999: 254). As significant uncertainties or unknowns, therefore, both technology and terrorism are perceived as more ominous than known threats (Embar-Seddon 2002: 1034).

Fear of terrorism, conceived of as random, incomprehensible and uncontrollable violence, may strike one as relatively 'normal'; fear of technology perhaps less so. However, as Mark Pollitt points out, for those unfamiliar with high technology, it is arcane, complex, abstract and indirect in its impact on individuals. Many people are therefore fearful that technology will become the master and humankind the servant. Couple this relatively new fear with the age-old fears associated with apparently random violence and the result is a truly heightened state of alarm. Pollitt contends that the media have further upped the ante by hyping the concept of convergence (1998: 8): the idea that all of the functions controlled by individual computers will connect to form a singular system such that, eventually, our entire existence will be managed by an all-powerful, but uncontrollable, network (see also Sandwell 2006: 47). The convergence represented by the reliance on uninterrupted systems of electrically powered computer networks to support all other infrastructures makes attacks on the electrical power grid, one of the key critical infrastructures of society, appear particularly fearsome. The result is that many people now feel themselves to be 'hostages to electricity' (as quoted in Graham 2004: 8). These feelings are reinforced by the prevalence of so-called 'shut-down-the-power-grid scenarios' in the mass media.[3] Two of the best-known scenarios[4] are those designed by the prominent analyst of information warfare, John Arquilla of the Naval Postgraduate School in Monterey, California and technology journalist Dan Verton.

Shut-down-the-power-grid scenarios

John Arquilla's 'The great cyberwar of 2002' first appeared in *Wired* magazine in February 1998. In the scenario, 'Liddy Dole faces the biggest crisis of her presidency: the first global cyberwar, where the enemy is invisible, the battles virtual, and the casualties all too real' (Arquilla 1998). The electric grid is one of the first infrastructures to be targeted by the attackers and cascading power failures ensure that the body count escalates rapidly caused by everything from traffic accidents to the explosion of a chemical plant. Who are the perpetrators of this mayhem, according to Arquilla's scenario? A group known as the Dove of Jihad claim responsibility, but this is quickly dismissed; China and Russia are then held responsible, followed by a shadowy figure operating out of Afghanistan(!). Eventually, however, the perpetrators are identified as a coalition of states including North Korea, Vietnam, Iraq and Libya, aided by the Cali drug cartel in Colombia and various Asian triads.

Arquilla's scenario is somewhat tongue-in-cheek, and eventually – the scenario runs to over 20 printed pages – he identifies a coalition of states, and not terrorists, as those responsible. This outcome is foreshadowed by the scenario's title: 'The great cyberwar'. Arquilla and his collaborator David Ronfeldt distinguish in their work between 'cyberwar' and 'Netwar'; 'cyberwar' is the domain of states, while cyberterrorism may be viewed as a category of 'Netwar', which is the domain of non- or sub-state actors (Arquilla and Ronfeldt 1993, 1996). Nonetheless, there is a cyberterror component to the scenario in that a number of real and fictional terrorist groups are mentioned, and the coalition of states that is eventually found to be behind the attacks seeks to conceal itself by taking on the name 'People For a Free World', which is reminiscent of the names of a number of terrorist organizations, including the Weatherman group and the New People's Army, amongst others.

François Debrix's choice of Fox TV documentary *Dangers on the Internet Highway: Cyberterror* (broadcast in the US in autumn of 1999) to illustrate his argument regarding the hype surrounding the subject of cyberterrorism is interesting from our perspective because the programme is developed around the scenario of 'the world's first cyber or Netwar'. The programme makers argue that the US reliance on ICT is the country's 'Achilles' heel', insisting that 'the cyber frontier is the next venue for war' and that 'cyberwarfare is taking the Internet to its most lethal level' (2001: 154). Various infowar specialists, including John Arquilla, sketch the impacts of a hypothetical series of escalating cyber-attacks: the collapse of air traffic control systems, resulting in multiple airplane crashes; overloaded digital networks, resulting in the collapse of finance and e-commerce networks; and collapsed power grids, non-functioning telephone networks, widespread car and train crashes, and nuclear meltdowns. In the television scenario, even the US's ability to fight a conventional war is wiped out due to the coordinated hacker attacks. 'Meanwhile, the perpetrators of the war remain undetected behind their distant, encrypted terminals, free to bring the world's mightiest nation to its knees with a few keystrokes in total impunity' (Graham 2004: 18).

Fox TV's scenario bears some strong resemblances to Arquilla's contribution to *Wired* just a few months earlier, but there are also some striking differences. On the one hand, the described outcomes of the cyber-attack(s) are very similar. On the other, while cyberterrorism is explicitly referred to in the programme's title, the perpetrator of the attacks is unveiled as a little-known country previously thought to have little IT capacity. This does not square with Arquilla's academic analyses of potential cyber-threats, which make an explicit distinction between the activities of hostile states (cyberwar) and those of sub-state organizations (Netwar, a sub-set of which is cyberterrorism).

Over the course of the next few years, the emphasis in terms of the cyber-threat image shifts from states to terrorists and back again. Nobody in the media seems quite sure whether states or terrorists pose the greater threat. Many journalists deliver a mixed message and warn that both types of actors are equally threatening.[5] In May 2001, no less august a publication than the *New Yorker* assured its readers that 'sophisticated terrorists (or hostile governments) now have the ability to crash satellite systems, to wage economic warfare by unplugging the Federal Reserve system from Wall Street, even to disrupt the movements of ships at sea' (Specter 2001). While in June 2001 an article in *USA Today* entitled 'Cyberspace: the next battlefield' asserted that:

> an adversary could use ... viruses to launch a digital blitzkrieg against the United States. It might send a worm to shut down the electric grid in

Chicago and air traffic control operations in Atlanta, a logic bomb to open the floodgates of the Hoover Dam and a sniffer to gain access to the funds-transfer networks of the Federal Reserve.

(Stone 2001)

After 11 September 2001, however, the spectre of cyberterror took on a new urgency.

In 2003, Dan Verton, a technology journalist,[6] wrote *Black Ice: The Invisible Threat of Cyberterrorism*, an analysis of the cyberterrorist threat aimed at the mass-market. The first chapter of Verton's book describes a coordinated series of virtual and physical attacks on critical infrastructures in the US Pacific North-west (2003: 1–16). The attackers carry out a series of suicide bombings using conventional explosives and anthrax-laced powder, they unleash malicious soft-ware code which targets Internet root servers and mobile phones, they deface the webpages of a number of major news organizations, and they set off an electro-magnetic pulse (EMP) bomb. Verton is clear as to the perpetrators: a collection of sub-state actors comprising a core group of al-Qaida members, aided by Russian hackers and a number of disgruntled energy company employees with right-wing sympathies. The effects of the attacks are described as lasting for weeks in some areas, months in others. Emergency services, medical facilities, businesses, banks, government offices, industrial plants and manufacturing firms are all depicted as susceptible to failures and disruptions to such an extent that some are forced to close their doors for good (Verton 2003: 14f.). One sceptical reader describes Verton's work as 'paranoid speculation' and lambastes Verton for his contention that 'we can safely discard the opinions of those who argue that cyberterrorism ... is impossible' (Greene 2004; Verton 2003: 96).[7] However, such contentions are accepted and acceptable because in our media-saturated world, events can be at once true and false, real and fictional. Verton concludes his scenario with the following observation:

> This is the face of the new terrorism. It is a thinking man's game that applies the violent tactics of the old world to the realities and vulnerabilities of the new high-tech world. Gone are the days when the only victims are those who are unfortunate enough to be standing within striking distance of the blast. Terrorism is now about smart, well-planned indirect targeting of the electronic sinews of a nation.
>
> (Verton 2003: 15f.)

He thus transforms his imaginings from prediction to reality and evokes the ulti-mate threat to the key assets of modern societies. In a similar fashion, the narra-tor of Fox TV's *Dangers on the Internet Highway* assures viewers that the information contained therein 'is not science fiction' (Debrix 2001: 154), inti-mating that it is thus 'science fact'. Jean Baudrillard has labelled this condition of undecidability of the event and uncertainty of meaning 'hyperreal' modernity. Hyperreality occurs when the media uses its technological capabilities to paint something as being more true to life than the object it is purporting to represent (Baudrillard 1983; see also Der Derian 1995: 37–41).

François Debrix suggests that Verton's and Arquilla's musings, along with other, similar scenarios, give the impression that the next spectacular terrorist act will occur both everywhere and nowhere at the same time through the use of the Internet, which is presently employed as an object of leisure or a necessary support for work, but which will very soon mutate into the world's deadliest weapon (2001: 156). Barry Sandwell concurs, adding that 'the most extreme manifestations of cyberfear are articulated around metaphors of boundary dissolving threats, intrusive alterities, and existential ambivalences created by the erosion of binary distinctions and hierarchies that are assumed to be constitutive principles of everyday life' (2006: 40). Some of the distinctions that continue to be eroded and which are invoked in the media to justify the continued hyping of the cyberterror threat include those separating the inside from the outside, the offline versus the online world, and the 'real' or physical from the virtual or imagined. This fits with Debrix's assertion that popular fears have taken on a new gravity and emergency responses have become everyday realities in media-saturated societies, but particularly in the US after 11 September 2001. Debrix goes on to suggest that 'in a generalised context of uncertainty, common anxiety and more or less planned strategies of emergency give rise to social epiphenomena like cyberterror, its at once real and imagined dangers, and its often paranoid responses' (2001: 153). In an age where information becomes knowledge, it is increasingly difficult to distinguish cyberterrorism from its media representations.

The exaggerated nature of the scenarios imagined by Verton, Arquilla and others is further highlighted when one considers that blackout, failure and accident are part of the normal operating environment of networked computer and critical infrastructure systems. It is worth keeping in mind that system failures – widespread water contamination, power failures, chronic flight disruptions and other cyberterror scenarios – are events that occur routinely and without affecting national security. In a relatively sober analysis that appeared in *Jane's Intelligence Review* in 1999, it was observed that:

> There is undoubtedly a lot of exaggeration in this field. If your system goes down, it is a lot more interesting to say it was the work of a foreign government rather than admit it was due to an American teenage 'script-kiddy' tinkering with a badly written CGI script. If the power goes out, people light a candle and wait for it to return, but do not feel terrified. If their mobile phones switch off, society does not instantly feel under attack. If someone cracks a web site and changes the content, terror does not stalk the streets.
>
> (Ingles-le Noble 1999)

Thus far, cyber-*error* has proved more frequent and more debilitating than cyberterror. With respect to electrical power, most outages occur due to natural phenomena such as severe weather, as attested, for example, by the impact of

2005's Hurricane Katrina on New Orleans. Nevertheless, the hitherto purely speculative threat to critical infrastructures from politically motivated and cyber-savvy foes continues to animate far more people than the proven, albeit non-purposeful and even quotidian, destructive capacity of operator error, acts of nature, and similar.

Reasoning by analogy

The importance of basic conceptions is illustrated, within cognitive research, by explanation by analogy, which is a problem-solving method in which knowledge of previous problems with allegedly similar structures is used to find the best way to solve current problems. Within the cyberterror threat discourse, the most prevalent analogy is the possibility of an 'electronic Pearl Harbor'. The comparison of so-called 'weapons of mass disruption' with 'weapons of mass destruction' is another popular play on words.

Electronic Pearl Harbor

Winn Schwartau of infowar.com first used the term 'Electronic Pearl Harbor' in testimony before the US Congress as early as 1991 (see Schwartau 1994: 43).[8] The Pearl Harbor analogy has since been used with startling frequency in the media as a shorthand description of the likely consequences of a cyberterrorist attack on the US. A LexisNexis search of major world newspapers found 105 mentions of this and related terms[9] in the ten years between 1994 and 2004. The function of this analogy is to link the cyber-security debate to a 'real' and successful surprise attack on critical US military infrastructures during the Second World War while, at the same time, warning against the idea of the US being invulnerable due to its geographical position. The analogy has immediate resonance and attracts wide understanding, which is perhaps unsurprising given that Pearl Harbor has become linked in popular consciousness with the events of 11 September 2001, to which it is often compared, which is again unsurprising considering that the story and visuals associated with the Japanese attack were doubtless fresh in the minds of many Americans in September 2001 given the release of the blockbuster movie *Pearl Harbor* in May of that year. However, while the Pearl Harbor analogy works very well, in terms of immediately conjuring up images of a sudden crippling blow against critical infrastructures resulting in chaos and destruction, it doesn't actually explain anything about cyberterrorism,[10] but works instead to manufacture fear in the simplest and most direct way possible.

Weapons of mass disruption

In the wake of 11 September 2001, threats to the integrity of the US information infrastructure have been ascribed a level of urgency analogous to nuclear and biological threats, which has galvanized the relationship between IT and security as a primary policy consideration in the US (Yould 2003: 75). In September 2002, Richard Clarke, former special White House adviser for Cyberspace Security, told ABC News: '[Cyberterrorism is] much easier to do than building a weapon of mass destruction. Cyberattacks are a weapon of mass disruption, and they're a lot cheaper and easier' (Wallace 2002). Howard Schmidt, Clarke's one-time deputy, has also repeatedly referred to the threat from 'weapons of mass disruption' (see, for example, McGray 2003). But even before 11 September 2001, the American 'cyber-angst' was palpable (Bendrath 2003).[11] As early as 1999, Congressman Curt Weldon (R-Pennsylvania) had placed cyberterrorism at the top of his list of modern threats to the American way of life. Speaking at the InfoWarCon conference to an audience of uniformed military personal, corporate IT managers, computer security consultants, and at least one screenwriter, Weldon said: 'In my opinion, neither missile proliferation nor weapons of mass destruction are as serious as the threat [of cyberterrorism]' (Poulsen 1999). In May 2001, Senator Robert Bennett (R-Utah) stated that '[attacks against the US banking system] would devastate the United States more than a nuclear device let off over a major city' (Porteus 2001). At around the same time, Michael Specter (2001), the author of *The New Yorker* article mentioned above, predicted: 'The Internet is waiting for its Chernobyl, and I don't think we will be waiting much longer'.

In her seminal article on the role of linguistic metaphors, puns and acronyms in the field of nuclear defence strategy, Carol Cohn demonstrated how specific uses of language were used to de-dramatize threats (see Cohn 1987). With regard to the cyberterrorist threat, exactly the opposite is happening. Far from de-realizing the threat, the discourse of cyberterrorism mobilized by the media and assorted 'experts' makes the threat seem real and palpable. Mediatized discussion of just about any topic fosters the formulation of buzzwords and catchy phrases. The designation of cyber-threats as 'weapons of mass disruption' directly analogous to 'weapons of mass destruction' – that is nuclear, biological or chemical weapons – is, however, both inaccurate and unhelpful in terms of advancing an understanding of the relationship between national security and IT. This is true whether one believes such threats are imminent (see Yould 2003: 84–8) or is sceptical of the cyberterrorist threat. For sceptics, equating the effects of a cyber-attack on the US banking system with the effects of the Chernobyl disaster is not only an exaggeration that defies corroboration, but is extremely disingenuous, suggesting as it does that the physical (and continuing) death of not just large numbers of people, but literally of an entire vast territory, is less significant than its digital disconnection (see Cohen 2003: 9f.).

Identifying antagonistic actors

Exploring the mediation of threat construction also requires analysis of the identification of specific hostile actors. Traditionally, the focus in security policy analysis has been on potentially threatening states or governments, but in debates about terrorism and information warfare, it has been emphasized that non-state actors may also pose a threat. The idea that anonymous adversaries may attempt to penetrate information systems from anywhere in the world breaks with the traditional understanding of security – that the identity, location and goals of the enemy are known – and increases the sense of fear and insecurity. 'The introduction of *non-state enemies* in security thinking implies opening up Pandora's box, as the number of potential enemies in "cyberspace" is virtually unlimited' [italics in original] (Eriksson 2001: 218). In terms of IT security, Denning has posited six different types of antagonistic actors: insiders, hackers, criminals, corporations, governments, and terrorists (1999: 26f.). The media have concerned themselves, for the most part, with just two of these: hackers and terrorists.

Terrorist hackers

In the cyberterror scenarios described here, governments and terrorists were portrayed as the main threats, but hackers were also mentioned. Before 11 September 2001, the media were fixated on hackers as antagonistic actors. Hackers, conceived of as computer abusers, had a history of being demonized in movies, on TV and in the press. As 'familiar, even archetypal characters' (Entman 2000: 15), when the cyberterrorist threat image was being constructed, they were the perfect candidates for identification as potential perpetrators. This development constitutes a classic case of the emergence of 'the worst-case result [out] of a dialectic between what is observed and what is imagined' (Lipschutz 1995: 2).

The threat of hackers infiltrating the world's most sensitive military systems is one of the most enduring and popular themes associated with hacking. It was first brought to the public's attention by the 1983 film *War Games*. In the film, a teenage boy hacks into the computer that monitors and controls the US nuclear and defence system. Believing that it is simply a game-playing machine, the teenager begins a game with the computer. However, the computer believes the game is 'real' and begins the countdown to a Third World War.

WIGAN (FBI): The kid claims he was looking for a toy company. Ha! Ha! That's great!

MCKITTRICK (SYSTEM MANAGER): There is no way a high school punk can put a dime in a telephone and break into our systems. He has got to be working for someone else. He's got to be!

WIGAN: He does fit the profile perfectly: he is intelligent but an underachiever, alienated from his parents, has few friends, a classic case for recruitment by the Soviets. Now what does this say about the state of our country? Have you got any insight into why a bright boy like this would jeopardize the lives of millions?

FBI AGENT: No, Sir, he says he does this sort of thing for fun!

(*War Games* 1983)

This scenario resonated deeply with the US public. On his arraignment on charges related to hacking, Kevin Mitnick was denied access not only to computers, but also to a phone, because the judge believed that, with the aid of a phone, Mitnick could set off a nuclear attack (Skibell 2002: 342; see also Ryan 2004: 8f.).

In his book *Hackers*, Paul Taylor describes a 1991 episode of the US chat show *Geraldo* (1999: 178f.). The show's introduction featured excerpts from the film *Die Hard II*, in which terrorists take over the computers of an airport, while the studio section of the show included an interview with Craig Niedorf (aka Knight Lightning), who was the subject of a US court case for having allegedly received the source code of the emergency services' telephone computer programs. During the course of the programme, show host Geraldo Rivera repeatedly referred to Niedorf as the 'Mad Hacker'. The prosecuting attorney in Niedorf's case also appeared on the show. Below is an excerpt of the dialogue that ensued:

RIVERA: Don, how do you respond to the feeling among so many hackers that what they're doing is a public service; they're exposing the flaws in our security systems?

PROSECUTOR: Right, and just like the people who rape a co-ed on campus are exposing the flaws in our nation's higher education security. It's absolute nonsense.

And on the issue of punishment of hackers:

PROSECUTOR: I don't think they're being punished very much at all. We're having trouble even taking away their gear. I don't know one of them [who] has done hard time in a prison ... even Mitnick who is a real electronic Hannibal Lecter ... did not get near any of the punishment that what he was doing entitled him to.

(as quoted in Taylor 1999: 178)[12]

At the very end of the show, Rivera asks the prosecutor to give a brief worst-case scenario that could result from the activities of hackers. He replies: 'They wipe out our communications system. Rather easily done. Nobody talks to anyone else, nothing moves, patients don't get their medicine. We're on our knees' (as quoted in Taylor 1999: 179).

Hackers get a lot of bad press. In terms of the hyping of the cyberterrorist threat, the portrayal of hackers as potential adversaries was not restricted to film and television; they were also repeatedly identified in the press as the most likely threat actors. The following quote from a 2003 *Newsweek* article entitled 'Bringing down the Internet' is typical:

If you wanted to write a science-fiction thriller about the day the Internet crashed, you'd start with a computer geek. Armed with nothing but a laptop and a high speed Internet connection, he releases a fast spreading computer virus that in a matter of minutes gives him control of thousands, perhaps millions, of personal computers and servers throughout the world. This drone army launches a silent and sustained attack on computers that are crucial for sending around the billions of packets of data that keep e-mail, the Web and other, more basic necessities of modern life humming. At first the attack seems to be an inconvenience – e-mail traffic grinds to a halt, Web browsing is impossible. But then the problems spread to services only tangentially related to the Internet: automated-teller machines freeze up, calls to emergency numbers fail to get routed to police stations and ambulance services, airport- and train-reservation systems come down. After a few hours, the slowdown starts to affect critical systems: the computers that help run power grids, air-traffic control and telephone networks.

(Adams and Guterl 2003)

According to the authors of this particular scenario, the cascading failures are not just regional or national in scope, but global. And within a few lines of text, the perpetrators morph from 'hackers' to 'geeks' to 'terrorists'. The problem is that even if 'hackers' managed such a feat, it would not constitute cyberterrorism unless they engaged in the act for political purposes. Most journalists are either unaware of this caveat or ignore it, with the result that the press have labelled some unlikely acts of computer abuse as 'cyberterrorism'.

According to newspaper reports, sending pornographic e-mails to minors, posting offensive content on the Internet, defacing webpages, using a computer to cause US$400 worth of damage, stealing credit card information, posting credit card numbers on the Internet, and clandestinely redirecting Internet traffic from one site to another all constitute instances of cyberterrorism (see Conway 2003: 34f.). And yet, none of these actions could be described as terrorism – some of them are not even criminal – had they been accomplished without the aid of computers (see Ross 2000: 255). Admittedly, terrorism is notoriously difficult to define; however, the addition of computers to plain old crime certainly does not fall in this category. So what then are the functions of these sorts of reports? They result in a widening of the category of 'cyberterrorism', which is crucial, as no 'true' act of cyberterrorism, narrowly defined, has ever yet occurred. In order to make the cyberterrorist threat image credible, therefore, the cyberterror scenarios must be represented as paroxysmal versions of a cyberterror that starts all the way from the teenage hacker.

It seems that even hackers themselves – albeit probably of the script kiddie variety – have begun to be influenced by their portrayal in the media. The anonymous defacement of two US government websites, carried out in late November 2001, read as follows: 'we are not hacker, we are just cyberterrorist'. Elsewhere, the defacers referred to themselves as 'mujihadeens' and threatened 'the greatest cyberterrorist attack against American government'. The culprits were almost certainly neither mujahideen nor terrorists, and were evidently more familiar with media portrayals of cyberterrorism than with any 'real' cyberterrorists.

It has been observed that all the various ways of abusing computers and IT can hardly be deemed existential threats to sovereign states (Erikkson 2001: 218). Nonetheless, the discourse surrounding computer hackers belabours the

potentially catastrophic economic and national security threats posed by malicious intruders, while for a long time identifying the subject of this threat as
young, self-trained computer geeks. This raised the fundamental question of
how obsessive, self-taught teenagers could overcome the security devised by
governments and corporations that together have spent billions of dollars
seeking to safeguard those same systems and cracking down on cyber-criminals
(Skibell 2002: 336)? In fact, more recently, the media have reassessed the
hacker-as-terrorist discourse, which had begun to appear increasingly uncon-
vincing, and in the wake of 11 September 2001, this discourse was superseded
by the terrorist-as-hacker approach.

Hacker terrorists

The 11 September 2001 attacks resulted in a complete change in threat perceptions, both in terms of the threat from conventional terrorism and its cyber
dimension. Ralf Bendrath details how, in the immediate aftermath of the attacks,
newspaper articles addressing the threat of cyberterrorism proliferated (2003:
59f.). A LexisNexis search of major US newspapers showed that in the US
newspapers of record, the *Washington Post* and *New York Times*, mentions of
cyberterrorism doubled in the aftermath of 11 September 2001. The question on
many people's lips was 'Is Cyber Terror Next?' (Denning 2001).

Once Osama bin Laden and al-Qaida had been fingered as the perpetrators of
the 11 September 2001 attacks, a steady stream of newspaper articles began to
appear suggesting that the latter were now engaged in planning a major cyberterrorist attack. So although there was no evidence available by which to measure
al-Qaida's IT literacy, more and more people came to believe and fear that it
was substantial. This resulted in the creation of a hyper-mediated vicious circle:
the media dramatized the intelligence estimates, and the politicians in turn
picked up media quotes, which they then relayed back in other media fora, and
so on. Within a very short time, unsubstantiated fears had transformed into fore-
casts (Bendrath 2003: 63).

In November 2001, an article appeared in *Information Security* magazine that
made the jump from 'might' or 'could' to 'will certainly':

> Though we have yet to see terrorist groups – such as Hizbollah, HAMAS,
> Abu Nidal and Al Qaeda – employ hacking or malware to target critical
> infrastructures, their reliance on information technology and acquisitions of
> computer expertise are clear warning signs. While damage caused by hack-
> tivists – and even cyberterrorists – has been minimal thus far, security
> experts predict that the nation's IT infrastructure *will certainly* be a target in
> the future [my italics].
>
> (McAlearney 2001)

Furthermore, in May 2002, an article appeared in *Newsweek* that was headlined
'Islamic cyberterror: not a matter of if, but of when' (Hosenball 2002). In late

June 2002, Roger Cressey, who was at that time chief of staff of the President's Critical Infrastructure Protection Board, made a (remarkably) similar claim: 'Al Qaeda spent more time mapping our vulnerabilities in cyberspace than we previously thought. An attack is a question of when, not if' (Borger 2002; Gellman 2002a and 2002b). This statement resulted in a deluge of press reports musing upon al-Qaida's alleged cyber-attack plans in 2002:

- 'Report: US fears possible Al Qaeda cyber attacks'. *Reuters*, 27 June.
- 'Cyber-attacks by Al Qaeda feared'. Barton Gellman in the *Washington Post*, 27 June.
- 'US "fears al-Qaeda hack attack"'. Kevin Anderson in *BBC News Online*, 27 June.
- 'Qaeda cyberterror called real peril'. Barton Gellman in the *International Herald Tribune*, 28 June.
- 'US fears al-Qaida will hit vital computer networks'. Julian Borger in the *Guardian* (UK), 28 June.
- 'Al Qaeda cyber alarm sounded'. William Mathews in *Federal Computer Week*, 25 July.[13]

William Matthews' article in *Federal Computer Week* included a prediction by Congressman Lamar Smith (R-Texas) that 'There is a 50 percent chance that the next time al Qaeda terrorists strike in the United States, their attack will include a cyberattack'.

The switch in the cyberterrorist threat image, from 'terrorist hackers' to 'hacker terrorists', highlights two things: first, guarding against, as well as combating, security threats is clearly made easier if one is able to identify the actors responsible. It is suggested that the process of introducing a threat image onto the political agenda is facilitated by the ability to identify the actor or actors constituting the threat (Livingston 1994: 4). Structurally-based threats have greater difficulty attracting attention than those portrayed as actor-based (Eriksson and Noreen 2002: 5f.). So while the identification of the cyberterrorist threat with an amorphous category such as that of 'hackers' is preferable to the latter, the ability to identify Osama bin Laden and/or al-Qaida as the source of the cyberterrorist threat is clearly preferable to both of these. Second, certain dramatic events may also have an impact on the resonance of a threat image. The events of 11 September 2001 acted as a trigger factor, revitalizing the cyberterrorist threat discourse and the idea of the 'hacker terrorist' in particular.

Conclusion

Finally, what were some of the effects of the cyberterror threat image as constructed in the US media and described in the foregoing? While so-called 'cyberpanics' may have imaginary origins, they can also have very real consequences (Sandwell 2006: 46).

The risk of a massive *conventional* terrorist attack on the US was emphasized by a small number of academics and others before the events of 11 September 2001, but was dismissed by the media (see Nacos 2002: 1f.), which chose to focus on cyberterrorism instead. Key decision-makers were therefore much more attuned to the latter threat than the former. Marcus Sachs,[14] who served in the White House Office of Cyberspace Security and was a staff member of the President's Critical Infrastructure Protection Board, had this to say in 2003 about the convergence of policy-makers' fear of technology with their fear of terrorism:

> We were very shocked in the federal government that the attack didn't come from cyberspace ... Based on what we knew at the time, the most likely scenario was an attack from cyberspace, not airliners slamming into buildings ... We had spent a lot of time preparing for a cyber attack, not a physical attack.
>
> (Poulsen 2003)

People's sense of what issues are of political relevance is always an ongoing process, which requires an emphasis on how threat images are discursively constructed, maintained and altered. This points to why particular emphasis needs to be placed upon the processes whereby (national) security issues communicatively emerge, and the central role of the media in such emergences. The political communication/threat image environment shapes both the information available and the ways in which not just ordinary people, but also political elites, use it in thinking about politics and national security.

Demonstrating the effects of the media's influence on publics and decision-makers is always difficult due to the indirect and complex dynamics involved; clearly, however, the US media has been highly successful in 'speaking' cyberterrorism into existence. Their reliance on '(hyper-)reality-producing dramas' (Debrix 2001: 153), Pearl Harbor analogies, comparisons of the effects of cyberterrorism with those of WMD, portrayal of hackers as a menace to national security, and general widening of the concept of cyberterrorism, in conjunction with the policy window opened by the events of 11 September 2001 and, consequently, the ability to cast Osama bin Laden and al-Qaida as certain future cyberterrorists has resulted in the hyping of an (imagined) fatal connection between virtual networks and critical infrastructures that, to date, has very little real form or substance.

This conclusion may not be quite as disturbing as it might first appear, however, for François Debrix it suggests that all of the various apocalyptic scenarios, televised simulations and musings as to the greater lethality of virtual over nuclear attacks have, in fact, ensured that a virtual Pearl Harbor will never materialize. The reason is that the fear of cyberterrorism has been spread so widely and with such success that should a 'real' attack ever occur, it couldn't match expectations: 'Being conditioned to such a degree of generalised panic, any real cyberterrorist attack that does not follow the simulated scenario and produce the anticipated amount of casualties will fall short of being worthy of people's attention and worry' (Debrix 2001: 156).

Notes

1 Vixie was, at that time, president of the Internet Software Consortium (an industry group). See Adams and Guterl 2003.

2 The survey was conducted before the blackout across the northern United States and eastern Canada on 14 August 2003.

3 A number of academic analyses of cyberterrorism also include such scenarios, see Collin 1998b; Devost *et al.* 1997.

4 Postmodernists prefer the term 'simulations' (see Baudrillard 1983).

5 In June 2001, Lawrence K. Gershwin, a top CIA official, took a similar stance in a statement to the Joint Economic Committee of the US Congress. Gershwin told the committee that foreign governments, rather than terrorists, were the most significant threat to US computers for the next five to ten years. 'Terrorists really like to make sure that what they do works ... They do very nicely with explosions, so we think largely that they're working on that'. Nonetheless, Gershwin warned that a terrorist organization could surprise intelligence officers and mount a cyber-attack within the following six months (Joint Economic Committee 2001: 6–10).

6 This is not to suggest that all journalists, without exception, are guilty of hyping the cyberterrorist threat. It is possible to point to the efforts of some journalists – technology journalists, in particular – to de-hype cyberterrorism. See, for example, Declan McCullagh's contributions to *Wired* and *{C:Net} News*; Thomas C. Greene and others in *The Register*; Bruce Schneier in his books, articles and *Cryptogram* newsletter (http://www.schneier.com/crypto-gram.html); and a significant amount of the commentary on cyberterrorism produced by *ZDnet* ('Information resources for IT professionals').

7 For an article which takes up many of the incidents outlined in the scenarios above, interrogates the likelihood of their successful occurrence, and finds them wanting, see Cohen 2003.

8 Ralf Bendrath describes Schwartau as 'the rock manager turned preacher of "information warfare"' (Bendrath 2003: 49). In the aftermath of 11 September 2001, Schwartau re-released his 1991 novel *Terminal Compromise* under the new title *Pearl Harbor Dot Com*. The following description of the novel is provided on Amazon.com:

> It used to take an entire nation to wage a war. Today it takes only one man. Taki Homosoto survived the hell of Hiroshima. Now, more than 50 years later, the time has come for the Americans to feel the flames of his revenge, using his personal army of terrorists and intelligence agents. The US Government and a network of somewhat reluctant allies – invisible and anonymous hackers join forces to battle this powerful enemy. The devastating climax of this one man's plan ... this powerful, bitter survivor of ayamachi, The Great Mistake, is certain to bring global chaos and economic meltdown. A terrifying thought provoking tale.

9 The search was undertaken on 18 August 2004 and used the terms 'electronic Pearl Harbor' (68), 'digital Pearl Harbor' (35) and 'cyber Pearl Harbor' (2).

10 A team at the Center for Strategic and International Studies has pointed out that the term 'electronic Waterloo' is more accurate, but it is much less used (see CSIS 1998: 2).

11 François Debrix uses the term 'e-anxiety' (Debrix 2001: 165), while Barry Sandwell refers to 'cyberphobia', 'cyberfear' and 'cyberparanoia' (Sandwell 2006: 40 and 47).

12 In the movie *Silence of the Lambs* (1991), Hannibal Lecter (as played by Anthony Hopkins) is a respected psychiatrist turned murderous cannibal.

13 In *The Register*, Thomas C. Greene contributed the tongue-in-cheek article 'Soon Al-Qaeda will kill you on the Internet' (Greene 2002).

14 Sachs collaborated on a fiction book entitled *Zero-Day Exploit: Countdown to*

Darkness (Rob Shein 2004, Syngress Media) detailing yet another cyberterror scenario. This time a 0-day vulnerability in a particular line of SCADA Master products that are widely used in petrochemical facilities is exploited by attackers, resulting in gas stations running out of gas, followed shortly by freight carriers, private individuals and local police and fire departments. Disaster can only be prevented by Reuben, an elite cyber-security researcher who stumbles across the plot while contracting for the federal government (from Amazon.com product description).

References

Adams, J. and Guterl, F. (2003) 'Bringing down the internet', *Newsweek*, 3 November 2003. Online. Available at: msnbc.msn.com/id/3339638/ (accessed 17 August 2007).

Arquilla, J. (1998) 'The great cyberwar of 2002', *Wired*, 6, 2. Online. Available at: www.wired.com/wired/archive/6.02/cyberwar.html (accessed 17 August 2007).

Arquilla, J. and Ronfeldt, D. (1993) 'Cyberwar is coming', *Comparative Strategy*, 12: 141–65.

—— (1996) *The Advent of Netwar*, Santa Monica: Rand. Online. Available at: www.rand.org/publications/MR/MR789/ (accessed 17 August 2007).

Baudrillard, J. (1983) *Simulations*, New York: Semiotexte.

Bendrath, R. (2003) 'The American Cyber-Angst and the real world: any link?' in Latham, R. (ed.) *Bombs and Bandwidth: The Emerging Relationship Between Information Technology and Security*, New York: The New Press, pp. 49–73.

Borger, J. (2002) 'US fears al-Qaida will hit vital computer networks', *The Guardian*, 28 June 2002.

Buzan, B. (1991) *People, States, and Fear: An Agenda for International Security Studies in the Post-Cold War Era*, 2nd edn, New York: Harvester Wheatsheaf.

Buzan, B., Wæver, O. and de Wilde, J. (1998) *Security: A New Framework for Analysis*, Boulder and London: Lynne Rienner.

Cohen, F. (2003) 'Cyber-risks and critical infrastructures', *Strategic Security*, 2. 27: 1–10.

Cohn, C. (1987) 'Sex and death in the rational world of defense intellectuals', *Signs: Journal of Women in Culture and Society*, 12, 4: 687–718.

Collin, B.C. (1996) 'The future of cyberterrorism', paper presented at the 11th Annual International Symposium on Criminal Justice Issues, University of Illinois at Chicago. Online. Available at: afgen.com/terrorism1.html (accessed 17 August 2007).

Conway, M. (2003) 'What is cyberterrorism? The story so far', *Journal of Information Warfare*, 2, 2: 33–42.

Cook, T.E. (1998) *Governing with the News*, Chicago: University of Chicago Press.

CSIS (Center for Strategic and International Studies) (1998) *Cybercrime, Cyberterrorism, Cyberwarfare: Averting an Electronic Waterloo*, Washington, DC: CSIS Press.

Debrix, F. (2001) 'Cyberterror and media-induced fears: the production of emergency culture', *Strategies*, 14, 1: 149–68.

Deibert, R.J. (2002) 'Circuits of power: security in the internet environment', in Rosenau, J.N. and Singh, J.P. (eds) *Information Technology and Global Politics*, Albany: SUNY Press, pp. 115–42.

Denning, D. (1999) 'Activism, hacktivism, and cyberterrorism: the internet as a tool for influencing foreign policy', in Arquilla, J. and Ronfeldt, D. (eds) *Networks and Netwars*, Santa Monica: Rand. Online. Available at: www.rand.org/publications/MR/MR1382/MR1382.ch8.pdf (accessed 17 August 2007).

—— (2001) 'Is cyber terror next?' in Calhoun, C., Price, P. and Timmer, A. (eds) *Under-*

standing September 11, New York: The New Press. Online. Available at: www.ssrc.org/sept11/essays/denning.htm (accessed 17 August 2007).

Der Derian, J. (1995) 'The value of security: Hobbes, Marx, Nietzsche, and Baudrillard', in Lipschutz, R. (ed.) *On Security*, New York: Columbia University Press, pp. 24–45.

Devost, M.G., Houghton, B.K. and Pollard, N.A. (1997) 'Information terrorism: political violence in the information age', *Terrorism and Political Violence*, 9, 1: 72–83.

Embar-Seddon, A. (2002) 'Cyberterrorism: are we under siege?', *American Behavioral Scientist*, 45, 6: 1033–43.

Entman, R.M. (1993) 'Framing: toward clarification of a fractured paradigm', *Journal of Communication*, 43, 4: 51–8.

—— (2000) 'Declarations of independence: the growth of media power after the Cold War', in Nacos, B.L., Shapiro, R.Y. and Isernia, P. (eds) *Decisionmaking in a Glass House*, New York: Rowman & Littlefield.

Eriksson, J. (2001) 'Cyberplagues, IT, and security: threat politics in the information age', *Journal of Contingencies and Crisis Management*, 9, 4: 200–10.

Eriksson, J. and Noreen, E. (2002) 'Setting the agenda of threats: an explanatory model', *Uppsala Peace Research Papers*, 6. Online. Available at: www.pcr.uu.se/publications/UPRP_pdf/uprp_no_6.pdf (accessed 17 August 2007).

Gellman, B. (2002a) 'Cyber-attacks by Al Qaeda feared', *Washington Post*, 27 June 2002. Online. Available at: www.washingtonpost.com/ac2/wp-dyn/A50765–2002Jun26 (accessed 17 August 2007).

—— (2002b) 'Qaeda cyberterror called real peril', *International Herald Tribune*, 28 June 2002.

Graham, S. (2004) 'War in the "weirdly pervious world": Infrastructure, demodernisation, and geopolitics', paper presented at the conference on Urban Vulnerability and Network Failure, University of Salford, UK, 29–30 April 2004. Online. Available at: www.surf.salford.ac.uk/documents/UrbanVulnerability/Graham.pdf (accessed 17 August 2007).

Greene, T.C. (2002) 'Soon Al-Qaeda will kill you on the internet', *The Register*, 28 June 2002. Online. Available at: www.theregister.co.uk/2002/06/28/soon_alqaeda_will_kill_you/ (accessed 17 August 2007).

—— (2004) 'Cyber-terror drama skates on thin black ice', *The Register*, 25 February 2004. Online. Available at: www.theregister.co.uk/2004/02/25/cyberterror_drama_skates_on_thin/ (accessed 17 August 2007).

Gronke, P. and Cook, T. (2002) 'Disdaining the media in the post 9/11 world', paper presented at the Annual Meeting of the American Political Science Association APSA, 29 August – 1 September 2002, Boston. Online. Available at: people.reed.edu/~gronkep/docs/apsa2002.pdf (accessed 17 August 2007).

Hosenball, M. (2002) 'Islamic cyberterror: not a matter of if, but of when', *Newsweek*, 20 May 2002. Online. Available at: archive.infopeace.de/msg01346.html (accessed 17 August 2007).

Ingles-le Noble, J. (1999) 'Cyberterrorism hype', *Jane's Intelligence Review*. Online. Available at: www.iwar.org.uk/cyberterror/resources/janes/jir0525.htm (accessed 17 August 2007).

Joint Economic Committee (2001) *Wired World: Cyber Security and the US Economy*, Washington, DC: US Government Printing Office. Online. Available at: www.house.gov/jec/hearings/6–21–01.pdf (accessed 17 August 2007).

King, B. (2002) 'Fear and lockdown in America', *Wired*, 25 July 2002. Online. Available at: www.wired.com/news/digiwood/0,1412,54099,00.html (accessed 17 August 2007).

Laqueur, W. (1999) *The New Terrorism: Fanaticism and the Arms of Mass Destruction*, Oxford: Oxford University Press.

Lipschutz, R.D. (1995) *On Security*, New York: Columbia University Press.

Livingston, S. (1994) *The Terrorism Spectacle*, Boulder: Westview Press.

McAlearney, S. (2001) 'Cyberspace braces for escalation and war', *Information Security*, 3, 89. Online. Available at: archive.infopeace.de/msg00639.html (accessed 17 August 2007).

McGray, D. (2003) 'The minister of net defense', *Wired*, 11, 5. Online. Available at: www.wired.com/wired/archive/11.05/schmidt.html (accessed 17 August 2007).

Nacos, B.L. (2002) *Mass-Mediated Terrorism. The Central Role of the Media in Terrorism and Counterterrorism*, New York: Rowman & Littlefield.

Pew Internet and American Life Project (2003) *Survey with Federal Computer Week Magazine About Emergencies and the Internet*. Online. Available at: www.pewinternet.org/pdfs/PIP_Preparedness_Net_Memo.pdf (accessed 17 August 2007).

Pollard, N.A. (2004) 'Indications and warning of infrastructure attack', in Nicander, L. and Ranstorp, M. (eds) *Terrorism in the Information Age: New Frontiers?* Stockholm: National Defence College, pp. 41–57.

Pollitt, M.M. (1998) 'Cyberterrorism: Fact or fancy?', *Computer Fraud and Security*, February: 8–10.

Porteus, L. (2001) 'Feds still need to define role in tackling cyberterror, panelists say', *GovExec.com*, 15 May 2001. Online. Available at: www.govexec.com/dailyfed/0501/051501td.htm (accessed 17 August 2007).

Poulsen, K. (1999) 'Info war or electronic sabre rattling?' *ZDNet*, 8 September 1999. Online. Available at: zdnet.com/2100–11–515631.html?legacy=zdnn (accessed 17 August 2007).

—— (2001) 'Cyber terror in the air', *SecurityFocus.com*, 30 June 2001. Online. Available at: www.securityfocus.com/columnists/6 (accessed 17 August 2007).

—— (2003) 'Official: Cyberterror fears missed real threat', *SecurityFocus.com*, 31 July 2003. Online. Available at: www.securityfocus.com/news/6589 (accessed 17 August 2007).

Ross, A. (2000) 'Hacking away at the counter-culture', in Bell, D. and Kennedy, B.M. (eds) *The Cybercultures Reader*, London & New York: Routledge, pp. 254–67.

Ryan, P.S. (2004) 'War, peace, or stalemate: wargames, wardialing, wardriving, and the emerging market for hacker ethics', *Virginia Journal of Law & Technology*, 9, 7: 1–57. Online. Available at: ssrn.com/abstract=585867 (accessed 17 August 2007).

Sandwell, B. (2006) 'Monsters in cyberspace: cyberphobia and cultural panic in the information age', *Information, Communication & Society*, 9, 1: 39–61.

Schwartau, W. (ed.) (1994) *Information Warfare. Cyberterrorism: Protecting Your Personal Security in the Electronic Age*, New York: Thunder's Mouth Press.

Skibell, R. (2002) 'The myth of the computer hacker', *Information, Communication & Society*, 5, 3: 336–56.

Specter, M. (2001) 'The doomsday click: how easily could a hacker bring the world to a standstill?', *The New Yorker*, 28 May 2001. Online. Available at: www.michaelspecter.com/ny/2001/2001_05_28_doomsday.html (accessed 16 October 2007).

Stone, A. (2001) 'Cyberspace: the next battlefield', *USA Today*, 16 June 2001. Online. Available at: www.usatoday.com/tech/news/2001–06–19-cyberwar-full.htm (accessed 17 August 2007).

Taylor, P.A. (1999) *Hackers: Crime in the Digital Sublime*, London: Routledge.

Verton, D. (2003) *Black Ice: The Invisible Threat of Cyberterrorism*, New York: McGraw Hill.

Wæver, O. (1995) 'Securitization and desecuritization', in Lipschutz, R. (ed.) *On Security*, New York: Columbia University Press, pp. 48–55.

Wallace, C. (2002) 'Internet as weapon: experts fear terrorists may attack through cyberspace', *ABC News.com*, 16 September 2002. Online. Available at: www.911 jobforums.com/archive/index.php/t-14870.html (accessed 23 September 2007).

West, D.M. (2001) *The Rise and Fall of the Media Establishment*, New York: Bedford/St. Martins.

Yould, R. (2003) 'Beyond the American fortress: understanding homeland security in the information age', in Latham, R. (ed.) *Bombs and Bandwidth: The Emerging Relationship Between Information Technology and Security*, New York: The New Press, pp. 74–98.

6 Homeland security through traceability

Technologies of control as critical infrastructures[1]

Philippe Bonditti

Every war that the United States has fought has been different from the last, and different from what defense planners had envisioned.

(Aspin 1993: section 3)

The major institutions of American national security were designed in a different era to meet different challenges. They must be transformed.

(The White House 2006: 43)

Since the mid-1990s, the issue of 'critical infrastructure' (CI) has become increasingly security-centred in the US. Through the *Presidential Directive Decision 39 on Counter-Terrorism Policies* (1995), President Bill Clinton first ordered the creation of a cabinet committee to 'review the vulnerability of government facilities in the United States and the nation's critical infrastructure' (Clinton 1995). The group, chaired by Attorney General Janet Reno, identified eight national critical infrastructures (telecommunications, transportation, emergency services, banking and finance, electrical power systems, water supply systems, gas/oil storage and transportation, and continuity of government) and two categories of threats to these infrastructures, 'physical and cyber-threats'. This led to the elaboration of a first national plan to defend the US against cyber-attacks: *Defending America's Cyberspace. National Plan for Information Systems Protection Version 1.0. An Invitation to a Dialogue*. This document defines infrastructure protection as the sum of all 'proactive risk management actions intended to prevent a threat from attempting to or succeeding at destroying or incapacitating critical infrastructures' (Clinton 2000: 148).

Two structuring elements still prevail today in any political decisions or commitments in relation to the protection of CI. More than ever, CIs are dealt with in close relation to 'terrorism' – even if not exclusively – and they remain divided into these two categories of 'physical and cyber', being potential targets of two major types of attacks: physical attacks, such as bombings against buildings, on the one hand, and electronic 'cyber-' attacks against computer systems on the other. Two major documents relating to CIP recently published by the White House still bear witness to these continuities. The first one, *The National Strategy to Secure Cyberspace* (2003), deals with the protection of the particular space composed of computer systems, cables and flows of digital information that is described as 'the control system of [the] country', 'the nervous system' (Bush 2003a: vii) of public and private institutions in the crucial sectors listed above. This document is an extension of the *National Plan for Information Systems Protection* issued in 2000.

The second document, the *National Strategy for the Physical Protection of Critical Infrastructure and Key Assets* (2003), deals with the critical infrastructure in the wider sense of all physical infrastructures that facilitate the continuity of work in the crucial sectors of agriculture and food, water, public health, emergency services, the defence industrial base, telecommunications, energy, transportation, banking and finance, chemicals and hazardous materials, postal service, and shipping (Bush 2003b). Here, and following the initial propositions of the mid-1990s, critical infrastructures are defined as ranging from railroads, highways and bridges to ports and historical buildings, and from pipelines and dams to water, power and computer systems. In all of these documents, critical infrastructures constitute both paths of communication and exchange, as well as sites of production, distribution and redirection of various materials (food, electricity, digital bytes etc.). Of all these critical infrastructures, the one we will focus on in this chapter is the network of computing systems and databases known as 'cyberspace', also defined in Annex D of the *National Plan for Information Systems Protection Version 1.0* as 'the world of connected computers and the society that surrounds them. Commonly known as the INTERNET' (Clinton 2000: 146).

The aim of the present chapter is to show that the convergence between the intensification of counter-terrorism policies on the one hand, and the progressive rise of CI(P) issues on the other, has a deep impact both on the traditional spatio-temporal demarcations that have hitherto prevailed and on the 'art of governing people'. The progressive merging of the figure of the enemy with constructs of unpredictable and shadowy 'terrorist networks' corresponds to the progressive integration of the national defence and protection system in a networked assemblage connected through digital systems. This causes Western societies, which are now at an intersection of strong 'security-driven' policies and deep processes of digitalization, to move progressively toward a new mode of governmentality determined by traceability, the crucial tool of which is the *digital* trace. In this chapter, it is argued that the current counter-terrorism policies, particularly when juxtaposed with how critical infrastructure is conceptualized, can not only be understood as functional responses to the transformation of transnational violence, i.e. so-called 'terrorism'. They are also a particular actualization of the underlying logics of inclusion and exclusion, which, as Michel Foucault explained, have historically been rendered operative through two major technologies of power, positive and negative.

Two main ideas underline the arguments in this chapter. First, it is argued that, as part of a long-term historical trend, the developments in counter-terrorism in the US accelerate and deepen the process of convergence in which coercive agencies have long been engaged. Second, I argue that the bureaucratic dimension of the security assemblage, mainly in the application of authoritative texts or claims, is experiencing a reconfiguration of its prerogatives, missions and internal power struggles around the computer networks and the digital trace. This process of reversing and changing the roles and activities of security agencies (cf. Bigo 2000) is itself reinforced by two sets of elements:

1   the exchange of agents between agencies as a result of the establishment of coordinating structures between them;
2   the progressive integration of various agencies' databases and the sharing of technical knowledge over which none of the agencies can pretend to have a monopoly.

An analysis of catalysts for all these convergences reveals the progressively networked nature of a state apparatus now governed by a concern for information-sharing and geared towards the protection of the homeland.

The first part of the chapter focuses on the Foucauldian perspective that is adopted. I will argue for the use of the Foucauldian disposit if as a methodological tool that helps to capture discursive formations, institutional adaptations and technological insights as working together, and resonating with one another. The aim of the second part is to show how narratives on terrorism have attempted to spatialize transnational political violence, organizing particular and specific conditions of possibility for the implementation of counter-strategies that can be observed in the geo-spatial prerogatives of the counter-terrorist agencies. While considering the sociological transformations at play in the bureaucratic architecture specifically commissioned to fight transnational violence, the chapter shows how the spatialization of the threat operated by linguistic practices actually resonates with that of the prerogatives of the state's counter-terrorism apparatus.

The approach of this chapter is derived from a reconciliation of the positions of Bourdieu and Foucault, as highlighted by Deleuze (Deleuze 1986: 43) and re-actualized for our problem by Didier Bigo (Bigo 2005). But it is also important to focus on the technological aspects of the assemblage and to deal with all the computing tools that security agencies are resorting to on a massive scale in the name of the sovereign. A 'socio-technical study' of the mechanisms at play is required (Deleuze 2003b: 246). That is the purpose of the third part of the chapter, in which I will highlight the recent transformation regarding counter-terrorism in the US with a particular focus on some computer-based techniques, such as biometrics and the massive resort to databases, so as to show how they transform the sites and modalities of the sovereign power, re-centring and re-spatializing the art of governing people around the digital trace. Subsequently, the chapter aims to show how these technologies of the digital trace in themselves become critical infrastructures.

Critical approach to security and methodology: Foucault and the dispositif

The Foucauldian perspective adopted in this chapter helps to readjust the traditional debates, which are generally 'security-centred' and far too deeply rooted in the discipline-structured form of the academic world. It not only helps to highlight the evolution in narratives on 'terrorism'/'counter-terrorism' and/or 'critical infrastructures' on the one hand, or the organic transformation of the state and of the particular modalities through which the legitimate use of violence is exercised, on the other, but is also useful for demonstrating how the sites and modalities of the sovereign decision are reconfigured by computing technologies. This approach thus facilitates a better understanding of the multi-levelled and multifaceted transformation at play in the 'art of governing people'.

Foucault proposed a particularly powerful theoretical framework for studying what is generally discussed as security and more fundamentally the adaptations in the practices of governmentality. His approach implies that security be comprehended not only in regard to the object/subject of security – establishing whether it is the state, the people, the individual, society, or another object that must be secured (first) – or just as a series of speech acts and securitization processes (Wæver 1995), but in terms of political technologies, space, and distribution of heterogeneous elements in time and space. For Foucault, the particular space of security is that of a series of probable events that will have to be regulated. It refers to a certain temporality and a certain distribution of events in time that must be inscribed in space through discursive and non-discursive formations to regulate singular events that constitute ruptures in everyday life.

A crucial notion in this task is what Foucault called the dispositif, which he defines as a particular formation in a given historical sequence 'a crucial function of which is to respond to a particular emergency' (Foucault 2001: 299). It is a networked complex of heterogeneous elements linking discourses, institutions, architectural dispositions, legal decisions, laws and administrative measures, as well as scientific, philosophical or moral claims. The dispositif is a system of light and shadow that illuminates pre-existing objects or situations in particular ways and that must be closely correlated to the regimes of narratives it constitutes. It consists of lines of forces and lines of subjectivation through which power operates and thus has to be closely correlated to what is constituted and institutionalized as knowledge. Deleuze even talked about a 'philosophy of the dispositif' with 'a change in the orientation, which turns it away from the eternal toward the new' (Deleuze 2003a: 321). Clearly, the dispositif can be understood as a complex and demultiplied apparatus by which power circulates and thus operates.

Foucault's notion of dispositif provides a systematic way of analysing 'security' and the underlying transformations that is attentive to both its discursive and non-discursive formations. It allows us to consider not only the rationalities at play in securing and securitizing moves through discursive and non-discursive practices, but also the lines along which they are developed and supported.

Discursive formations and the performativity of language actually imply not only observation of how they create conditions of possibilities for further developments, but also that they have material, physical, biological, technical, historical and social conditions of possibility. These possibilities need to be articulated in our analysis in order to grasp their multifaceted aspects and to transcend the state-centred framework of analysis.

Thinking in terms of the dispositif helps transcend the dualities between discursive and non-discursive formations and between theory and practice. It allows us to take into account the crucial role of language and of narratives, without reducing the world to textual and discursive procedures. It enables us to analyse discursive and non-discursive formations through the relational or networked space they constitute, and not just separately. The dispositif as concept enables us to observe how the demarcations established in various narratives between the good and the bad, the just and the unjust, but also in the law between the legal and the illegal, resonate and are implemented through particular architectural dispositions and specific computer-based technologies. This helps us to understand in new ways how all these aspects allow specific know-how and techniques to surface, but also and more generally to grasp the production of sense, meaning and knowledge in a particular historical sequence.

I propose to use the dispositif as an ontological and methodological tool. This will help us to decipher contemporary realities by penetrating their mechanisms and also enables us to engage with politics by not just observing it from a hypothetical external point. In that sense, my proposal differs slightly from the proposals of Didier Bigo, Thomas Mathiesen or David Lyon for the banopticon, the synopticon and the superpanopticon respectively (Bigo 2008; Mathiesen 1997; Lyon 1994). In my opinion, it is not only about actualizing, in the contemporary era, the 'dispositif panoptique' (taken as the particular principle of political organization of the disciplinary societies); but also about making the dispositif operational at the level of analysis by using it as a methodological tool. It is a way to make theory a practice, a practice of resistance against power, by 'making it visible where it is the less visible and the more insidious' (Deleuze 2002: 290). It is no surprise that Foucault has never really been 'classified' and that he always rejected any kind of affiliation with any particular discipline, defining himself primarily as a 'demolition expert'.[2] The analysis of the present Foucault engages in (Veynes 1971), and the toolbox he provides (Lascoumes 1993; Davidson 1997), should thus help us to capture how power operates, both at the micro levels and in the combination of these micro levels.

In the research for this chapter, various discourses and texts, congress hearings and reports, laws, directives and administrative regulations as well as organizational charts were analysed, all in relation to the fight against terrorism and to CIP. These narratives and texts are seen as points of entry to the security assemblage in the making. But they are also operational demarcations/distinctions and/or associations/junctions that need to be contextualized to highlight better how the jurisdictional, bureaucratic and technological evolutions resonate with one another. I consider these narratives and texts as traces of those who have pronounced, written, supported and disseminated them so as to establish their provenance; they are traces of the outside of language, traces of the non-linguistic dimension of all those practices in relation to the fight against 'terror-ism' and CIP issues. In this way, we follow another Foucauldian approach in a freely interpretative way:

> All these practices, these institutions and theories, I take at the level of traces, that is, almost always at the level of verbal [textual] traces. The ensemble of these traces constitutes a sort of domain considered as homo-geneous: no differences are established a priori between traces, and the problem thus is to find, between these traces of different order, enough common traits to constitute what logicians call 'classes', aestheticians call 'forms', social scientists call 'structures', which are the invariant common denominator of a certain number of those traces.
>
> (Foucault 1966: 527)[3]

Discourses and texts are thus both objects and points of entry to the object of our study – active agents/discursive lines (Deleuze 2003a: 320) – and at the same time, they constitute traces of other active agents of the security assemblage we have considered. Beyond intertextuality, we are facing the necessity to come back to social practices and sociological dispositions to highlight the very social mechanics from which, and within which, those narratives surface, and not only the performative capacity of language and discursive regimes.

In this chapter, the aim is to enter into the microphysics of power by explor-ing the structure of the bureaucratic apparatus and how it resonates with the system of demarcation established in and by narratives. This chapter aims to localize the speakers who produce those texts and discourses, in order to better visualize the bureaucratic dimension of the assemblage in its very dynamic and in its hierarchical structure, to retrace the genealogy of those bureaucratic units, and to establish the synaptic correspondences between linguistic and non-lin-guistic practices, between enunciation procedures and the structural forms of the state apparatus. Furthermore, I will try to bring to light the successive actualiza-tion of the bureaucratic order so as to understand what kind of actualization of threats corresponds to it in the discursive order. The analysis therefore focuses on the nature of the link that exists between these heterogeneous elements.

I do not pretend here to apply fully the above proposal of using the dispositif as a tool. The objective is rather to highlight the heterogeneity of the elements involved, which are, for now, homogenized by the normative security narratives. This proposal works with broader implications and, first of all, demands that the academic world abandon its traditions of axiomatic neutrality and of individual research agendas for research engaging with politics and with collective work (cf. C.A.S.E. Collective 2006). Indeed, this would contribute to advancing acad-emia beyond its disciplinary structured – and at times confining – form. Opera-tionalizing the dispositif would help to articulate perspectives in terms of linguistic/discursive/textual analysis with a sociology of strategies (so as to highlight the sociological conditions that work with narration), with an anthropology of the bureaucratic apparatus (which supports particular narratives, know-how and power technologies), with law-oriented analysis that would help highlight the legal dispositions, or for some more recent studies, like surveillance studies, computer-oriented analysis to better understand the impact of the increased recourse to computer language on the contemporary system of demarcations (algorithmic techniques in control matters, for example).

Linguistic and textual formations: claiming the particular space of the terrorist threat and of the collective self before 11 September 2001

Let us now examine the narratives on transnational political violence more closely. Since the end of the 1960s, transnational political violence and the US counter-terrorist state apparatus have usually followed the logics/rationale of territorial mechanics. Until the mid-1990s, the terrorist threat was mainly regarded through the inside/outside prism. A given act of violence was enounced, qualified and treated differently depending on whether it had occurred on the national territory or abroad. This was partly due to ideological reasons, which had long caused political violence to be conceived as being related to hostile activities of the USSR during the Cold War, and subsequently as related to the so-called Rogue State paradigm. From the mid-1990s onwards, however, the idea of a networked threat became dominant in the narratives on terrorism. The paradigm of globalization succeeded that of the inside/outside dichotomy, which is seriously challenged by the focus on new technologies and their de-territorialized nature.

This is not to say that these narratives are mutually exclusive. These two trends have always co-existed in discourses and texts describing terrorism. The first one, which tends to territorialize the threat, to strongly associate it with geographical areas or specific countries, was dominant until the mid-1990s, while the second, which deterritorializes the threat to connect it to social (terrorist cells) or technical (cyberterrorism) networks, has had much more structuring force since then. Corresponding to these two ways of spatializing the threat is an extensive temporality that not only concerns the effectivity of political violence, but its potentiality as well. Most of the documents analysed expose a definition of terrorism as 'the *threat* or *use* of violence': a distinction that not only opens the possibility of reaction, but also of anticipation; in other words, the possibility not only of reactive measures (police, investigation) against terrorism, but also of proactive measures (surveillance).

It also becomes apparent that in the period between 1945 and 2006, the attempt to localize (and not just spatialize) the terrorist threat, so as to anticipate it, is all the stronger the more it is described in global terms, as existing virtually anywhere at anytime. And the more the threat is said to be organized in the particular form of the network, the more the bureaucratic structure itself becomes involved in a networked dispersal of its bureaucratic units through the massive resort to technology.

Territorializing the threat, organizing the state apparatus for collective self-defence

These spatio-temporal considerations on transnational political violence are supported by a large set of texts. They can be observed in the *Patterns of Global Terrorism* series issued annually by the State Department (DoS); in the military doctrine documents of the Pentagon (Department of Defense, DoD) and in the National Security Strategies published by the White House. They can also be observed in various administrative regulations (National Security Decisions, Presidential Decision Directives), and even in law. In 1978, while defining the threats that could justify domestic counter-intelligence activities by the Federal Bureau of Investigation (FBI) against a supposed threat, Congress actually introduced for the first time a definition of international terrorism in the US Civil Code:

> 'International terrorism' means activities that ... occur totally outside the United States, or transcend national boundaries in terms of the means by which they are accomplished, the persons they appear intended to coerce or intimidate, or the locale in which their perpetrators operate or seek asylum.
> (US Civil Code, Title 50, Chapter 36, subchapter 1, 1801)[4]

This nicely illustrates the particular way in which the US has traditionally perceived itself in relation to terrorism. Under this definition, international terrorism was understood to occur outside the US. This perception implicitly prevailed in research programmes on terrorism initiated at the end of the 1960s at the RAND Corporation and within the CIA's Office of Policy Research. These programmes aimed at listing all 'terrorist' acts registered outside of the national territory. The CIA first issued the results of this research in 1976 in a document titled *International and Transnational Terrorism: Diagnosis and Prognosis*. The production of this document later became the responsibility of the Office for Combating Terrorism of the State Department and is now a well-known annual publication entitled *Patterns of Global Terrorism*.

These documents on terrorism drew a series of demarcations: first, between a relatively pacified national arena and a dangerous outside, and second, between international terrorism and domestic terrorism. These divisions resonated with the actors who had long governed the counter-terrorism state apparatus (and more generally any state security apparatus in the Western world), and it is precisely these distinctions that are challenged by the various reforms initiated after 11 September 2001. From the early 1970s onwards, the structure of this counter-terrorism state apparatus had been organized along those same traditional demarcations, implemented by National Security Decisions (NSD) 30 and 207 respectively, which were issued in 1982 and 1986 by then-president Ronald Reagan. These NSD designated the State Department as the lead agency for the fight against international terrorism (i.e. terrorism occurring outside of the US), the FBI as lead agency for the fight against domestic terrorism (i.e. terrorism occurring on the national ground), and the CIA as the lead agency for gathering intelligence in relation to terrorism abroad. This reveals a mimetic relation between the perceived threat and the counter-threat to be organized: the distinction established between international and domestic terrorism is mirrored by a corresponding division between the entities of the state apparatus commissioned to fight terrorism abroad and those tasked with fighting terrorism domestically. The threat and the counter-threat are articulated on and within the spatial categories of sovereignty, and the mimetic relation that encompasses both of them remained governed by the idea of the state and by the symbolic order of the line taken as demarcation.

Another interesting aspect can be observed in this spatialization of the terrorist threat. It is particularly tangible when considering the State Department's *Patterns of Global Terrorism*. This annual report aims at describing the evolution of so-called 'terrorism'. On a statistical basis, the analysis is organized around the main geographical areas (South America, Europe, Middle East, Central Asia etc.) and identifies issues of major concern regarding political violence. During the 1980s, a hierarchy was established between them: the first three areas in order of importance were Europe, South America and the Middle East until 1985; the Middle East, South America and Europe (the latter mainly as affected by the 'Middle East terrorism spillover') in the late 1980s; and in the 1990s, the main focus was on the Middle East. A close reading of *Patterns of Global Terrorism* reveals that the geographical space of terrorism progressively moved from Europe to the 'South', and especially to the Middle East. In the 1980s, these analyses resonated with those developed within the Pentagon by high-ranking military officials who were arguing for the necessity to adapt US military forces to a new kind of war they called low-intensity conflicts (LIC) and that were to be mainly located in the 'unstable Third World', or the 'South', which was perceived as being threatened by Soviet expansionist interests. In the 1980s, those high-ranking officials from the Pentagon reactivated the counter-insurgency doctrine applied in Vietnam in the 1960s as part of the LIC doctrine, in which counter-terrorism activities became one of the six fields of military concern (Klare and Kornbluh 1987).

Taken together, those analyses drew the picture of a geographical shift that was supposed to correspond to a move from an ideological (Communism) to a religious (Muslim) motivation of terrorism. This move was rendered possible by a particular perception of transnational violence by US agencies that have long tended to understand it as a tool of foreign policy. There was a tendency in the late 1970s/early 1980s to accuse the USSR of being the main instigator of worldwide terrorist attacks. From 1979, and under the requirement of the Export Administration Act, the State Department identified so-called 'State Sponsored Terrorism' in a list available in *Patterns of Global Terrorism*. Thus was institutionalized a list of entities banned from the inter-state system because of their support of 'terrorism'. In addition to countries such as Cuba, Nicaragua or North Korea, which were listed in the 1980s, four of the six states listed in 1990 were Muslim countries: Iran, Iraq, Syria and Libya (in addition to Cuba and North

Korea). These were subsequently designated as so-called 'rogue states', new enemies of the free world in the globalized post-bipolar era of the 1990s. This association between political violence and some particular states can be understood as the product of the historical necessity that works with sovereignty. For the military forces to be engaged in the fight against 'terrorism', the Pentagon actually requires clear state enemies, just like the State Department requires states to engage in a diplomatic process aiming at curbing political violence. This is also our understanding of the designation of the Axis of Evil by President George W. Bush after 11 September 2001 (see also Brunner, Chapter 7, this volume).

Crucial evolutions within the Pentagon have to be considered in parallel to the double move of the relocalization of the terrorist threat – from Europe to the Middle East, and from ideological to religion-based terrorism – that was achieved by the promulgation of specific narratives. Two major military commands were established within the Department of Defense in the 1980s: the Central Command (USCENTCOM) and the Special Operations Command (USSOCOM). USCENTCOM became the fourth geographical command in charge of the Middle East area. From the point of view of grand strategy, this development marks a new concern for the Middle East. USSOCOM was created to coordinate the special operations forces of the main US armed services (Air Force, Navy, Marines and Army). It was to become the unified command of smaller and more adaptive, highly trained and well-equipped forces that had been built up in the 1950s and 1960s to face guerrillas and that were to intervene in low-intensity conflicts later in the 1980s.

The implementation of this new command in 1986 furthered a fundamental strategic evolution that can be interpreted as the discretization of the battlefield.[5] The discretization of the battlefield had been initiated within the Army during the 1950s in the Special Warfare Doctrine, which challenged the traditional representation of war governed by the idea of a single linear frontline. This representation still prevailed during the bipolar era, with a major front envisaged in Europe against the military forces of the Warsaw Pact. At the turn of the 1990s, the Lake Doctrine marked a new step in this move by envisaging the conduct of operations in not just one but two (and then four) major war theatres simultaneously in different parts of the world. As we will see, narratives on Network Centric Warfare and Force Transformation later in the 1990s would mark another step in the discretization of the front.

Deterritorializing the threat and re-organizing the collective self-defence apparatus of the state

A second move is to be observed in those accounts that have attempted to define, qualify and spatialize the terrorist threat. This is especially the case, even if not exclusively, in Congressional hearings and reports by the representatives of intelligence and counter-intelligence agencies (especially CIA and FBI). Those accounts of the terrorist threat tend to deterritorialize it. This does not mean that it is removed from Euclidian space, but rather that these narratives re-inscribed the threat in the mechanisms of the social order. They put the emphasis on networks that allegedly linked terrorist cells dispersed around the world. In addition to the list of 'state-sponsored terrorism', a list of terrorist organizations has been issued annually since 1996 in a specific section. Narratives on violent activities orchestrated by the USSR, the opposing force of the US during the bipolar era, progressively merge into narratives on the threat of Muslim extremism embodied in the al-Qaida network, the networked antagonist of the state apparatus claiming a monopoly on legitimate violence on a specific territory. Since then, the geographical space is not necessarily and inevitably the tool through which the terrorist threat can be apprehended. The rationality and imagery of the network thus spread, informing the narratives about the 'terrorist' threat with the image of globalization.

During the 1990s, and particularly from the mid-1990s onwards, the rationale of the network was extended and reinforced by the association progressively established between terrorism and technology. Since then, the representation of the threat has no longer only been geographical and informed by the territorial imagery rooted in the fifteenth century (Walker 1991), but by the technical imagery governed by speed, invoking different spatial and temporal coordinates. This later move not only articulates the threat against the structure of geographical borders, but also against that of computerized systems, which cause this double characteristic to be both rooted in the physical order (servers, hard drives, memory sticks, routers, detectors, captors, acquisition stations, scanners, digital cameras located in buildings dispersed across multiple locations) and completely emancipated from it at the same time. These systems actually generate non-Euclidian spaces of exchange and communication in which packets of digital data circulate with high speed. Likewise, the terrorist threat consists not only of networked dispersed cells of people. In narratives and reports, the threat of political violence is actualized in two different forms: the now almost classical ones like bombings, and the ones directed against the computer system as such, like virus attacks. The idea that the US as a sovereign state, as well as its citizens, being coextensive biological entities of the nation, is confronted by transnational political violence exclusively outside of the national territory, is seriously challenged. Analysis of terrorism, driven by an ontology of the worst-case scenario, now oscillates between the bacteriological threat and that of an 'electronic Pearl Harbor'.

These developments are part of a wider evolution in the perception of threat by security agencies that are increasingly taking into account the digital element. In the early 1980s, the Immigration and Naturalization Service of the Department of Justice implemented the Lookout System to filter immigration to the US, while the Department of State was setting up the TIPOFF programme. Later, the FBI established the Computer Analysis and Response Team (CART), and later in the 1990s set up the Critical Investigations and Infrastructure Threat Assessment (CIITAT). It also developed computer-based surveillance programmes such as the Omnivore programme, regularly issued 'Cyber notes', and actively participated in the elaboration of a new category of crime: cyber-crime. The military, which had been developing its own cybernetics strategies since the end of the 1960s and the early years of the Defense Advanced Research Program Agency (DARPA), uses its own idiosyncratic vocabulary, which is centred on Information and Cybernetic Warfare. Both of these were developed in addition to older types of warfare like Transnational Infrastructure Warfare (TIW), Asymmetric Warfare and Asynchronous Warfare, all of which were steps toward the current developments in Network Centric Warfare. In this context, CIP became an issue of national security (see Dunn Cavelty, Chapter 2, this volume). In 1998, following Presidential Directives 38 and 63, the National Infrastructure Protection Center was set up within the FBI and a 'National Coordinator for Security, Infrastructure Protection, and Counter-Terrorism' was appointed. The following year, the White House issued *Defending American Cyberspace*. The notion of cyber-attacks directed against digital systems coexists in the discourse with concepts of more conventional attacks directed against critical infrastructures, seen here as technical support and structures of 'cyberspace', which is conceived as consisting of waves and cables.

But the threat that was actualized on 11 September 2001 was not at all like the one that had been postulated in the previous years. The attacks consisted not of an 'Electronic Pearl Harbor', nor of a bacteriological attack, but of three hijacked planes that crashed into the Twin Towers and the Pentagon. In this sense, a threat is always something potential, something virtual that finds a first actualization in the linguistic and textual/verbal order (see also Conway, Chapter 5, this volume and Der Derian and Finkelstein, Chapter 4, this volume). This must be what then-secretary of defence Les Aspin meant in 1993 when he wrote: 'Every war that the United States has fought has been different from the last, and different from what defense planners had envisioned' (Aspin 1993). All claims about the source, the form, and the space of 'terrorism' after 11 September 2001 have accelerated and deepened these trends of de-territorialization and 'technologization' of the threat that I have tried to highlight above. But the coexistence of these two narratives implies the articulation of two different spatiotemporal conceptions: the first one governed by fixity, geographical territory and the skeleton of geographical borders in which lines work as lines of demarcation; the other governed by mobility/fluidity, the particular space of technology made of digital bytes, the proper skeleton of computerized systems made of cables and waves in which lines work as junction enabling the point as the primary location for the exercise of the sovereign authority. It is at the crossroads of these two images that the current (re-)configuration process of the US national counter-terrorism apparatus is to be located.

Organizing the defence of the homeland in the digital age: networking the state apparatus and protecting cyberspace

The various National Security Strategy documents published by the White House over the last five years, both individually and collectively, still bear witness to this historical and continuing pattern of spatialization and territorialization of the threat. Like *Patterns of Global Terrorism* and the military doctrines, they give powerful expression to the permanent and continuous attempt to articulate the threat. This pattern includes a discontinuous space that is to be secured and is now centred on the geographical homeland extended beyond its 'smart borders' by its citizens, soldiers, civilian infrastructures, military bases abroad, and by cyberspace. These new national security strategies entail significant and worrying transformations for the US administration due to the concern for homeland security.

The notion of homeland security is not a new one. It had already surfaced in various political arenas during the 1990s in relation to the diminished efficiency of borders – here understood as the historical regulative technology of flows of people and goods. But the strong perception of the American territory as an inviolate sanctuary had relegated these debates to the political background until the conception was violently destroyed on 11 September 2001, after which it was replaced by a perception of the nation's territory as being extremely vulnerable (see also Brunner, Chapter 7, this volume). Today, homeland security can be regarded as the protective dimension of the global US strategy pursued in the aftermath of 11 September 2001. Defined as 'a concerted national effort to prevent terrorist attacks within the US, reduce America's vulnerability to terrorism, and minimize the damage and recover from attacks that do occur' (Office of the Homeland Security 2002: 2), homeland security as a concept is the result of a focus on the vulnerability of the US that surfaced under the Clinton administration. Homeland security is now the responsibility of the Department of Homeland Security (DHS), which became the first major bureaucracy in the world specifically commissioned to respond to uncertainty and emergency. The DHS has been justified by the necessity to improve the protection of the national territory and the population through better coordination of the agencies involved in this task. It is the result of an 'extensive rationalization' of the activities aimed at reducing the vulnerability of the US. It is extensive in that the territory is not only geographical, consisting of soil, air and water, but also made up of cables and waves transporting digital data and supported by integrated computer networks: the critical infrastructures of the digital age. This extensive rationalization operates on the underlying logic of anticipation that fundamentally alters the modalities of sovereign power in controlling people (pro-active policing, remote control, surveillance) and in making war (pre-emptive war).

Integrating military force: transformation and the new modalities of war

The changes in the US apparatus of national defense to adapt to the contemporary necessities of protecting the homeland in the digital age are particularly telling when trying to understand the adaptations as corresponding to narratives about US territorial vulnerability and catastrophic terrorism. Two examples of these adaptations are the reorganization of the Unified Command Plan at the Pentagon with the creation of a fifth geographical command, Northern Command (NORTHCOM) in April 2002, and the creation of the Marines Special Operation Command (MARSOC) within USSOCOM. NORTHCOM is now in charge of the North American geographical area. It is responsible for the territorial, aerospace and maritime defences of the US. It commands US forces that operate within the territory of the US in support of civil authorities and act as a coordinating organ. It is the agency, within the Pentagon, where the military dimensions of homeland security activities (homeland defence) are conceived, implemented and coordinated. It is presented as 'an integral part of the rapidly expanding interagency network supporting Homeland Defense' (Myers 2003) and is evidence of a powerful military investment in the defence of the national territory.

MARSOC is the major command of the Marine Special Forces. Its location within the USSOCOM not only re-establishes a balance in the power struggle between USSOCOM and the US Marine Corps. It is also a further step in the reconceptualization of warfare. Established specifically to wage unconventional warfare in the 1950s, the Special Forces are now envisaged as the basis of non-linear armies. The creation of MARSOC is a prime example of the long trend of US military force transformation that works with an evolving perception of conflicts and war. It has to be understood in relation to the discretization of the front mentioned above and the doctrinal adaptations known as *Force Transformation*, which aim to integrate forces into a synchronous military apparatus. Transformation is not an objective, but a method, the implementation process of the Revolution in Military Affairs. Supported by the Office of the Secretary of Defense, the doctrine was developed by high-ranking military officers in the second half of the 1990s (Cebrowski and Garstka 1998). It shows the move from a conception of war in terms of Platform Centric Warfare to a vision in terms of Network Centric Warfare in which the linear front is substituted by potential 'points of confrontation'. Instantaneity and simultaneity are the keywords of transformation, which puts information and the idea of networked forces at the very heart of military strategies and tactics. It aims at ensuring that information surfacing in a point p of the networked US military forces engaged in a theatre of war be instantaneously available in every point of the network. Today, this programme intriguingly resonates with narratives on the new worldwide terrorist enemy: 'the Al-Qaida network is adaptive, flexible, and arguably more agile than we are' (Jacoby 2003: 3), which makes 'the War on Terror a war against networks and not nations' (Office of the Assistant Secretary for Public Affairs 2005). The underlying logic of the Pentagon is to network military forces in order to better protect the homeland against a networked enemy. It challenges scales and induces a progressive de-differentiation of strategy and tactics. It makes a central and absolute necessity of gathering, keeping and providing relevant information so as to make it instantaneously available on a large scale. This necessity also drives the transformation of the intelligence community for the particular purpose of the protection of the homeland.

Integrating intelligence: information and the homogenization of modalities of control and surveillance

Intelligence has always been perceived as the primary tool for the fight against terrorism. Since the beginning of the 1970s, it was presented as the means of gathering information so as to facilitate efficient protection against the terrorist threat. Following the intelligence logic, being efficient when dealing with a threat means being able to act before the threat is actualized. Therefore, the fundamental aim of the intelligence logic is anticipation. Because 11 September 2001 revealed the inability of the US intelligence community to deal with the terrorist threat appropriately, the main issue now is that information-sharing should make it possible for the relevant agency to anticipate and act in time. The Uniting and Strengthening America by Providing Appropriate Tools Required to Intercept and Obstruct Terrorism (USA PATRIOT) Act has eliminated judicial control over intelligence activities and broken down the barriers between law enforcement and intelligence established by the Foreign Intelligence Surveillance Act (FISA) in 1978 (Cole and Dempsey 2002: 159–65). The integration of the FBI's counter-intelligence and counter-terrorist divisions under a single heading, the various bureaucratic units built up to bring together agents from the various agencies of the intelligence community (like the NCTC), and the focus on upgrading information technology are among the many measures recently adopted to improve information-sharing. The keywords of these transformations are information and integration. The circulation of information now has to be ensured through the integration of bureaucracy, which is to be achieved through two main avenues: the creation of coordination units and the upgrading of information technology.

> The reform of the intelligence community initiated after 11 September 2001 aimed at silencing power struggles by the creation of a new power position above them. Indeed, the new director of National Intelligence, a position until now occupied by the director of the CIA, currently reports directly to the White House. This restructuring of the intelligence community with the creation of a new superordinate power position also gives strong coordination prerogatives to the DNI and to key units such as the National Counter-Terrorism Centre (NCTC). The NCTC is a mixed structure composed of agents from the agencies of the intelligence community, including the FBI, the CIA, the DHS, and the intelligence agencies of the DoD (National Security Agency (NSA); Defense Intelligence Agency (DIA); National Geospatial Agency (NGA)). It now serves, in its own words, as the primary organization in the United States Government for integrating and analyzing all intelligence pertaining to terrorism possessed or acquired by the United States Government (except purely domestic terrorism); as the central and shared knowledge bank on terrorism information; it provides all-source intelligence support to government-wide counterterrorism activities; it establishes the information technology (IT) systems and architectures

within the NCTC and between the NCTC and other agencies that enable access to, as well as integration, dissemination, and use of terrorism information.

(NCTC 2007)

The NCTC is the first modality through which integration is to be rendered operative: the setting up of close cooperation between agents whose daily work is organized by and within a single coordination structure.

The other modality is the upgrading of information technology through which these agents not only work together, but also share access to the same databases. Within the NCTC, agents from the FBI, the CIA, the DHS and the DoD have access to 'NCTC online', a classified repository which hosts 6,000 users and six million documents, and is used by over 60 contributing departments and agencies. Within the DHS, the DHS Operation Center manages the HSIN, a computer-based counter-terrorism communications system connecting all 50 states, five territories, Washington, DC, and 50 major urban areas. The FBI has also developed a new 'Top Secret/Secret Compartmental Information (SCI)' network known as 'SCION' which connects FBI headquarters and field offices to the CIA and other members of the intelligence community (Office of the Inspector General 2004). The use of such technical systems makes the question of their compatibility a primary issue, which has caused the FBI to work in close relation with the DHS chief information officer while implementing its own systems, and also to choose the 'Oracle 9i Relational Database' to make it compatible with the CIA systems (FBI 2005: 45). For eight of the major US administration networks, the DHS is also developing the Homeland Secure Data Network (HSDN) connected to the Pentagon secured network (SIPRNET). The HSDN is intended to facilitate secure sharing of classified information that would provide instantaneous knowledge at every point of a progressively networked administration (GAO 2004).

While considering the upgrading of the information focus, particular attention should also be paid to such agencies as DARPA or the NSA. DARPA is the central research and development organization of the DoD. It developed the controversial Terrorism Information Awareness Program (TIA, initially called Total Information Awareness). TIA research and development efforts are supposed to

demonstrate that some or all of the tools under development really do contribute to the successful accomplishment of the counterterrorism mission – in particular, dramatically improve the predictive assessments of the plans, intentions, or capabilities of terrorists or terrorists groups. If successful, TIA and its components tools would … enable ad hoc groups to form quickly within and across agency boundaries to bring relevant data, diverse points of view and experience to bear in solving the complex problems with countering terrorism.

(Poindexter 2003)

The NSA is the Pentagon's cryptology organization. It 'must live on the network to perform both its offensive and defensive mission' (NSA/CSS 2000: 31). It is currently in charge of the Terrorist Surveillance Program (TSP), as part of which it wiretaps the phone and e-mail communications of US citizens within the US. Such surveillance programmes, informed by the vision of total technological control, redesign the modalities through which intelligence-gathering is conducted. They reinforce the move from Human Intelligence (HUMINT) to Technological Intelligence (TECHINT), seriously challenging the inside/outside paradigm and the protection of individual privacy. But they also actively promote turning cyberspace itself into a surveillance tool. The latter is becoming a digital area that needs to be permanently scrutinized in search of suspicious communications and that also contains databases full of information that security agencies gather on individuals while pretending to protect territory and populations.

Protecting the homeland: securing cyberspace

The protection of the nation is the main mission of the DHS. Among other tasks, such as the management of activities in case of natural catastrophes, the DHS is in charge of collecting, treating and disseminating relevant information about threats against the homeland. It manages border control (through the TSA and the BCP), immigration policy (in close relation with the DoS and the FBI), and the protection of critical infrastructures. Within the scope of its border control and immigration control missions, the DHS also relies heavily on databases in the three major programmes it manages. The first one of these, the Computer Assisted Passenger Prescreening System (CAPPSII), is a limited, automated pre-screening system of passengers. The second one, the National Security Entry–Exit Registration System (NSEERS), establishes a national registry for temporary foreign visitors (non-immigrant aliens) arriving from certain countries, or who meet a combination of intelligence-based criteria, and are identified as presenting an elevated national security concern. The programme collects detailed information about the background and purpose of an individual's visit to the US, the periodic verification of their location and activities, and departure confirmation. The third one, the US VISIT programme, is 'a continuum of security measures that begins overseas and continues through arrival and departure from the United States to ensure the person crossing our border is the same person who received the visa' (DHS 2007). Through its Bureau of Immigration and Customs Enforcement (ICE), the DHS also conducts programmes such as the Student and Exchange Visitor System (SEVIS), and through the Bureau of Customs and Border Protection, which focuses on the transit of people and goods across the border, it administers the personal data on passengers (PNR) flying to the US and coming from the EU.

The combined analysis of the DoS and the DHS is very revealing in considering the main hypothesis of this chapter: that a progressive networking and re-spatialization of the US anti-terrorism state apparatus is underway in order to protect the territory 'from a distance'. Through the Antiterrorism Assistance

Program, which was established in the 1980s to train civilian security and law enforcement personnel from friendly governments in police procedures that deal with terrorism, the DoS now 'helps with the implementation of biometric identification systems'.[6] As one of the oldest agencies involved in counter-terrorism and in immigration control, the DoS has progressively developed a large panoply of programmes to control mobility at a distance. Through its widespread network of employees, the DoS issues visas and manages the Consular Consolidated Databases, the TIPPOFF Program and the Terrorist Interdiction Program. It participates, both within and beyond the territory of the US, in the accumulation of a massive reservoir of computerized knowledge on people going to or simply passing through the US.

All of these developments work together in the US with reinforced visa policies and new technological insights that support this logic of defending the homeland. Here, biometry establishes the crucial link between the two skeletons of the geographical borders and of computer systems, between the control of people in a specific location and the digital databases in which referent identities are registered, and to which the agencies are connected. These systems draw the lines of a multilevel assemblage of control over people; a control that allows the enforcement of spatial demarcations by linking distant points of control through the network of databases that work with biometrics. It is in this sense that the term 'globalized control' must be understood. This illusion works on the assumption that permanent control of people attempting to enter and exit a territory generates knowledge as to who precisely is inside. The complex computer-based systems and huge digital databases containing information on people allow for simultaneity in the act of controlling and the enforcement of sovereign decisions. At the core of these developments are networked computer systems that are fast becoming the most crucial tool through which the state security apparatus now protects territories and populations from the 'new', equally networked terrorist threat. Those computer systems are entirely part of cyberspace as the wired site of accumulation and conservation of the digitalized state knowledge on people. For this reason, cyberspace itself requires protection first and is called on to become its own tool of protection (Bonditti 2004). The DHS now also has the mission of integrating and securing the 34 major computer networks of the US administration, which are also considered part of the homeland. This vision of a cyberspace to be secured first establishes a hierarchical relation between the security of the homeland and that of cyberspace (Bonditti 2004; Dillon 2003), the security of the latter becoming the condition of the security of the first. Cyberspace becomes the most critical of critical infrastructures, being in turn both part of, and differentiated from, the territorial homeland. Security by traceability can only be achieved by mastering and securing cyberspace.

Conclusion

The above has described the forms of US counter-terrorism efforts, and these forms actually mirror the state's own description of terrorism. In other words, the counter-terrorism state apparatus is itself making a networking move. It is connected to – and dependent upon – computerized networks, tasked with the protection of the homeland at a distance and legitimized by a narrative on terrorism as a networked enemy. Therefore, homeland security is not just the reactivation of the symbolic and affective roots of patriotism in the US. It is a strong sociological reality connected to a strange form of 'overwhelming retreat'. It is overwhelming in that the national space to be secured is not just geographical, but also embodied in computerized networks and informational spaces of exchange that need to be protected. It is overwhelming because the will to protect these territories/spaces activates mechanisms to control people, through efforts that are not only actualized within or at the limits of these territories, but on a global scale. It also redesigns the modalities of war, now conceived as pre-emptive. It reflects a retreat in that it relocalizes and respatializes the collective self, (re-)defining its limits while defining those of the homeland, and transforming the border into a set of globally dispersed points, an ensemble of biometric checkpoints. It creates possibilities for global traceability; a traceability aimed at controlling potential realities in order to better anticipate their actuality. This works with a kind of politics progressively organized along the symbolic order of the *point of control* (the discretization of the 'front' in warfare and the discretization of the border), to succeed the order following the *line of demarcation*.

All these developments – which are to be observed in the US, but are also partially visible in Europe – can be reinscribed in Foucault's wider analysis of the historical move of Western societies from a territorial pact to a security pact between the state and the population. This slow drift draws on three successive historical sequences. The first is one in which the state of justice is born from a feudal territoriality where the crucial role of law and power is codified as the power to kill. The second sequence characterizes the administrative state that surfaced during fifteenth and sixteenth centuries, marked by its administrative regulations and the territoriality of sovereignty. The third sequence appeared at the turn of the seventeenth century with the state of government and the 'security dispositifs' as primary mechanisms of power and power codified as the power *'to make live'*. The governmentalized state is not only defined by its territoriality, nor only by its administrative apparatus, but equally by the living population with both volume and density which it manages in its biological determinant. In each of these historical periods, power has operated through different techniques: mainly legal and juridictional techniques for the first one, disciplinary techniques for the second, and techniques of security for the third. This is not to say, as Foucault explains, that security techniques have replaced the techniques of discipline, which in turn have replaced the legal and juridictional mechanisms. Foucault distinguishes the mechanisms or techniques from the political technologies, so that in attempting to catch those transformations, all these singular mechanisms tell particular stories. However, they simultaneously tell the wider story of how they have come to work together, each of these singular mechanisms integrating and (re)activating, in their own logic, different elements of the others. As for the mechanisms, Foucault analysed those of cellular confinement – hospitals, barracks, industrial firms, prisons and schools – to observe disciplinary effects of power. While considering current political technologies, the challenge is to observe a network so as to decipher how various techniques work together, how they resonate with one another, and how the activation of one particular technique induces adaptations in the others.

The move described by Foucault from a territorial to a security pact works through a process of nomadization, which is the reverse process of the sedentarization process that gave rise to the territorial pact (Deleuze and Guattari 2004). It is a move that tends to allow for mobility and even nomadism, but under the condition of the security of flows (flows of people, goods and capital) that are vital to capitalism and increasingly secured through the technology of traceability. It is thus no surprise if the major figure of the threat is now presented in the particular form of the network, and it is no surprise that the modalities of the counter-threat are now progressively networked. These elements do not work univocally, however. There is strong resistance to this move, which explains why the terrorist threat can still be territorialized in some narratives (rogue states, state-sponsored terrorism, 'Axis of Evil'), while being deterritorialized in others (networked terrorist cells) and even abstracted from the geographic coordinates (cyberterrorism). Two main political rationalities hang in the balance here: the traditional and historical Western one on the one hand, in which lines primarily work as demarcations (borders), and the technological one on the other, in which lines primarily work as junctions. This is what we have to observe and understand in order to catch the meaning of what Foucault called 'security societies' (Foucault 2004: 12), in which critical infrastructure, especially computer systems, are seen as the central nervous system. Critical information infrastructure expresses both the potential and the actual, the territorialized and the deterritorialized. It is located at the conjunction between the territorial and the security governmentalities of Foucault. This is what we have to analyse to understand what is progressively replacing disciplinary societies that are going through a critical historical sequence (Deleuze 2003b: 246). While Western human institutions structured in the particular form of closed entities – from the state itself to the psychiatric hospital – which enact political demarcations delineating the inside from the outside, the normal from the abnormal, the threatened from the threat, the identical from the different, are imploding everywhere, we think such a perspective will help to grasp the actualization of what has historically been discussed as security, and from which counter-terrorism efforts based on and in close relation with CIP policies are now proliferating.

Notes

1 My thanks to Andrew Neal and Chris Findlay for turning the chapter from virtual to actual English and to Christian Olsson for the permanent and stimulating discussion.
2 Michel Foucault (1975) in an interview with Roger Pol Droit: 'I am a bomb demolition expert (artificier). I built something that ultimately serves for a siege, a war, destruction. I am not for destruction, but I defend the idea that one should be able to go

through, to go ahead, that one should be able to make the walls crumble' [my translation].
3 My translation; for an alternative translation, see Foucault *et al.* (1998).
4 This definition has been introduced by the Foreign Intelligence Surveillance Act of 1978.
5 In mathematics, 'discretisation concerns the process of transferring continuous models and equations into discrete counterparts. This process is usually carried out as a first step toward making them suitable for numerical evaluation and implementation on digital computers' (see Wikipedia, 2007, s.v. 'discretisation').
6 Interview with a high-ranking official of the State Department (November 2003): 'all our efforts are now guided by the worry to catch the threat before it reaches the national territory'.

References

Aspin, L. (1993) 'Forces to implement the defense strategy', in *Report to the Bottom Up Review*, Chapter 3, Washington, DC. Online. Available at: www.fas.org/man/docs/bur/part03.htm (accessed 30 October 2007).

Bigo, D. (2000) 'When two become one', in Kelstrup, M. and Williams, M.C. (eds) *International Relations Theory and the Politics of European Integration: Power, Security and Community*, London: Routledge, pp. 171–204.

—— (2005) 'Gérer les transhumances. La surveillance à distance dans le champ transnational de la sécurité', in Granjon, M.C. (ed.) *Penser avec Michel Foucault. Théorie critique et pratiques politiques*, Paris: Karthala, pp. 130–60.

—— (forthcoming, 2008) 'Globalized (in)security: the field and the ban-opticon', in Bigo, D. and Tsoukala, A. (eds) *Terror, Insecurity and Liberty: Illiberal Practices of Liberal Regimes*, London: Routledge.

Bonditti, P. (2004) 'From territorial space to networks: a Foucauldian approach to the implementation of biometry', *Alternatives*, 29, 4: 465–82.

Bush, G.W. (2003a) *The National Strategy to Secure Cyberspace*, Washington, DC: US Government Printing Office.

—— (2003b) *The National Strategy for Physical Protection of Critical Infrastructures and Key Assets*, Washington, DC: US Government Printing Office.

C.A.S.E. Collective (2006) 'Critical approaches to security in Europe: a networked manifesto', *Security Dialogue*, 37, 4: 443–88.

Cebrowski, A.K. and Garstka, J.J. (1998) 'Network-centric warfare: its origins and future', *US Naval Institute Proceedings*, 124, 1: 28–35.

Clinton, W.J. (1995) *US Policy on Counterterrorism*, Presidential Decision Directive 39, Washington, DC, 21 June 1995. Online. Available at: www.fas.org/irp/offdocs/pdd39.htm (accessed 30 October 2007).

—— (2000) *Defending America's Cyberspace: National Plan for Information Systems Protection. An Invitation to a Dialogue.* Version 1.0, Washington, DC: US Government Printing Office.

Cole, D. and Dempsey, J.X. (2002) *Terrorism and the Constitution*, New York: The New Press.

Davidson, A.I. (1997) *Foucault and his Interlocutors*, Chicago/London: The University of Chicago Press.

Deleuze, G. (1986) *Foucault*, Paris: Les Editions de Minuits.

—— (2002) 'Les intellectuels et le pouvoir' (interview with Michel Foucault, 1972), in Deleuze, G., *L'île déserte*, Paris: Les Editions de Minuits, pp. 288–300.

—— (2003a) 'Qu'est ce qu'un dispositif?' (1st edn 1987), in Deleuze, G., *Deux régimes de fous*, Paris: Les Editions de Minuit, pp. 316–25.

—— (2003b) 'Post-scriptum sur les sociétés de contrôle' (1st edn 1990), in Deleuze, G., *Pourparlers*, Paris: Les Editions de Minuits, pp. 240–7.

Deleuze, G. and Guattari, F. (2004) 'Treatise on Nomadology – The War Machine', in Deleuze, G. and Guattari, F., *A Thousand Plateaus*, London/New York: Continuum, pp. 387–468.

DHS (Department of Homeland Security) (2007) *Travel Security and Procedures*. Online. Available at: www.dhs.gov/xtrvlsec/ (accessed 30 October 2007).

Dillon, M. (2003) 'Virtual security: a life science of (dis)order', *Millenium*, 32, 3: 531–58.

FBI (Federal Bureau of Investigations) (2005) *Report to the National Commission on Terrorist Attacks upon the United States, The FBI Counterterrorism Programme since September 2001*. Online. Available at: fl1.findlaw.com/news.findlaw.com/hdocs/docs/terrorism/mueller41404stmt.pdf (accessed 30 October 2007).

Foucault, M. (1966) 'Les mots et les choses', in Foucault, M., *Dits & Ecrits I*, Paris: Quarto-Gallimard.

—— (1975) 'Interview with Roger Pol Droit', *Le Point*, 1659: 82.

—— (2001) 'Le jeu de Michel Foucault' (interview with D. Colas, A. Grosrichard, G. Le Gaufey, J. Livi, G. Miller, J.-A. Miller, C. Millot, G. Wajeman), in Foucault, M., *Dits & Ecrits II. 1976–1988*, Paris, Gallimard, pp. 298–329.

—— (2004) *Sécurité, Territoire et Population, Cours au Collège de France, 1977–1978*, Paris: Gallimard/Seuil.

Foucault, M., Rabinow, P. and Hurley, R. (1998) *Aesthetics, Method and Epistemology. Essential Works of Michel Foucault 1954–1984*, vol. 2, New York: The New Press.

GAO (Government Accountability Office) (2004) *Information Technology: Federal Homeland Security Networks*, GAO-04–375, Washington, DC: Government Accountability Office.

Jacoby, L.E. (2003) 'Current and projected national security threats to the US', Statement for the Record, prepared by Vice Admiral Lowell E. Jacoby, US Navy, Director, Defense Intelligence Agency, for the Senate Select Committee on Intelligence, 11 February 2003.

Klare, M.T. and Kornbluh, P. (1987) *Low Intensity Warfare. Counterinsurgency, Proinsurgency and Antiterrorism in the Eighties*, New York: Pantheon Books.

Lascoumes, P. (1993) 'Foucault et les sciences humaines, un rapport de biais. L'exemple de la sociologie du droit', *Criminologie*, 26, 1: 35–50.

Lyon, D. (1994) 'From big brother to electronic panopticon', in Lyon, D. (ed.) *The Electronic Eye: The Rise of Surveillance Society*, Minneapolis: University of Minnesota Press, pp. 57–80.

Mathiesen, T. (1997) 'The viewer society. Michel Foucault's "panopticon" revisited', *Theoretical Criminology*, 1, 2: 215–34.

Myers, R. (2003) *Defense Subcommittee Hearing: Statement of General Richard Myers*, Washington DC: US Senate Committee on Appropriations, 5 March 2003.

NSA/CSS (National Security Agency/Central Security Service) (2000) *NSA/CSS Manual 123–2*. 24 February 1998.

NCTC (National Counterterrorism Center) (2007) *About the National Counterterrorism Center*. Online. Available at: www.nctc.gov/about_us/about_nctc.html (accessed 30 October 2007).

Office of the Assistant Secretary for Public Affairs (Pentagon) (2005) *Facing the Future:*

Meeting the Threats and Challenges of the 21st Century. Highlights of the Priorities, Initiatives, and Accomplishments of the U.S. Department of Defense 2001–2004, Washington, DC, February 2005.

Office of the Homeland Security (2002) *National Strategy for Homeland Security*, Washington, DC: US Government Printing Office.

Office of the Inspector General (2004) *A Review of the FBI's Handling of Intelligence Information Related to the September 11 Attacks: Special Report*. Online. Available at: www.usdoj.gov/oig/special/s0606/app.3.htm (accessed 30 October 2007).

Poindexter, J.M. (2003) *Report to Congress regarding the Terrorism Information Awareness Program*. Washington, DC: US Department of Defense, 20 May 2003. Online. Available at: w2.eff.org/Privacy/TIA/TIA-report.txt (accessed 30 October 2007).

Veynes, P. (1971) 'Foucault révolutionne l'histoire', in Veynes, P., *Comment on écrit l'histoire*, Paris: Seuil; trans. Davidson, A.I. (1997) 'Foucault revolutionizes history', in Davidson, A.I., *Foucault and His Interlocutors*, Chicago: University of Chicago Press, pp. 116–82.

Wæver, O. (1995) 'Securitization and desecuritization', in Lipschutz, R.L. (ed.) *On Security*, New York: Columbia University Press, pp. 46–87.

Walker, R.B.J. (1991) *Inside/Outside*, Cambridge: Cambridge University Press.

White House, the (2006) *The National Security Strategy of the United States of America*, March 2006. Online. Available at: www.whitehouse.gov/nsc/nss/2006/nss2006.pdf.

Wikipedia contributors (2007) 'Discretization', *Wikipedia, The Free Encyclopedia*. Online. Available at: en.wikipedia.org/w/index.php?title=Discretization&oldid=159319238 (accessed 30 October 2007).

7 The gendered narratives of homeland security

Anarchy at the front door makes home a haven

Elgin M. Brunner

It is commonly acknowledged in both theory and practice that the logic of security is undergoing significant change. The longstanding and inherently binary organizing principles of security are under pressure or even in the process of dissolving. It is increasingly difficult to unambiguously identify both the enemy and the subject of security, to distinguish between civilian and military tools and targets, to separate peace from war and defensive from offensive means, and to assure civil liberties as well as to provide protection from potential terrorist attacks. Most fundamentally – and cutting across all these elements – the delineation between the inside and the outside is crumbling. From these observations, the following question arises: if 'security politics is located right on the border between inside and outside and is therefore involved in keeping the distinction' (Hansen 1997: 329), what does it mean for the politics of security that the delineation between inside and outside is becoming increasingly volatile? Specifically, and in the context of this volume, how are such efforts crystallized in what can be called the *politics of securing the homeland*?

It is another commonplace observation that dichotomous organizing principles that have traditionally been constitutive of discourses and practices of security, statehood and identity are pervasively gendered. They reinforce mutual hostilities through gendered and racialized depictions of friend and foe (Tickner 2002), they generate support on the 'home front' and motivate soldiers for combat (Goldstein 2001), they warrant 'differentiated forms of carnage and destruction' (Milliken and Sylvan 1996: 323), they prevent gendered insecurities from being noticed as either the consequence of an incapacity to voice insecurity or as the consequence of the intimate inter-linkage between the subject's gendered identity and other aspects of its identity, such as religion (Hansen 2000). However, if – as a consequence of the changing setting of security becoming manifest in the politics of securing the homeland – these dichotomies are breaking down, one could expect that the resulting 'new' security discourses and practices would simultaneously undergo change as regards their gendered underpinnings. In the following, we will examine whether that is in fact the case.

Based on the combination of these two sets of problems, the analysis undertaken in this chapter strives to answer two related sets of questions. First, how are the characteristics of the changing logic of security manifested in the US narratives constitutive of the practices that aim to reestablish 'homeland security' in the immediate aftermath of the terrorist attacks of 11 September 2001? Related to this question, the chapter will enquire how the commonly assumed erosion of the conceptual boundaries between inside and outside, civil and military, peace and war, normal and exceptional is discernible in the speeches advocating the major recent institutional change undertaken in order to secure the US homeland, namely the creation of the Department of Homeland Security (DHS). This chapter thus looks at one defining moment in the history of critical infrastructure protection (CIP), understood broadly as a central part of 'homeland security'. This helps us to understand how CIP is situated in the wider discourse of homeland security and how '9/11' as a defining moment has shaped the direction of CIP. Second, this chapter will discuss whether the changing logic of security transforms its gendered underpinnings to become less virulent. It will attempt to establish whether and how these narratives draw on gendered tropes, and whether and how they rely on, refer to, and thereby instantiate stereotypical conceptions of gender and power. It is the contention of the chapter that the argumentative interlocking of the official '9/11' narrative with the discursive endorsement of the DHS moves the 'new' practices of security into the domestic space while drawing on 'old' gender stereotypes.

On the one hand, the current transformation of the practices of security is widely recognized, and a wide range of theoretical and practical attempts are being undertaken to cope with this development – as shown in the contributions in this volume. On the other hand, the gendered aspects of this discourse have not yet come under widespread scrutiny, and the extant analyses (e.g. Young 2003; Hunt and Rygiel 2006; Shepherd 2006) remain relatively marginalized, notwithstanding the pervasive importance of gender issues for societal security narratives. A particularly striking example of the latter is this extract from an editorial of the *Wall Street Journal*:

> ... men are back ... I am speaking of masculine men ... Men who are welders, who do construction, men who are cops and firemen ... we are experiencing a new respect for their physical courage, for strength and for the willingness to use both for the good of others ... I think that sense is coming back into style because of *who saved us on Sept. 11*, and that is very good for our country. Why? *Well, manliness wins wars*. Strength and guts plus brains and spirit win wars.
>
> (Noonan 2001, emphasis added)

Such stories often go unnoticed and unexamined in the mainstream debate about the politics of securing the homeland. Moreover, in the unfolding of the so-called homeland security discourse after 11 September 2001, the constitutive productivity of discourse – the endowment of the world with meaning – or, as defined by Fairclough, 'the text's [and/or speeches'...] effects upon ... people (beliefs, attitudes, etc.), actions, social relations, and the material world' (2003: 8), also remains relatively unappreciated. Therefore, it is apposite to analyse how the narratives of '9/11' link to the practices of homeland security, and what logic is followed by the discursively created meanings of the homeland security concept.

Hence, this contribution undertakes a discourse analysis of the high-level policy-narratives of '9/11' and of the endorsement of the DHS. It aspires to unmask some of the gendered constructions within the early stories about the securing of the homeland. Due to the constitutive consequentiality of discourse, such an analysis enables us to make propositions about the gendered practices of homeland security. If, as Gregory holds, 'the mistake that logocentrism makes is in not seeing the cultural contingency of its philosophical categories' (1989: xvi) that makes 'meaning' a dynamic process, it is argued that this mistake further includes the refusal to see the androcentric contingency of these very categories. Therefore, it is the aim of this chapter to 'expose the constructed, but [suppos-edly] effective, character of masculine hegemony' (Zalewski 1998: 5) in the dis-cursive construction of the practices of homeland security between the immediate aftermath of 11 September 2001 and the creation of the DHS. Such an analysis of 'discourses as systems of meaning production' (Shepherd 2006: 20) is suitable for unmasking one of the intimate linkages between 'storytelling' and the practices of power. While this link is at the core of patriarchy and its reproduction, it also points to the contingency of the latter. Sharing with Kris-tensen (Chapter 3, this volume) the observation that security practices are shift-ing into society, this contribution focuses on how gendered narratives are in fact underpinning this very move and thereby proposes a complementary insight to the 'important consequences for how to make security strategies'. The difference to Kristensen's contribution is that this chapter looks at how the 'external' and the allusion to the overwhelming threat of terrorism is used to push for 'internal' measures securing 'the homeland', whereas Kristensen looks at the domestic CIP discourse. Thus, in a way, the two are complementary: the external dis-course is a pre-condition for what Kristensen looks at.

The chapter first briefly establishes the empirical setting of the changing poli-tics of homeland security, in order to develop the appropriate analytical tools, namely the concepts of discursive agency and of gender. Against this theoretical backdrop, the second section reconstructs in a compact manner the two separate bodies of narrative evidence under scrutiny: the discourses establishing the '9/11' story and those endorsing the DHS. The third section analyses how these narratives are argumentatively interlocked and how they draw on gendered con-structions. In the context of this argument, it becomes evident that many binaries of the security logic are crumbling, while the gendered underpinnings of the same very logic are strengthened. This allows us to conclude that the securitiza-tion of the political space 'inside' rests on gendered dichotomies. In other words, the attempt to effectively 'manage' the crumbling of the other dichotomies does depoliticize the problematization of gender.

The setting of homeland security politics, discursive agency, and gender

In the immediate aftermath of the terrorist attacks and the shocking experience of crucial vulnerability within the nation's borders, homeland security as a keyword and concept gained a highly politicized profile in the US almost overnight.[1] On 20 September 2001, the president, in his seminal 'freedom and fear at war' speech (Bush 2001i), announced the creation of the Office of Homeland Security (OHS) and the appointment of Pennsylvania Governor Tom Ridge as its director in order to improve the security of the US homeland. Ridge was sworn in three weeks later to head the institution that was responsible for 'the implementation of a comprehensive national strategy to secure the United States from terrorist threats and attacks' (Bush 2001k). In July 2002, the *National Strategy for Homeland Security* elaborated by the OHS was ready for publication. While the president in his preface alleges that 'the need for homeland security is not tied solely to today's terrorist threat' (Bush 2002c), it is nevertheless precisely this terrorist threat that forges the document's strategic objectives: first, to prevent terrorist attacks within the US; second, to reduce the vulnerability of the US to terrorism; and third, to minimize the damage and allow the nation to recover as quickly as possible from attacks that do occur (OHS 2002). Hence, as a consequence of '9/11', the focus of providing security at home shifted almost entirely towards protection from terrorism. One year after the attacks had occurred, the OHS was merged into the DHS, which was created by the Homeland Security Act 2002 (White House 2002). In parallel to the National Security Council, the Homeland Security Council was established.

The creation of the Department of Homeland Security can indeed be regarded as the 'most extensive reorganization of the federal government in the past fifty years' (OHS 2002). It is often characterized as representing the acknowledgment that the provision of security no longer follows the logic of the conceptual pairs of inside/outside, war/peace, civil/military or normal/exceptional, which have traditionally been constitutive of discourses and practices of security, statehood and identity. Due to the duly internalized claim that the US is 'today a nation at risk to a new and changing threat' (Bush 2001c) that is both deadly and omnipresent, it is now easier for policy-makers to take recourse to extraordinary means for combating this threat. This mechanism is due to what Hansen (2006: 35) calls the dual political dynamic of security discourses: 'they invest those enacting security policies with the legitimate *power* to undertake decisive and otherwise exceptional actions, but they also construct those actors with a *responsibility* for doing so'. As a consequence, the term 'homeland security' has become an expression that is representative of changing security practices as exemplified by CIP, insofar as its specific undertakings increasingly operate across the blurred boundaries between the military and the civilian domains, adopting both measures that traditionally are seen as defensive as well as such that are regarded as offensive, semantically confusing the terminologies between

the state of war and the state of peace, and notably operating in close cooperation with both private and public entities.

On the practical level, it often is argued, the terrorist attacks on New York
and Washington have made it clear to 'the West' that indeed, the traditional and
exclusively military practices of security projected abroad are no longer sufficient. Instead, in the face of terrorism, new practices concurring with the above-
mentioned characteristics have to be developed and implemented.[2] The stronger
focus on the protection of critical infrastructures can be seen as a practical governmental attempt to adapt to the changing security environment and to the vulnerabilities generated by its linkage with the so-called information revolution.
While the process of conceptually rescheduling security has been under way at
least since the end of the Cold War, this change has only relatively recently
gained high-profile attention in the political establishment, and increasingly, this
transformation is politically instrumentalized. In the realm of military doctrine,
the blurring of delimitations can be observed mainly with regard to the delin-
eations between war and peacetime operations (civilian/military), on the one
hand, and with regard to the subjects/objects (as in critical infrastructures) targeted in these operations (home/abroad), on the other. The US doctrine on psychological operations, which is explicitly designed to 'influence attitudes,
perceptions and behaviors ... *during peacetime and in times of conflict*' (USAF
2003: ixf., emphasis added), may serve as a showcase example of such doctrinal
and operational blurring. On the theoretical level, the concept of societal security tries to seize the new challenges and threats that stem from the changing
environment. The labelling of society's identity as being 'relevant in itself and
not only as an element of state security' (Wæver 1993: 27) can be understood as
the absorption of the enhanced awareness that military threats represent only one
dimension of the threat landscape (Hamilton 2005). Having briefly displayed the
empirical context of this analysis, the following section will sketch the theoretical backdrop by outlining the major analytical tools, namely the concepts of
discursive agency and of gender.

Discursive agency

There are different ways of paying tribute to the importance of written and/or
spoken language in social science research, but a common feature is the focus on
the defining moment of interrelatedness between power, knowledge and discourse. This interrelatedness is manifested in different ways, such as in the
establishment and maintenance (disciplining) of knowledgeable practices
(norms) or in the development of commonly accepted historical narratives.

The phenomenon of 'discourses as being productive (or reproductive) of
things defined by the discourse' (Milliken 1999: 229) includes a complex
process in which knowledgeable practices are defined and where disciplining
techniques and practices are elaborated and applied. The societal production of
meaning (truth) is the nexus linking power and discourse; to be the holder of discursive agency is empowering.[3] It is the linguistic practice of discursive framing

that mediates meaning between objects and subjects (Der Derian 1992, cited in Huysmans 1997). Frames are to be understood as central basic perception categories and structures through which actors perceive their environment and the world (Dunn and Mauer 2006). These categories have a pre-existence in the perception of collective culture and in the memory of the actors. Therefore, the actors attribute meaning to the things they recognize as corresponding to the previously structured world (Donati 2001). In short, discursive framing is the rhetorical (written and spoken) allusion to such pre-existing cognitive models, while simultaneously, through these iterative references, the particular cognitive models are shaped and perpetuated. When this is done successfully -- with resonance – discursive framing leaves an impression on social reality. To put it differently, through the framing mechanism, discourse imparts meaning to the material world by paying tribute to the earlier absorbed meanings. In this way, discourse is constitutive of reality.

Equally important, because discourses 'work to define and to enable, and also to silence and to exclude ... by ... endorsing a certain common sense, but making other modes of categorizing and judging meaningless, impracticable, inadequate or otherwise disqualified' (Milliken 2001: 139), the analytical relevance of such mechanisms becomes evident. By exposing them, the analysis has the potential to denaturalize dominant meanings and practices and to disclose their contingency. The constitutive consequentiality, or performativity, of discourse points to the importance of examining both the homeland security narrative and the role of gendered underpinnings therein.

Conceptualizing gender

Like wars, 'gender norms ... help ... to constitute the norms of statecraft' (Campbell 1992: 11). The analogy is significant: since the body – which is traditionally conceived of as an essential aspect of the gendering of identity – has to be 'understood as historically well-established analog for the constitution of state identity' (Campbell 1992: 11), the gendered body has an evident value for an analytical examination of how identity is forged (not only) in times of war. The concept of gender builds on the general understanding that opposes gender to sex, in that it refers to the social classifications of what is 'feminine' and what is 'masculine'.[4] While the latter relates to the physiological distinction between men and women, gender is conceived of as a 'set of variable, but socially and culturally constructed relational characteristics' (Tickner 2002: 336). These characteristics are dichotomous and often mutually exclusive: notions such as power, autonomy, rationality, activity and the public sphere are stereotypically associated with the masculine, while their opposites, such as weakness, dependence, emotionality, passivity and the private sphere are associated with the feminine. What has seduced men and women to accept the rationale of war since times immemorial has been the very fundamental gender formulation of 'beautiful souls' and 'just warriors', according to which women are seen as life-givers and men as life-takers (Elshtain 1987). This shows that 'men and women, protectors and protected, are constructed in relation to each other, just as, or as part of, the related construction of masculinity and femininity' (Pettman 1996: 99). It is inherent to the characteristics stereotypically associated with masculinity and femininity that they construct a hierarchical gendered social relationship between the 'male' and the 'female'. This culturally original dichotomy imparts a qualificative character to all dichotomies, which are always, even if implicitly, hierarchical (Derrida 1972; Hansen 1997; Milliken 1999). Thus, gender is used here to 'refer to a symbolic system, a central organizing discourse of culture, one that not only shapes how we experience and understand ourselves as men and women, but that also interweaves with other discourses and shapes *them*' (Cohn 1993: 228). It is this interweaving of the stereotyped and binary gender conceptions with other discourses that *produces a gendered discourse.* By iteratively referring to explicit and implicit gender stereotypes, these discourses establish qualificative dichotomies empowering the one side and disempowering the other, valorizing and devalorizing, and thereby constitutively reproduce a relation of power and subordination along the lines of unproblematized gender stereotypes.

This depiction of the concept of gender points to yet another relevant feature, which is the inherent aim to strive towards democratic gender relations, defined by Connell (2000) as moving toward equality, non-violence and mutual respect. Since identities – including gender – are susceptible to shaping, the exposure of the often pervasively stereotypical referencing is indispensable for the forging of transformation. Nonetheless, 'gender identities are neither totally self-created nor completely determined ... nor can they be separated from other factors of identity formation; notably, class, race, and sexuality' (Hooper 2001: 38). Moreover, such conceptions and identities are neither static nor monolithic. As Hooper shows, gender identities are 'fluid and always in the process of being produced through the interaction between ... the three dimensions' of embodiment, institutional practices, and language/discourse (Hooper 2001: 40). Simultaneously, the dichotomously gendered identities mask 'more complex social realities and reinforce ... stereotypes' (Hooper 2001: 45). The alternative is to document the diversity of both femininities and masculinities (Connell 2005) in order to transcend one of the pervasive origins of dichotomous thinking, while avoiding the essentialist attempt to proceed to the reverse assessment within the very same dichotomies.

This chapter – by adopting gender as a central category of analysis – thus looks at the US discourse that was creative of the homeland security practices in the aftermath of 11 September 2001. It aspires to unmask some of the gendered narratives underpinning the changing practices of security. It is argued that these narratives disclose how the longstanding conceptual pairs of security are disintegrating. In particular, the concepts of inside/outside, civil/military and defence/offence become semantically and argumentatively intertwined. The narratives of security take over the domestic space. While one aspect hereof is indeed the privatization of security (Dunn Cavelty, Chapter 2, this volume), another is that simultaneously, the private is securitized (Kristensen, Chapter 3, this volume). Focusing on this latter feature reveals that the crumbling of the longstanding conceptual pairs of security does not transform the 'new' security narratives to become less gendered. While moving the practices of security into the domestic space, and thereby contributing to the semantic militarization of the inside, the 'new' narratives of security draw on 'old' gender stereotypes and manifold unproblematized gendered dichotomies.

Interlocking narratives of securing 'the homeland'

This analysis focuses on two 'clusters' of public utterances by the US president that were jointly constitutive of the homeland security discourse. The first engages the statements of George W. Bush in the immediate aftermath of 11 September 2001. The second is made up of instances of presidential speeches arguing in favour of judicial and institutional homeland security initiatives – the creation of the Office of Homeland Security, the adoption of the USA PATRIOT Act, the publication of the *National Strategy for Homeland Security* and the creation of the DHS through the Homeland Security Act of November 2002. In the following sections, both the discourses establishing the '9/11' narrative and those advocating the creation of the DHS are reconstructed in condensed form and displayed separately.

The '9/11' narrative

Events are imbued with meaning and acquire a long-term existence through the way in which they are narrated. There can be no question that as a consequence of the events of 11 September 2001 in New York and Washington, international terrorism immediately became perceived as the single most threatening feature to the national security of the US. Hence, the narration of terrorism as the single most threatening feature is intimately bound to the way in which the subjects authorized to speak and act told the story of '9/11'.

On 11 September 2001 at 8:30 p.m., US President George W. Bush addressed the nation. This statement is the very first official interpretation[5] of what had happened that day. To a nation under shock and in deep grief, the US president expresses a sense of 'disbelief, terrible sadness', but also 'a quiet, unyielding anger'. Moreover, the president claims that 'these acts of mass murder were intended to frighten our nation into chaos and retreat. But they have failed; our country is strong'. And, further on, in a fitting play of words, he notes that 'these acts shattered steel, but they cannot dent the steel of American resolve'. In the face of 'evil, the very worst of human nature … we responded with the best of America – with the daring of our rescue workers'. Moreover, Bush declares that 'our military is powerful, and it's prepared … We will make no distinction between the terrorists who committed these acts and those who harbor them … we stand together to win the war against terrorism' (Bush 2001a). Only one day later, on 12 September, the 'acts of mass murder' have changed into 'more than acts of terror. They were acts of war'. The perpetrators of the attacks are 'a different enemy than we ever faced. This enemy hides in shadows, and has no regard for human life ... an enemy who preys on innocent and unsuspecting people, then runs for cover ... tries to hide' (Bush 2001b). In short, this enemy is composed of 'faceless cowards' (Bush 2001c). But, since 'we will be steadfast in our determination', the united nation will win this new and 'monumental struggle of good versus evil' (Bush 2001b). For the US, the heroes at hand are the police, the firemen and the rescue workers, whom the president thanks from atop a burned-out fire truck (Mral 2004: 26) 'for your hard work ... and for making the nation proud' (Bush 2001d) by 'running up the stairs and into the fires to help others' (Bush 2001e), letting the US and the world 'see our national character in rescuers working past exhaustion ... and in eloquent acts of sacrifice [such as] one man who could have saved himself [but] stayed until the end at the side of his quadriplegic friend'. Such behaviour is supposed to show 'an abiding love for our country', whose 'responsibility to history is already clear: to answer these attacks and rid the world of evil'. The war 'waged against us by stealth and deceit and murder' provokes this 'peaceful nation [to become...] fierce when stirred to anger' (Bush 2001e). On 15 September, a new wording with regard to the self and the enemy other, which would prove to be highly persistent, was introduced: on the one hand, 'we will find those who did it; we will smoke them out of their holes; we will get them running' (Bush 2001f), making clear that, on the other hand, 'this was an assault not just against the United States, but against civilization' (Powell in Bush 2001f), 'this is the fight of all who believe in progress' (Bush 2001i).

The phrasing was largely in place by 15 September. Nevertheless, the words would still undergo some elaboration and, of course, they would be repeated constantly. In this view, the 'amazing spirit of sacrifice and patriotism and defiance' is as important as the definition of 'American courage – [as] the courage of firefighters and police officers' (Bush 2001g). At the same time, the enemy is cast increasingly as being cowardly and cruel. Not only is the adversary 'an enemy that likes to hide and burrow in ... [but there are also] no rules. It's barbaric behavior. They slit throats of women ... they like to hit, and then they like to hide out', but again it is stated that 'we're going to smoke them out' since 'this is a fight for freedom ... and we will not allow ourselves to be terrorized by someone who thinks they can hit and hide in some cave' (Bush 2001h).

Advocating the creation of homeland security institutions

The themes and frames established in the narratives of 11 September 2001 prominently reverberate in the discourses framing the internal measures in reaction to the terrorist attacks and thereby reveal how the supposed firmly distinct inside and outside intertwine, how defence and offence blur, and how a military logic and vocabulary conquers the domestic space. Moreover, it will become clear that, while these traditional dichotomies of the security logic crumble, the binary and gendered stereotypization does persist.

On 8 October 2001, Pennsylvania Governor Tom Ridge was sworn in to lead the Office of Homeland Security. In his speech at the ceremony (Bush 2001j), the US president elaborates on the main themes that will determine the home-land-security discourse. Not only does he contend that 'the best defense against terror is a global offensive against terror' in order to promote the start of the 'war on terror' abroad with the conventional military operation which the US began at this very moment in Afghanistan, but he also praises Secretary of Defense Donald Rumsfeld and Attorney General John Ashcroft, as well as George Tenet (CIA) and Bob Mueller (FBI) for working aggressively and being 'fine Americans who understand the nature of the conflict, and [who] are pre-pared to join me in doing whatever it takes to win the war'. Only then does he turn to the domestic aspect of so-called 'homeland security' by first thanking Ridge and his family for 'your sacrifice' to America in accepting the post, and then praises Ridge as a 'patriot who has heard the sound of battle', since he is a 'decorated combat veteran of the Vietnam War'. Moreover, as the US 'face[s] new threats and, therefore ... need[s] new defenses', this is the right man. His mission will be 'to design a comprehensive, coordinated national strategy to fight terror here at home'. On the same occasion, remarks by Ridge himself sim-ilarly blur the spaces in which the 'war on terror' takes place as he encourages the entire American people to be grateful to those 'men and women in uniform, who are courageously defending our nation today'. They represent the very best of America's 'shared sense of duty and mission'. He proclaims that the effort of assuring the security of the homeland 'will begin here [and] it will require the involvement of America at every level' (Ridge in Bush 2001j).

On 26 October 2001, Bush signed the USA PATRIOT Act. On this occasion, he addresses the public and announces that 'this law will give intelligence and law enforcement officials important new tools to fight the present dangers' (Bush 2001l) and to face a 'threat like no other nation has ever faced'. The ter-rorists who 'recognize no barrier of morality ... have no conscience ... [and] cannot be reasoned with ... must be pursued, they must be defeated, and they must be brought to justice'. Moreover, the president presents what he identifies as the linchpins of the new law: it changes 'the laws governing information-sharing', it 'will allow surveillance of all communications used by terrorists, including e-mails, the Internet, and cell phones', it enables the US to 'better meet the technological challenges posed by this proliferation of communications technology', and 'finally, the new legislation greatly enhances the penalties that will fall on terrorists'. It is important to the argumentation of the president that 'this legislation is essential not only to pursuing and punishing terrorists, but also [for] preventing more atrocities in the hands of the evil ones. This govern-ment will enforce this law with all the urgency of a nation at war' (Bush 2001l).

In June 2002, the administration began its campaign pushing for the estab-lishment of the Department of Homeland Security. In an address to the federal employees working in the area of homeland security, the president states:

> You know, the amazing thing about America is our nation is stronger today
> than it was before the enemy hit. I like to remind people, they must have not

understood who they were dealing with. They probably thought we m
file a lawsuit or two – (laughter) – but they didn't understand the charact
of the American people, the strength and resolve of our great land.

(Bush 2002a)

In a way that is identical to the '9/11' narrative, he draws a picture of the 'outside'
as being populated by barbaric killers hiding in caves and shadows: 'we're hunting
down these killers wherever they try to hide'. This task is heroically pursued by
'our great military'. Quite casually, the president addresses the issues of the inside:
'we're making progress overseas, we're making progress at home'. Without
further elaboration, he lists the measures taken – increased aviation security, the
tightening of the borders, the stockpiling of medicines against biological agents,
the improvement of information-sharing and new steps to protect critical infrastructure – only in order to insist again on the overall theme of the 'war on terror',
which 'we will win ... thanks to the heroism of our fighting troops, and thanks to
the patriotism of our people'. This patriotism is exemplified in actions such as
those of a member of the armed forces, of whom Bush claims that 'in the mist of
chaos, he was a calm and steady soldier, at one point carrying a woman to the
safety of a nearby emergency vehicle'. Those working for the newly created DHS
'understand, that a full life is one that serves something greater than yourself ...
and that something is the greatest country on the face of earth' (Bush 2002a).

Releasing the *National Strategy for Homeland Security*, the US president
argues that, in the face of a threat that is deadly and omnipresent, 'the current
structure of our government is a patchwork, to put it best, of overlapping
responsibilities and it really does hinder[6] our ability to protect the homeland'
(Bush 2002b). It follows that there is need for a strategy that 'can deal with the
true threats of the 21st century'. Moreover, in order to achieve this goal, 'our
unity is a great weapon in this fight'. Nevertheless, because 'we're in new times
in America, and that requires new thinking ... this new Department must have
every tool it needs to secure the homeland' (Bush 2002d). As the creation of the
DHS approaches, the president takes recourse to strong words as he declares that
'America now is the battlefield' (Bush 2002e). In view of this semantic militarization of the home front, it is no surprise that he addresses the chief of police
of Washington, DC, by stating that 'you and your troops do a fabulous job here'.
As more than a year has passed since the attacks occurred, the reiteration of the
war theme is prominent in the series of six consecutive phrases:

Our nation was confronted by a new kind of war. See, we're at war. This is
a war. This isn't a single isolated incident. We are now in the first war of the
21st century. And it's a different kind of war than we're used to. I explained
part of the difference is the fact that the battlefield is now here at home.

(Bush 2002e)

Similarly, the images of courage and sacrifice recur, as does the unprecedented
nature of the war and the allegation that '[t]he threats to the Homeland are

s establishes the rationales that 'to meet the threats to our
ʜust have authority … to waive certain rights for national
ʾbecause] it makes no sense in a time of war to diminish
sident'. Of course, it is no coincidence that the argument
ʜ us or with the enemy' follows immediately. When Bush
ʜmminent creation of the DHS by the adoption of the
 ̣̣̣ ̣ecurity Act in his weekly radio address, he even introduces the 'disarmament' of Iraq in order to display the advantages of the new department,
because 'we're committed to defending the nation. Yet wars are not won on the
defensive' (Bush 2002f). On 25 November 2002, finally, he states that America
is 'taking historic action to defend the United States and protect our citizens
against the dangers of a new era'. The president repeatedly recapitulates that:

> we recognize our greatest security is found in the relentless pursuit of these
> cold-blooded killers. Yet … the front of the new war is here in America …
> The Homeland Security Act of 2002 takes the next critical steps in defend-
> ing our country. The continuing threat of terrorism, the threat of mass
> murder on our own soil will be met with a unified, effective response.
>
> (Bush 2002g)

Note that the second set of statements examined as evidence in this part is
explicitly uttered in relation to the measures required at home in order to re-
establish homeland security.

Battlefield America – the semantic militarization of the domestic space

These two bodies of reconstructed and condensed discursive evidence demonstrate that the changing practices of security are manifest in the presidential discourses both of the immediate aftermath of '9/11' and of the narrative
endorsement of so-called homeland security, and that these discourses simultaneously rest on unproblematized gender stereotypes and gendered dichotomies.
The following section will highlight the commonalities of the two discourses
separately displayed above, as well as discrepancies between them, in order to
show how they are argumentatively intertwined while drawing on gendered
underpinnings.

It is the argument of this chapter that the binary organizing principles of
security are in a process of dissolution. This is also apparent in the presidential
discourses. The domestic scene of the attacks is particularly important. One of
the founding binaries – the safe inside (home) as opposed to the anarchic and
dangerous outside (abroad) – has crumbled. The homeland is no longer a safe
haven. The anarchic and dangerous outside has intruded. This experience causes
the US president to state that the US is confronted with a declaration of war. The
reciprocal declaration of the 'war on terror' does, at first sight, operate within
the clearly drawn boundary separating peacetime from conditions of war. But it

has also become clear immediately that this is no traditional war. The repetitive insistence on the novelty of both the war and the threat not only creates a situation of emergency, but also one of exceptionality, and thereby establishes a rationale that calls for the application of new means and measures in order to face the danger, i.e. it demands the acceptance of 'whatever it takes to win the war'. This observation applies on both levels, at home and abroad; the rationale of exceptionality is invoked by the US in order to legitimize the transgression of norms and rules of both international and domestic law.

While the second body of evidence examined here constitutes the primary adoption of domestic measures in order to restore 'homeland security' to the US, it is striking how the external realm is used in order to promote and legitimate these very measures at home. Offence is explicitly proposed as the best defence, and Ridge's military experience in Vietnam is invoked as the central qualifying characteristic for the leader of the Office of Homeland Security. Furthermore, the semantic interweaving of military and civilian terms becomes evident in certain moments such as when the US president refers to the Washington police force as *troops*, or to a firefighter as a *soldier* who heroically saved a helpless woman by carrying her to the nearby emergency vehicle. Such phrasing, which seems legitimate in times of exceptional strain, is also indicative of how easily the supposed neutrality, and institutional benevolence, of police forces in liberal states evaporates at critical historical moments and gives way to a hegemonic militarized response. Military language seizes the inside and conquers the domestic space. As President Bush puts it: America is now the battlefield; the front of the new war is here in America. In such a situation, of course, no one would want to obstruct the government's ability to protect the homeland – hence, who would deny the president the authority to waive certain rights for national security purposes? Because the war is won through the patriotism and the unity of the American people, it is clear that someone who is not 'with us' can only be with the enemy. Such utterances not only 'discipline' the objects of security (the population), but also do they raise the pressure on the private sector to cooperate (see, e.g. Kristensen, Chapter 3, this volume). The rationale of exceptional circumstances allows for the semantic militarization of the domestic space and simultaneously forestalls any potential challenge to the narrative chosen and the responses adopted. In sum, the traditional binary pairs structuring discourses of security – exemplified in the homeland security discourse – have indeed come under pressure: inside and outside are argumentatively intertwined, offensive measures are undertaken in the name of defence, and military language and logic is increasingly intruding into the civilian domestic space by invoking the rationale of exceptional circumstances.

Simultaneously, these narratives draw on manifold hierarchical gendered dichotomies and dualistic metaphors in their attempt to encapsulate the events they refer to. Predominantly, these are grouped into the categories of 'us', who are civilized, progressive (since 'our' women are free from oppression), technologically advanced, cultured, courageous, benign, strong and firm, and 'them', who are barbarian, uncivilized, morally and developmentally retarded, and cowardly but brutal. Besides the establishment of an explicit and morally saturated hierarchy, these classifications also correspond to the differing temporal perspectives that are characteristic of the inside and the outside. Inside, the temporal conception is governed by progress, while outside, the progressive project is indefinitely delayed, since the reign of anarchy leads to conflict and war (Walker 1993; Hansen 1997). There can be no doubt that dualistic thinking is deeply rooted in our cognitive strategies in general, and in structuring discourses in particular. Binary oppositions such as normal/pathological, educated/ignorant, modern/traditional are only a few of the pairs that structure our perception of the world. As discursive framing must refer to pre-existent perception categories, dichotomies and dualistic concepts are predestined for structuring our framing mechanisms. Dichotomous thinking and framing proceeds through a double move of homogenization within the categories and a simultaneous insistence on the (supposedly qualitative) differences between the categories. As indicated above, the focus on such dichotomies is essential for the analysis of gender aspects. In the discourses analysed here, dichotomous framing complements the mechanisms driving the rationale of exceptional circumstances and unambiguously establishes which feature is preferable over the other, which meaning or interpretation is more valuable, and which response should be adopted and which one dismissed. Thus, in instantiating the hegemonic discourse, both the exceptionality mechanism and the dichotomous framing mechanism are discernible in the official narrative that attempts to seize '9/11', its aftermath, and the consequences drawn in order to endorse the measures of securing the homeland. Both processes are highly relevant for facilitating the chosen policy responses.

The moral evaluation of the events that is palpable in the discourses analysed here is established in highly qualifying terms, the framing of the self and the other, and the depiction of the necessary response. The US national identity is intimately linked to the actors framed as having 'saved us on 9/11'. The glorification of an ethos of masculine bravery and action, sacrifice, brotherhood, and responsibility is implicitly contrasted against a pre-'9/11' identity supposedly inspired by personal gain and decadence. The fact that the role of men as heroic protectors regained its full force within US society as a consequence of '9/11' is manifested in the image of firefighters, police officers, politicians and defence specialists, and soldiers. These images of a stereotypical form of hegemonic masculinity represent the 'inherent force of good' and strength of the US nation. These official narratives show that:

> hardly anyone is confused about gender anymore. It's men we're sending into alien landscapes of Afghanistan, and we're praying they're tough and strong and mean. There's no confusion about leadership either. It's George W. Bush and his battle-savvy Cabinet we're grateful for, and we pray they're tough, strong and mean enough too.
>
> (Parker 2001)

This shows that the stereotype of masculinized toughness is again elevated 'to the status of an enshrined good' (Enloe 2000), implying not only the use of military means as the most appropriate response, but also the semantic militarization of internal police forces, firefighters and homeland security workers, since they call for conformity with the ideals of the stereotypical hegemonic masculinity – toughness, strength and sacrifice. In accordance with this finding of what we could call a 'remasculinization' of US official discourse as an immediate consequence of the events of 11 September 2001, Tickner judges that 'given the massive sense of insecurity generated by the first foreign terrorist attack on American civilians at home, there is something reassuring about "our" men protecting us from "other men"' (2002: 339). This is apparently even more true when these others are barbarians, uncivilized, primitive and evil – hence brutally hypermasculine – and capable of hitting anywhere at anytime, which facilitates the rationale of exceptional circumstances, before cowardly hiding in caves – exposing their defective manhood.

The concept of war – the novel quality and military language of which has intruded into the inside through the promotion of the 'war' paradigm – inherently draws on dichotomous thinking. It needs to do so in order to establish the rationale that the political purpose of securing the homeland can be achieved through violent means, namely through the 'war on terror'. Not only is war as opposed to peace the most efficient legitimation of the exceptionality rationale, but its 'us versus them' dichotomy is also a fundamental precondition for gaining support when nations fight an 'other'. Both of the major characteristics of dichotomous thinking, the homogenizing within the one category – the 'us' – and the insistence upon the qualitative difference between the categories – the assigning of inferiority to the 'them' – are conducive to conflict. What makes these rationales gendered is their operation through the mechanisms of pervasive referencing to, and the instrumentalization of, unproblematized gender stereotypes – as elaborated above. By separating the mechanisms in such a way, a differentiation can be introduced between how the measures of security are recurrently gendered and the gendering of the concepts of both war and peace, which through its essentializing draws on the very same (gendered) dichotomies.[7] As Goldstein (2001) has shown, the 'war system' and the unproblematized 'gender system' are mutually constitutive of each other; they illustrate the nature of the relation between foreign policy – the 'war system' – and identity – the 'gender system' – in poststructuralist theory (Hansen 2006). The 'beautiful souls/just warriors' formulation (Elshtain 1987) simultaneously requires war and gains legitimacy through the occurrence of wars. The gendered and dichotomized US narrative of '9/11', its aftermath, and the narrative endorsement of the 'new' politics of securing the homeland can therefore be qualified as being closely linked to the recourse to war in response to the terrorist attacks of 11 September 2001. It represents the standard hegemonic action in times of crisis. As David Campbell puts it:

> The response of the war machine is consistent with the logic of previous state responses to crises. The response that would have changed the world

would have seen Presidents and Prime Ministers stand before the cameras and say that because it was the principle of respect for civilian life that had been assaulted, we would unite with others in the laborious, step-by-step, time-consuming task of justice [to capture indicted suspects and bring them to an international tribunal], so that our actions would not be the ones which validated the terrorist logic of ends justifying means.

(Campbell 2002: 165)

This option, which is often mistaken as more 'feminine', whereas it is simply less gendered – two fundamentally different assertions – is explicitly ridiculed by the US president. On the one hand, in nearly every single utterance relating to the 11 September 2001 attacks, he claims that the 'evildoers' need to be brought to justice. In a democratic political system resting on the principle of the rule of law, such rhetorical framing unambiguously evokes the holding of a regular court trial. On the other hand, another phrase that recurs in manifold utterances of the US president in relation to homeland security is the following, which makes an obvious mockery of the rule of law concept: 'they probably thought we might file a lawsuit or two'. Each time, this phrase is followed by laughter (mentioned in the transcript). Not only is such silencing of alternative policy options powerful, but it also ridicules the principle of due legal process as a tool for the 'weak' that is incompatible with the 'strong and independent' self.

The changing security narratives exhibit another feature that operates through the constant references to the state of emergency while resting on a pervasively gendered binary, and which concerns the relation between the state and its citizens. The concept of so-called masculinist protection rests on multiple premises that determine the relationship between the protected (stereotypically the woman and children at home/inside) and the protector (stereotypically the man dealing with the anarchic and therefore dangerous environment/outside). This relationship rests as much on the willingness to make a sacrifice for the sake of others, and the related sense of gratitude, as it does on overt domination and claims of superiority. Moreover, it is a relationship that encapsulates the prevalent hegemonic gender relations. The prototypical unit that it is based upon is, of course, the nuclear family. In a 'Hobbesian' environment 'masculine protection is needed to make a home a haven ... in return ... the woman concedes critical distance from decision-making autonomy' (Young 2003: 4). The logic also applies to the relationship between the US state and its citizens as regards the adoption of the multiple measures which aim at re-establishing the security of the homeland in the immediate aftermath of the terrorist attacks. The constant reference to a condition of emergency – the evocation of a situation of 'Hobbesian' anarchy – serves to mobilize fear and thereby establishes the rationale according to which special measures such as surveillance, obedience and unity, to name but a few, are necessary in order to ensure protection. This protection is conditional on obedience; the populace has to concede critical distance from decision-making and succumb to the bargain inherent to the principle of masculinist protection. As Hunt and Rygiel (2006: 15) formulate it, gendered war 'stories are used to camouflage a politics of control'. The narrative instantiating these measures of homeland security unambiguously shows how 'the Bush administration has repeatedly appealed to the primacy of its role as protector of innocent citizens and liberator of women and children to justify consolidating and centralizing executive power at home and dominative war abroad' (Young 2003: 10). But, as this analysis shows, the borders between home and abroad have been dislocated in this 'novel' war. If the battlefield is in the US, anarchy is no longer relegated to the international arena, but has come to the front door, causing the 'inside' to go private. Hence, in addition to the framing of the collective self as concurring with stereotypical masculinity, the definition of the collective self through the technological policies of control (Bonditti, Chapter 6, in this volume), also rests on the gendered principle of masculinist protection.

Conclusions

On the one hand, changing practices of security are indeed manifested; longstanding conceptual pairs that structure discourses of security, statehood, and identity are in the process of dissolving, as becomes apparent in the early narratives establishing the measures for restoring the security of the US homeland. The narrative that is constitutive of the practices of homeland security shows how the crumbling boundaries between war and peace, inside and outside, and civil and military have contributed to moving the practices of security into domestic space and thereby lead to a semantic militarization thereof; the exceptional has become increasingly normal, which accounts for the demise of many of the traditional security binaries. In this part of the security discourse, multiple stereotypes of hegemonic masculinity are discernible. On the other hand and simultaneously, other equally longstanding and overtly gendered binary pairs are still constitutive of the security rationale underpinning the narrative endorsement of homeland security, including the civilized/barbarian, war/peace, and normal/exceptional dichotomies necessary for sustaining the stereotypical hegemonic masculinity and its 'protection' principle. This part of the analysis has shown that the mechanisms of framing '9/11', its aftermath, and the instantiation of homeland security by the US establish a (dis-)qualifying relation of power. I claim that, by doing so, these mechanisms utilized by the current US government generate a masculinized discursive hegemony over the definition of power. This masculinized hegemony over the definition of power is expressed in an exemplary manner in a statement by Susan Sontag: ' "Our country is strong," we are told again and again. I for one don't find this entirely consoling. Who doubts that America is strong? *But that's not all America has to be'* (2001, emphasis added). As shown, the tenets of heteronormative patriarchy are identifiable at multiple instances in these discourses. They define what is normal and what constitutes a deviation from the norm. The heroes are the strong and courageous soldiers, police officers and firefighters, and they represent the very best of the entire nation because they protect the people, depicted as being organized in the nuclear family unit. We might ask with Habermas (2004): who needs these 'heroes', and why? We may also do well to absorb his reference to Brecht's warning: 'Woe betide the country that needs heroes'. The hegemonic masculinity that is enforced time and again is a proxy for the steady reproduction of the gendered stereotypes, which are even more powerful in times of crisis and war. By linking the constant reference to a state of emergency (Agamben 2002) with the supposed male specialization in security (Young 2003), the instantiation of such stereotypical hegemonic masculinities powerfully secures the 'masculine' social construction of power.

While the problematization of gendered constructions is not nearly as mainstreamed as other critiques of hegemonic discourses of peace, war and security, the very same mechanisms apply when it comes to the silencing of dissent. The hegemonic attribution of meaning to '9/11' served not only to disqualify alternative interpretations, but also to foreclose certain questions. On the one hand, Judith Butler's pithy observation applies:

> the raw public mockery of the peace movement, the characterization of anti-war demonstrations as anachronistic or nostalgic, work to produce a consensus of public opinion that profoundly marginalizes anti-war sentiment and analysis, putting into question in a very strong way the very value of dissent as part of contemporary U.S. democratic culture.
>
> (Butler 2002: 1)

On the other hand, it is the constant reference to the existential nature of the threat that makes such proceedings possible in the first place. The mobilization of fear, operationalized by what Zehfuss (2003) has identified as the exhortation to remember, provokes widespread and unquestioned acceptance of the measures displayed in order to eradicate the source of the existential threat, and simultaneously serves to close the ranks and isolate those who dare to disturb the sense of unanimity. I agree with Zehfuss' view that, when the US president asked the citizens of his country on 20 September 2001 to 'live your lives and hug your children' (Bush 2001i), this implied a secondary level of meaning: 'Concentrate on your families. Do not concern yourselves with the difficult business of politics. The state will provide security' (Zehfuss 2003: 525). This double message represents both the heteronormative model about how to live private life and the urge not to meddle with the concrete task of restoring security. By acquiescing to this appeal, the public agrees to abide by the principle of masculinist protection provided by the ensuing security state 'that wages war abroad and expects obedience and loyalty at home' (Young 2003: 2), only that this war has come inside; the battlefield is at the front door. The politicization of gender falls by the wayside in this securitization of the domestic, 'inside' political space. This analysis has shown that, while gender is at the centre of security-related policies, the US politics of securing the 'homeland' have depoliticized the problematization of gender. The disciplinary power of 'homeland security' is intimately entwined with the continued naturalization of gendered dichotomies.

Notes

1 The latest major official published evidence of this development is the Joint Publication 3–27, Homeland Defense of 12 July 2007.
2 Such as the surveillance of citizens (wiretaps) at home without judicial oversight, or the creation of the allegedly new legal category of 'unlawful combatants' for hostile actors captured in the war abroad.
3 Logocentrism – derived form the Greek word *logos* meaning word, reason and spirit – has been 'the dominant operation for constructing meaning in Western thought' (Gregory 1989: xvi) from Ancient Greek philosophy through to present time. It refers to the belief that the assumed underlying bases of reality can be revealed by pure reason and truth, and it therefore implies a conflation and monopolizing of both truth and its production.
4 The articulation of the debate problematizing this dichotomy (Butler 1990 and 1993) goes beyond the scope of the present analysis.
5 An immediate interpretation was also, of course, provided by the media through the manner and words chosen while covering the events. In this particular case, the formative influence on the global perception of what had happened can be considered striking. The framing influence of the CNN headline 'America under attack' would be highly interesting for analysis – however, it goes beyond the scope of the issue treated here.
6 Only six days previous, it was stated that the country was stronger than before the enemy had struck.
7 I am convinced that this mechanism should absolutely be avoided, since it does not aim at transcending the power relations between the gendered individuals of both sexes, but at the inversion of the still stereotyped relation of power. This, I would argue, is neither desirable nor sustainable.

References

Agamben, G. (2002) 'Security and terror', *Theory & Event*, 5, 4. Online. Available at: muse.jhu.edu/journals/theory_and_event/toc/archive.html#5.4 (accessed 11 August 2007).

Bush, G.W. (2001a) *Statement by the President in His Address to the Nation*, Washington, DC, 11 September 2001. Online. Available at: www.whitehouse.gov/news/releases/2001/09/20010911–16.html (accessed 3 August 2007).

—— (2001b) *Remarks by the President in Photo Opportunity with the National Security Team*, Washington, DC, 12 September 2001. Online. Available at: www.whitehouse.gov/news/releases/2001/09/20010912–4.html (accessed 3 August 2007).

—— (2001c) *Honoring the Victims of the Incidents of Tuesday, September 11, 2001*, Washington, DC, 12 September 2001. Online. Available at: www.whitehouse.gov/news/releases/2001/09/20010912–1.html (accessed 3 August 2007).

—— (2001d) *President Bush Salutes Heroes in New York*, Washington, DC, 14 September 2001. Online. Available at: www.whitehouse.gov/news/releases/2001/09/20010914–9.html (accessed 3 August 2007).

—— (2001e) *President's Remarks at National Day of Prayer and Remembrance*, Washington, DC, 14 September 2001. Online. Available at: www.whitehouse.gov/news/releases/2001/09/20010914–2.html (accessed 3 August 2007).

—— (2001f) *President Urges Readiness and Patience, Remarks by the President, Secretary of State Colin Powell and Attorney General John Ashcroft*, Washington, DC, 15 September 2001. Online. Available at: www.whitehouse.gov/news/releases/2001/09/20010915–4.html (accessed 3 August 2007).

—— (2001g) *Radio Address of the President to the Nation*, Washington, DC, 15 September 2001. Online. Available at: www.whitehouse.gov/news/releases/2001/09/20010915.html (accessed 3 August 2007).

—— (2001h) *Guard and Reserves 'Define Spirit of America'*, Washington, DC, 17 September 2001. Online. Available at: www.whitehouse.gov/news/releases/2001/09/20010917–3.html (accessed 3 August 2007).

—— (2001i) *Address to a Joint Session of Congress and the American People*, Washington, DC, 20 September 2001. Online. Available at: www.whitehouse.gov/news/releases/2001/09/20010920–8.html (accessed 3 August 2007).

—— (2001j) *Gov. Ridge Sworn-In to Lead Homeland-Security*, Washington, DC, 8 October 2001. Online. Available at: www.whitehouse.gov/news/releases/2001/10/20011008–3.html (accessed 3 August 2007).

—— (2001k) *Executive Order Establishing Office of Homeland Security*, Washington, DC, 8 October 2001. Online. Available at: www.whitehouse.gov/news/releases/2001/10/20011008–2.html (accessed 3 August 2007).

—— (2001l) *President Signs Anti-Terrorism Bill*, Washington, DC, 26 October 2001. Online. Available at: www.whitehouse.gov/news/releases/2001/10/20011026–5.html (accessed 3 August 2007).

—— (2002a) *President Bush Thanks Homeland Security Workers*, Washington, DC, 10 July 2002. Online. Available at: www.whitehouse.gov/news/releases/2002/07/20020710.html (accessed 3 August 2007).

—— (2002b) *President Releases National Strategy for Homeland Security*, Washington, DC, 16 July 2002. Online. Available at: www.whitehouse.gov/news/releases/2002/07/20020716–2.html (accessed 3 August 2007).

—— (2002c) 'My fellow Americans', Preface to *National Strategy for Homeland Security*, Washington, DC, 16 July 2002: Office of Homeland Security, The White House. Online. Available at: www.whitehouse.gov/homeland/book/nat_strat_hls.pdf (accessed 3 August 2007).

—— (2002d) *Anti-Terrorism Technology Key to Homeland Security*, Washington, DC, 22 July 2002. Online. Available at: www.whitehouse.gov/news/releases/2002/07/20020722–1.html (accessed 3 August 2007).

—— (2002e) *President Bush Pushes for Homeland Security Department*, Washington, DC, 12 November 2002. Online. Available at: www.whitehouse.gov/news/releases/2002/11/20021112–1.html (accessed 3 August 2007).

—— (2002f) *President Discusses Dept of Homeland Security in Radio Address*, Washington, DC, 16 November 2002. Online. Available at: www.whitehouse.gov/news/releases/2002/11/20021116.html (accessed 3 August 2007).

—— (2002g) *President Bush Signs Homeland Security Act*, Washington, DC, 25 November 2002. Online. Available at: www.whitehouse.gov/news/releases/2002/11/20021125–6.html (accessed 3 August 2007).

Butler, J. (1990) *Gender Trouble Feminism and the Subversion of Identity*, New York and London: Routledge.

—— (1993) *Bodies that Matter On the Discursive Limits of 'Sex'*, New York and London: Routledge.

—— (2002) 'Explanation and exoneration, or what we can hear', *Theory & Event*, 5, 4, Online. Available at: muse.jhu.edu/journals/theory_and_event/toc/archive.html#5.4 (accessed 11 August 2007).

Campbell, D. (1992) *Writing Security. United States Foreign Policy and the Politics of Identity*, revised edn, Minneapolis: University of Minnesota Press.

—— (2002) 'Time is broken: the return of the past in the response to September 11', *Theory and Event*, 5, 4, Online. Available at: muse.jhu.edu/journals/theory_and_event/toc/archive.html#5.4 (accessed 11 August 2007).

Cohn, C. (1993) 'War, wimps, and women: talking gender and thinking war', in Cooke, M. and Woollacott, A. (eds) *Gendering War Talk*, Princeton: Princeton University Press, pp. 227–46.

Connell, R.W. (2000) 'Arms and the man: using the new research on masculinity to understand violence and promote peace in the contemporary world', in Breines, I., Connell, R.W. and Eide, I. (eds) *Male Roles, Masculinities and Violence: A Culture of Peace Perspective*, Paris: UNESCO, pp. 21–33.

—— (2005) 'Change among the gatekeepers: men, masculinities, and gender equality in the global arena', *Signs: Journal of Women in Culture and Society*, 30, 3: 1801–25.

Der Derian, J. (1992) *Antidiplomacy: Spies, Speed, Terror, and War*, Oxford: Blackwell.

Derrida, J. (1972) *Positions*, Paris: Les Editions de Minuit.

Donati, P.R. (2001) 'Die Rahmenanalyse politischer Diskurse', in Keller, R., Hirseland, A., Schneider, W. and Viehöver, W. (eds) *Handbuch der Sozialwissenschaftlichen Diskursanalyse, Band I: Theorien und Methoden*, Opladen: Leske & Budrich, pp. 145–75.

Dunn, M. and Mauer, V. (2006) 'Diskursanalyse: Die Entstehung der Nationalen Sicherheitsstrategie der USA', in Siedschlag, A. (ed.) *Methoden der sicherheitspolitischen Analyse: Eine Einführung*, Wiesbaden: VS Verlag für Sozialwissenschaften, pp. 189–217.

Elshtain, J.B. (1987) *Women and War*, New York: Basic Books.

Enloe, C. (2000) 'Masculinity as foreign policy issue', *Foreign Policy In Focus*, 5, 36. Online. Available at: www.fpif.org/fpiftxt/1502 (accessed 3 August 2007).

Fairclough, N. (2003) *Analysing Discourse Textual Analysis for Social Research*, London and New York: Routledge.

Goldstein, J.S. (2001) *War and Gender. How Gender Shapes the War System and Vice Versa*, Cambridge: Cambridge University Press.

Gregory, D.U. (1989) 'Foreword', in Der Derian, J. and Shapiro, M.J. (eds) *International/Intertextual Relations. Postmodern Readings of World Politics*, Lexington: Lexington Books, pp. xiii–xxi.

Habermas, J. (2004) *Der gespaltene Westen*, Frankfurt am Main: Suhrkamp.

Hamilton, D.S. (2005) 'The relevance of societal security for the United States', in Hamilton, D.S., Sundelius, B. and Grönvall, J. (eds) *Protecting the Homeland: European Approaches to Societal Security: Implications for the United States*, Washington, DC: Center for Transatlantic Relations, pp. 149–64.

Hansen, L. (1997) 'R.B.J. Walker and International Relations: deconstructing a discipline', in Neumann, I.B. and Waever, O. (eds) *The Future of International Relations Masters in the Making*, London and New York: Routledge, pp. 316–36.

—— (2000) 'The little mermaid's silent security dilemma and the absence of gender in the Copenhagen School', *Millennium: Journal of International Studies*, 29, 2: 285–306.

—— (2006) *Security as Practice: Discourse Analysis and the Bosnian War*, London and New York: Routledge.

Hooper, C. (2001) *Manly States, Masculinities, International Relations, and Gender Politics*, New York: Columbia University Press.

Hunt, K. and Rygiel, K. (2006) '(En)Gendered war stories and camouflaged politics', in Hunt, K. and Rygiel, K. (eds) *(En)Gendering the War on Terror. War Stories and Camouflaged Politics*, Aldershot: Ashgate Publishing Limited, pp. 1–24.

Huysmans, J. (1997) 'James Der Derian: the unbearable lightness of theory', in Neumann, I.B. and Waever, O. (eds) *The Future of International Relations Masters in the Making*, London and New York: Routledge, pp. 337–58.

Milliken, J. (1999) 'The study of discourse in International Relations: a critique of research and methods', *European Journal of International Relations*, 5, 2: 225–54.

—— (2001) 'Discourse study: bringing rigor to critical theory', in Fierke, K. and Jorgensen, K.E. (eds) *Constructing International Relations: The Next Generation*, Armonk: M.E. Sharpe, pp. 137–59.

Milliken, J. and Sylvan, D. (1996) 'Soft bodies, hard targets, and chic theories: US bombing policy in Indochina', *Millennium: Journal of International Studies*, 25, 2: 321–59.

Mral, B. (2004) *'We're a peaceful nation': War rhetoric after September 11*, Special Feature 5, Stockholm: Swedish Emergency Management Agency SEMA.

National Security Archive (2006) 'Rumsfeld's roadmap to propaganda', *National Security Archive Electronic Briefing Book*, 117, 26 January 2006. Online. Available at: www.gwu.edu/~nsarchiv/NSAEBB/NSAEBB177/index.htm (accessed 3 August 2007).

Noonan, P. (2001) 'Welcome back, Duke: from the ashes of Sept.11 arise the manly virtues', *The Wall Street Journal*, 12 October 2001, editorial page. Online. Available at: www.opinionjournal.com/columnists/pnoonan/?id=95001309 (accessed 3 August 2007).

OHS (Office of Homeland Security) (2002) *National Strategy for Homeland Security*, Washington, DC, 16 July 2002: The White House. Online. Available at: www.whitehouse.gov/homeland/book/nat_strat_hls.pdf (accessed 3 August 2007).

Parker, K. (2001) 'War puts truth back in vogue', *Chicago Tribune*, 24 October 2001.

Pettman, J.J. (1996) *Worlding Women, A Feminist International Politics*, London: Routledge.

Runyan, A.S. (1990) 'Gender relations and the politics of protection', *Peace Review*, 2, 4: 28–31.

Shepherd, L.J. (2006) 'Veiled references. Constructions of gender in the Bush Administration discourse on the attacks on Afghanistan post-9/11', *International Feminist Journal of Politics*, 8, 1: 19–41.

Sontag, S. (2001) 'Feige waren die Mörder nicht. Amerika unter Schock: Die Falsche Einstimmigkeit der Kommentare', first published in *Frankfurter Allgemeine Zeitung*, 215, 15 September 2001, p. 45. English original version: *Susan Sontag's words after the WTC tragedy*. Online. Available at: www.american-pictures.com/english/jacob/Sontag.htm (accessed 3 August 2007).

Tickner, J.A. (2002) 'Feminist perspectives on 9/11', *International Studies Perspectives*, 3: 333–50.

USAF (United States Air Force) (2003) *Joint Publication 3–53 Doctrine for Joint Psychological Operations*, 5 September 2003. Online. Available at: www.gwu.edu/~nsarchiv/NSAEBB/NSAEBB177/02_psyop-jp-3–53.pdf (accessed 3 August 2007).

—— (2007) *Joint Publication 3–27 Homeland Defense*, 12 July 2007. Online. Available at: www.fas.org/irp/doddir/dod/jp3_27.pdf (accessed 11 August 2007).

Wæver, O. (1993) 'Societal security: the concept', in Waever, O., Buzan, B., Kelstrup, M. and Lemaitre, P. (eds) *Identity, Migration and the New Security Agenda in Europe*, London: Pinter, pp. 17–40.

Walker, R.B.J. (1993) *Inside/Outside: International Relations as Political Theory*, Cambridge: Cambridge University Press.

White House, The (2001) *Uniting and Strengthening America by Providing Appropriate Tools Required to Intercept and Obstruct Terrorism (USA PATRIOT) Act,* adopted 24 October 2001. Online. Available at: thomas.loc.gov/cgi-bin/query/z?c107:H.R.3162. ENR:/ (accessed 3 August 2007).

—— (2002) *A Bill to Establish the US Department of Homeland Security, and for Other Purposes,* adopted 25 November 2002. Online. Available at: www.whitehouse.gov/deptofhomeland/bill/hsl-bill.pdf (accessed 3 August 2007).

Young, I.M. (2003) 'The logic of masculinist protection: reflections on the current security state', *Signs: Journal of Women in Culture and Society,* 29, 1: 1–25.

Zalewski, M. (1998) 'Introduction: From the "woman" question to the "man" question in International Relations', in Zalewski, M. and Parpart, J. (eds) *The 'Man' Question in International Relations,* Boulder/Oxford: Westview Press, pp. 1–15.

Zehfuss, M. (2003) 'Forget September 11', *Third World Quarterly,* 24, 2: 513–28.

8   Conclusion

The biopolitics of critical infrastructure protection

Julian Reid

This volume breaks new ground in contextualising the development of Critical Infrastructure Protection (CIP) historically, politically and strategically. The practices and techniques of, and the thinking that fuels the desire for, CIP, did not emerge from a vacuum. Nor do they constitute some kind of revolution in the thought, practice and technicalities of security. Strategically, Chapter 1 by Collier and Lakoff shows, CIP is underpinned by a way of thinking about security that has a vexed history, encompassing genealogical relations with techniques of warfare that emerged in the early twentieth century. Historically, as Chapters 2 and 5 by Dunn Cavelty and Conway show, it cannot be explained without reference to the processes of global interdependence, and especially the technological innovations that have fostered the growing transnationalisation of Western states and societies. And Brunner's contribution (Chapter 7) points to the fact that the 'new practices' associated with homeland security are not so new after all, especially if we analyse their gendered underpinnings. In political terms, it is related to a way of problematising security that is distinctly liberal. Chapter 3 by Kristensen provides a cutting-edge analysis of how CIP is enacting a shift in the security practices of Western states, leading from a concern with securing territorial borders to a concern with promoting a 'society-wide state of security' by working on the inside, 'with the grain of society', as Kristensen expresses it. As Bonditti's demonstrates in Chapter 6, the origins of the CIP approach can be traced to the eighteenth century with the rise of distinctly liberal approaches to the problems of security and governance, in which the life of individuals and populations became new targets for intervention and regulation on account of the desire to strengthen the vitality of the state. As Der Derian and Finkelstein show (Chapter 4), the strategies through which that vitality is being pursued today are constitutive of a condition wherein 'it is not humans that must be protected, but the network and the human as a node in the network that must be secured'. Liberalism, a political philosophy and a set of governmental practices based on a fundamental claim as to the capacity to protect the qualities of a distinctly human way of living, has given rise to regimes that privilege the security of their informational infrastructures over, and sometimes in direct conflict with, the human life that otherwise might be seen to depend on them.

As the volume also discusses in depth, and as the introductory chapter makes especially clear, we ought therefore to be circumspect about claims as to the distinctiveness of CIP as a response to new forms of threat, particularly that of terror. CIP is best understood not as a response to the emergence of terror. Rather, the declaration of the 'war on terror' has provided liberal regimes with an opportunity to extend, and invest more deeply in, approaches to the problem of security that have a substantial history. Nevertheless, in concluding this volume, it seems necessary to stress the importance of the inflections given to the phenomenon of critical infrastructure by the development of terrorism and the responses of liberal regimes to it. For it can be said that the tactical targeting of infrastructures by terrorist groups such as al-Qaida marks a fairly new era in terrorist strategy. What renders the new forms of terrorism distinct from previous forms is their dedicated targeting of the architectures of organisation, which is to say the critical infrastructures, of liberal regimes. The groups that liberal regimes aim to secure themselves against are regarded as significant threats precisely because they deliberately target the critical infrastructures that enable the liberality of these regimes, rather than simply the human beings that inhabit them. Indeed, intelligence agencies such as the FBI report that groups like al-Qaida are making the targeting of critical infrastructures their tactical priority (Likosky 2006: 89). In Iraq, the insurgency is defined by similar strategies involving the targeting of key infrastructure projects.

It is true that the targeting of infrastructures by political violence movements also has a long history. The Irish Republican Army conducted a campaign directly targeted against the transport and financial infrastructures of Britain during the late twentieth century (Belton 2006). However, infrastructure was targeted in that conflict primarily because it provided a means of applying violence by indirect means without substantial loss of life. In the case of the new forms of terrorism, critical infrastructures are choice targets for violent destruction. It is specifically these infrastructures, so fundamental to the capacities of liberal regimes and their societies to function in accordance with their own self-understandings of the quality of life and how to secure it, which terrorist groups such as al-Qaida are seeking to destroy, significantly on both strategic *and* moral grounds. The political representatives of liberal regimes, such as Tony Blair in Britain and George W. Bush in the US, were absolutely correct therefore, when they ascribed such *vital* stakes to the war on terror. For this is indeed, as both these state leaders asserted, a conflict over essential questions of 'how to live' and the propriety of different 'ways of life' (Blair 2005; Bush 2001). Not simply, however, one way of life defined by a commitment to essential liberties and freedoms versus another way of life defined by systems of oppression and prohibition. But a conflict between regimes empowered by their investment in the biological stuff of population versus political movements opposed on principal to the governance of societies via such materialist understandings of the conditions for life's security. Key ideologues of the current of political Islam that inspires these movements speak explicitly of this cleavage in their account of what they describe with enmity as 'Jahiliyyah' societies (see Qutb 2005: 46–51).

Therefore, the contemporary reification of critical infrastructure as an object for protection owes a significant debt to the development of new forms of political agency concerned with attacking liberal regimes by undermining specifically liberal sources of security and governance. All of these developments only serve to fuel liberal representations of the war on terror as a struggle between regimes tasked with promoting security for human life against enemies dedicated to its nihilistic destruction. Why would anyone seek to destroy infrastructure other than out of a profound antipathy for the fundamental conditions which human life requires for its prosperity and security? This volume, in opening up the debate on CIP to allow for the examination of the dehumanising dimensions and implications of the practices involved in CIP, and objectives at stake in it, throws a spanner into the works of such modes of representation. This is especially true for the chapters by Der Derian and Finkelstein (Chapter 4) as well as Bonditti (Chapter 6), both of which extend Michel Foucault's seminal analysis of the origins of liberal regimes in practices of discipline and biopolitics whereupon infrastructure was first objectified as a fundamental source of security to the state. Both of these chapters demonstrate in different ways why the rationalities informing CIP cannot be understood in simplistic terms of a desire for the protection of human beings from the risk of violent death at the hands of terrorists, but express a more technocratic will to defend infrastructures even at the cost and to the detriment of distinctly human capacities. Second they underline the fact that the waging of this war involves the deployment of tactics which, rather than simply securing the life of populations imperilled by terrorist tactics, deliberately target it with newly insidious techniques of discipline and control, all in the name of infrastructure protection. In doing so, the volume highlights what can justly be described as the *biopolitical* dimensions of the war on terror and the broader security strategies of liberal regimes that have been developed to prosecute it.

In concluding this volume, then, I would like to extend and draw out what I read as being its most valuable contribution to our knowledge of this lugubrious phenomenon. If we believe our governments and most of the academic literature on the subject, both the security and quality of life is inextricably dependent on the protection of the critical infrastructures through which liberal regimes are organised. But the provision of such infrastructure protection requires the deliberate targeting of the human life that inhabits critical infrastructures with increasingly invasive techniques of governance. As a consequence of the declaration of the war on terror, and more especially as a result of the ways in which the threat of terrorism is being interpreted and understood by its proponents, the investment of regimes in the development of new techniques and technologies for the control of human life is increasing rapidly. Strategies for critical infrastructure protection are affording significant advances in the development of scientific knowledge and technological control of the evolutionary capacities and adaptive capabilities of the human. Amid the creation of plans for the provision of critical infrastructure protection, and in the establishment of new governmental agencies for the execution of those plans, the biological sciences in particular are undergoing a major renaissance (Cooper 2006). The implications of these new forms of knowledge and security technologies for the quality of human life are profoundly paradoxical. Human beings themselves do, of course, rely significantly on the operability and maintenance of infrastructures themselves. But it is a fact that human beings within critical infrastructures are also regarded as posing the greatest danger to them (Dunn 2005). In this context, the human can be seen to have become both the rogue element against which liberal regimes are today seeking to secure themselves, as well as the central resource on which they are attempting to draw in pursuit of their security.

In order to afford their own protection, liberal regimes have learned historically to govern human life via its reduction to what I have called 'logistical life'. This term is apt because the techniques and practices of social control through which regimes of the eighteenth century learned to govern were drawn directly from the domains of war, military strategy, tactics and organisation (Reid 2006: 17–39). Logistical life is a life lived under the duress of the command to be efficient, to communicate one's purposes transparently in relation to others, to be positioned where one is required, to use time economically, to be able to move when and where one is told to, and crucially, to be able to extol these capacities as the values for which one will agree to kill and die for (Reid 2006: 13). In the eighteenth century, the deployment of techniques with which to increase the logistical efficiencies of societies was legitimised by regimes through the claim that it was necessary for the exceptional defence of the civil domain of society from its external enemies. Increased military efficiency and discipline was said to be necessary and beneficial to forms of civil life, the 'quality' of which was defined by their distinction from the warlike conditions that were said to prevail beyond the boundaries of the state. It is in critique of this type of legitimisation that Foucault's analysis, in its demonstration of the ways in which techniques for the increase of the logistical efficiency of armed forces impacted directly upon the everyday order of life within the civil domain of society, is so powerful. He exposes how the methods with which liberal regimes historically prepared for war with external enemies provided model templates with which to subject the life of their civilian populations to new insidious forms of control and manipulation, and how, in turn, liberal regimes have sought to legitimise their wars in the name of the defence and development of the very forms of logistical ways of living they were busy inculcating within and among their subjects.

Now, in the twenty-first century and in the context of the war on terror, we are witnessing precisely the same methods of legitimisation being employed by liberal regimes, but with a radical twist. Today, the argument being deployed is not, as it was in the eighteenth century, that the increase of the logistical efficiency of societies is a necessary sacrifice in the interest of defending an otherwise distinctly civilian population. Today, it is deemed necessary to defend the logistical life of society from enemies that are deemed dangerous precisely because they target life in its logistical dimensions. Amid the global campaign against terrorism, the capacities of societies to practice a logistical way of life have become indistinguishable from conceptions of the 'quality of life' for human beings. Throughout, for example, the seminal US *National Plan for Research and Development in Support of Critical Infrastructure Protection*, one finds the quality of human life construed in terms of its logistical capacities. The docility and plasticity of human bodies, the manipulability of human dispositions, and the many ways in which human behaviour can be subjected to techniques of control, are conceptualised not just as a means for the protection of liberal societies, but as qualities that distinguish the uniqueness of the human species. As the *Plan for Research and Development* states:

> Part of the challenge of infrastructure protection is how to take full advantage of human capabilities. The Social, Behavioral and Economic (SBE) Working Group in the National Science and Technology Council (NSTC) is focused on scientific research in the areas of sensory, motor, cognitive and adaptive capability of the human. Currently, the brain is unmatched by any technological system. The human brain is a semi-quantitative supercomputer that is programmable and reprogrammable by explicit training, previous experience, and on-going observations on a real-time, virtually instantaneous basis.
>
> (Department of Homeland Security 2004: 63)

The quality of human life, we are told in forthright terms, is reducible to its superior amenability to logistical transformation. Its greater capacity for adaptation and transformation is what distinguishes it from other life forms. Contemporary accounts of this form of human superiority, understood in terms of humans' amenability to logistical techniques of transformation, recall in their depth and specificity the expressions of wonderment at life's malleability to be found in military texts of the eighteenth century that Foucault's original exploration of the disciplinary and biopolitical underpinnings of liberal modernity first exposed (1991: 135–69).

> Human eyes are capable of high-resolution, stereo-optical vision with immense range, and, integrated with a highly plastic brain, make humans uniquely capable of discovery, integration, and complex pattern recognition. Human hands constitute a dexterous, sensitive biomechanical system that, integrated with the brains and eyes, are unmatched by current and near-future robotic technologies. Humans operate in groups synergistically and dynamically, adjusting perceptions, relationships and connections as needed on a real-time and virtually instantaneous basis. Human language capabilities exist and operate within a dimensional space that is far more complex and fluid than any known artificial architectures.
>
> (Department of Homeland Security 2004: 63)

As Foucault's original analysis of the development of liberal regimes of power revealed, the emergence of the military sciences in the eighteenth century was allied to as well as constitutive of the broader development of the life sciences. Developments in modern military science have consistently fed off and contributed to changes in the life sciences more generally. Now, in the twenty-first century, we can see this alliance being cemented in the development of new methods for the defence of liberal regimes in what is known as 'human factors engineering', or HF/E. HF/E is, as the *National Plan* describes, 'both a science of human performance and an engineering discipline, concerned with the design of systems for both efficiency and safety' (Department of Homeland Security 2004: 64). Developed since before the Second World War, its aim is to harness the 'cognitive, emotional and social capabilities of the human' in order to design more secure systems for the defence of critical infrastructures and to invest in such human capabilities with a view to creating systems of infrastructure that are resilient to 'deceptive behaviors', 'rogue activities', and to 'insider threats' said to endanger critical infrastructures (Department of Homeland Security 2004: 42).

But in engineering, the means with which to secure infrastructures against the 'deceptions', 'rogues' and 'insider threats' aimed at it, human life today faces increasingly intense threats to its integrity. The radical indeterminacy of the human, its capacity for error, its creative capacities for thought and expression, are directly endangered by the increasingly insidious forms of control being wielded and asserted in strategies for the securing of critical infrastructures against terrorism. As the *Plan* informs its readership, 'Anyone can be presumed to be a candidate for insider threat' (Department of Homeland Security 2004: 43). Indeed, everyone is suspect of constituting this form of threat. Research and development in response to the fear of insider threats is aimed at the creation of what is called a 'National Common Operating Picture for Critical Infrastructure' (COP) not simply in order to 'sense rogue behavior' in pre-identified sources of threats to life, but in order to be able to 'sense rogue behaviour in a trusted resource or anticipate that they may be a candidate threat' (Department of Homeland Security 2004: 41). It is therefore deemed necessary 'that we presume any insider could conduct unauthorised or rogue activities' (Department of Homeland Security 2004: 42). Consequently, the movement of human life, each and every possible human disposition and expression, is becoming the target of strategies construed paradoxically for the defence of human well-being. In this context, any action or thought that borders on abnormality is to be targeted as a potential source of threat. As the *Plan* states, 'the same anticipation of overt damaging action by a purposeful threat can be used to anticipate an unfortunate excursion in thought or action by a well-meaning actor' (Department of Homeland Security 2004: 44).

The development of technologies and techniques for the analysis of 'what people do' and their 'deceptive behaviours' runs the risk not simply of outlawing fundamental conditions for quality of human life. It creates and indeed instantiates the risk of the violent destruction of forms of life, of human populations and individuals, who through no fault of their own are deemed to exhibit signs of anomalous and threatening behaviour. The deliberate murder of Jean

Charles de Menezes, killed with five gunshots to the head fired at point-blank range by British police on 22 July 2005, is a case in point. This human being, described as an 'unidentified male' with 'dark hair beard/stubble', was targeted on account of the fact that his 'description and demeanour' 'matched the identity of a bomber suspect'. The simple fact of his leaving an apartment block thought to have been used by terrorist suspects, the simple fact that on his subsequent journey, he exited and re-entered the bus on which he travelled, and in spite of the fact that he walked and did not run, showed no sign of possessing weapons of destruction, and gave no signal of intent of any sort, was nevertheless deemed to represent a divergence from a normal pattern of behaviour so serious that he was targeted and killed with the most deliberate violence. In spite of the scale and intensity with which the aim of a complete mapping of human dispositions and behaviours has been pursued, and in spite of the urgency with which today it is being implemented, the most banal and everyday expressions of life continue to fall, tragically, outside its grasp.

As it was in the eighteenth century that the fantasy of a society which functions as a type of socio-military machine, and 'that would cover the whole territory of the nation and in which each individual would be occupied without interruption but in a different way according to the evolutive segment, the genetic sequence in which he finds himself' (Foucault 1991: 165) emerged, so at the beginning of the twenty-first century, we can see that fantasy being given new forms in the shape of critical infrastructure protection. Making sense of what is at stake in this phenomenon requires a complete reversal of the terms in which its utility is currently being articulated by liberal regimes of power. Rather than conceptualise this present struggle in terms of a war on terror in the defence of a common humanity against an enemy that is inimical to life, we can better conceptualise it as a conflict over the political constitution of life itself. When the methods with which regimes are seeking to secure the life of their societies demand an incremental targeting of life, to the point where the most ordinary expressions of life are rendered objects of strategic intervention, it is necessary to question the ways of valorising life that create such paradoxical conditions. This volume, in my reading, creates important openings for the further exploration of such a line of questioning.

References

Belton, P. (2006) 'Lessons to be learned from the British experience in critical infrastructure protection', in Forest, J.J.F. (ed.) *Homeland Security: Protecting America's Targets*, Westport: Praeger Security International.

Blair, T. (2005) 'Statement from Downing Street', 7 July 2005. Online. Available at: news.bbc.co.uk/2/hi/uk_news/4659953.stm (accessed 19 November 2007).

Bush, G.W. (2001) *Address to a Joint Session of Congress and the American People*, Washington, DC, 20 September 2001. Online. Available at: www.whitehouse.gov/news/releases/2001/09/20010920-8.html (accessed 19 November 2007).

Cooper, M. (2006) 'Pre-empting emergence: the biological turn in the War on Terror', *Theory, Culture & Society*, 23, 4: 113–35.

Department of Homeland Security (2004) *The National Plan for Research and Development in Support of Critical Infrastructure Protection*, Washington, DC: Department of Homeland Security. Online. Available at: www.dhs.gov/xlibrary/assets/ST_2004_NCIP_RD_PlanFINALApr05.pdf (accessed 19 November 2007).

Dunn, M. (2005) 'The socio-political dimensions of critical information infrastructure protection (CIIP)', *International Journal of Critical Infrastructure*, 1, 2/3: 258–68.

Foucault, M. (1991) *Discipline and Punish: The Birth of the Prison*, London: Penguin.

Likosky, M.B. (2006) *Law, Infrastructure, and Human Rights*, Cambridge: Cambridge University Press.

Qutb, S. (2005) *Milestones*, New Delhi: Islamic Book Service.

Reid, J. (2006) *The Biopolitics of the War on Terror: Life Struggles, Liberal Modernity and the Defence of Logistical Societies*, Manchester and New York: Manchester University Press.

Index